PENGUIN BOOKS

THE OCEAN

Sanjeev Sanyal is the prin_____nent of India and an internationa_____eorist. He writes on a wide array _____istory, and is the author of the b_____ _Seven Rivers_ and _The Indian Renaissan__. __ 2014, he was given the inaugural International Indian Achiever's Award for contributions to literature. He has been a fellow of the Royal Geographical Society, London; visiting scholar at Oxford University; adjunct fellow at Institute of Policy Studies, Singapore; and a senior fellow of the World Wide Fund for Nature.

Sanjeev spent two decades working in international financial markets and was named Young Global Leader 2010 by the World Economic Forum. In 2007, he was awarded the Eisenhower Fellowship for his work on urban issues. Sanjeev attended Shri Ram College of Commerce, Delhi, and St. John's College, Oxford, where he was a Rhodes Scholar. He lives in Delhi.

PRAISE FOR *THE OCEAN OF CHURN*

'A racy read that covers a whole range of theatres . . . A rare gift, a kaleidoscopic study of an ocean . . . deeply rewarding and constantly entertaining'—*The Hindu*

'Sanyal draws on an impressive array of sources and documents them carefully . . . His capacity for bringing history to the reader through a sharp eye for the most up-to-date material and their implications is commendable . . . Sanyal's chief achievement is to continually prise revelatory little nuggets out of history's unyielding rock'—*India Today*

'A compelling effort . . . packed with riveting stories and interesting characters . . . A highly captivating narrative history'—*Open*

'Compelling and original'—*Pioneer*

'The book challenges the history of India written by the victorious. It's a tough task, but [Sanyal's] efforts are valiant and praiseworthy' —*Mail Today*

'Fascinating . . . Indian historical narratives are dominated by the mountains. This is a rare perspective from the sea . . . [There is] no better contemporary introduction to our maritime heritage than this book'—*Livemint*

'Can put a lot of tomes to shame. What's more—it will leave readers with a wanton craving for more'—*Catch News*

'History is the art of researching facts well and building compelling narratives based on the said facts. Few modern scholars do this better than Sanjeev Sanyal. *The Ocean of Churn* is yet another triumph. Read it. You will have fun. More importantly, you will learn'—Amish

PRAISE FOR *LAND OF THE SEVEN RIVERS*

'A must-read'—*Indian Express*

'A reminder, a ledger of milestones and landmarks in a country steeped in stories . . . infused with both wit and intelligence'—*The Hindu*

'[A] gripping yet thought-provoking account of the rise and fall of urban civilizations in India'—*Business Standard*

'Highly enjoyable and provocative'—*India Today*

THE
OCEAN
OF CHURN

HOW THE INDIAN OCEAN
SHAPED HUMAN HISTORY

SANJEEV SANYAL

PENGUIN BOOKS

An imprint of Penguin Random House

PENGUIN BOOKS

USA | Canada | UK | Ireland | Australia
New Zealand | India | South Africa | China | Singapore

Penguin Books is part of the Penguin Random House group of companies
whose addresses can be found at global.penguinrandomhouse.com

Published by Penguin Random House India Pvt. Ltd.
4th Floor, Capital Tower 1, MG Road,
Gurugram 122 002, Haryana, India

First published in Viking by Penguin Random House India 2016
Published in Penguin Books 2017

25 24 23

ISBN 9780143429081

Typeset in Dante MT Std by Manipal Digital Systems, Manipal
Printed at Replika Press Pvt. Ltd, India

www.penguin.co.in

To the Dark One, Goddess of Time, She who ultimately devours the greatest of empires and the mightiest of kings

Contents

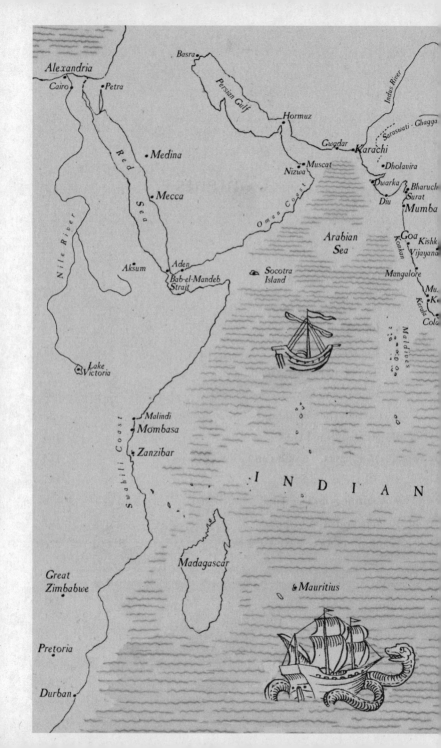

THE INDIAN OCEAN

River Brahmaputra

River Ganga

•*Patna*

Kolkata •*Chittagong*

•*Kohima*
•*Imphal*

Bhubaneswar •Konark

Odisha

•*Rangoon*

konda
derabad

Andhra

Chennai
agapattinam

*Bay
of
Bengal*

Port Blair

*Andaman
and Nicobar
islands*

affna
nuradhapura
olombo

nka

Ayutthaya

Angkor

Lake
Tonle Sap

•*My Son*

Ho Chi Minh
City

Mekong River

*Isthmus
of Kra*

Oc Eo

Kedah ?*Bhujang Valley*
Penang

Melaka Straits

•*Melaka*

•*Singapore*

B o r n e o

Sumatra

•*Palembang*

Sunda Strait
•*Jakarta*

Java

Borobudur
Bali

O C E A N

◦*Cocos Islands*

Australia

Author's Note

I have lived most of my life on the rim of the Indian Ocean. I was born in Kolkata and spent most of my adult life in cities like Mumbai and Singapore. Gradually, as I explored these cities and their surrounding countryside, I became aware of how the history and culture of the Indian Ocean people have been closely interconnected for thousands of years. Indeed, once you become conscious of it, it springs at you everywhere—in the narrow lanes of Zanzibar, the frankincense-perfumed bazaars of Muscat, the ancient temples of southern India and in the ruins of Angkor. At some point I began to systematically collect this information and a vivid, multicoloured picture began to emerge that was quite different from what existing books on the region seemed to suggest.

Almost all of the existing books on the Indian Ocean fall into one of two categories. The first category, which still accounts for the bulk, comprises of histories of the region written from a Western perspective. One would get the impression from these narratives that the history of the Indian Ocean came into being only after the Portuguese arrived on the scene and that it effectively stopped with the withdrawal of the colonial powers. Ancient Indian mariners, Arab merchants and Indonesian maritime empires are simply left out or are presented perfunctorily in an opening chapter as background material. The little that is mentioned is presented in terms of the supply of spices to medieval Europe, as if the Indian Ocean people existed only as part of a supply chain and did not have an independent way of life.

The second category comprises of books written by indigenous scholars who have begun to explore the past of their respective countries. This group has published an increasing number of books and papers in recent years as new material has emerged from archaeology and elsewhere. Their writings have introduced a local perspective to the narrative and restored some balance. However, one major shortcoming of their approach has been a narrow focus on a particular country or region rather than on the broader picture of the Indian Ocean. This is misleading in its own way as it does not fully acknowledge the interconnectedness of the region's history. This book is an attempt to remedy the shortcomings of both the above approaches.

As any writer will tell you, publishing a book is a team sport. This book would not have been possible without the support of many people. The first person I would like to thank is Gurcharan Das. I had been collecting material on the Indian Ocean for over a decade, but it was his encouragement that got me to start typing. Let me express my gratitude to scholars who provided valuable inputs: Patricia Groves, Deb Raj Pradhan, Saradindu Mukherji, Lalji Singh, Sakaya Truong Van Mon and P.J. Cherian. I would also like to mention Saurabh Sanyal, Ranajit Sanyal and other members of my extended family who helped me piece together lesser-known facts about Indian revolutionaries who had fought against British colonial rule.

As anyone reading my books will quickly realize, I try to visit most of the places that I write about. I strongly believe that one can never really understand history unless one visits the places where key events took place. Sadly, many writers do not bother with such ground-proofing and this perpetuates basic errors that are quoted from one book to another. Therefore, I would like to thank those who were kind hosts during my travels and, in some cases, accompanied me on my adventures: Ramesh and Madhvi Khimji, Mrinalini and Praveen Rengaraj, Vivekananda Kendra (Kanyakumari), Aurobindo Ashram (Puducherry), Nirmala Raja, Sujata and Nitesh Shetty,

Meena and Himanshu Shekhar Mohapatra, Akash Mohapatra, Payal Adhikari, Smita Pant, Lucas Dengel, Bikash Pattnaik, Maritime History Society (Mumbai), Mohan Narayan and Odakkal Johnson. I would also like to thank Ameya Nagarajan and Peter Ruprecht who read some of the early drafts and provided valuable comments.

I am also grateful for the support of my editors at Penguin—the cheerful enthusiasm of Udayan Mitra and the meticulous attention to detail of Richa Burman and Paloma Dutta. Thanks for putting up with my various quirks. I would also like to mention Jit Chowdhury for contributing the cartography and artwork. Finally let me thank my wife Smita who accompanied me on many of my research trips and patiently heard me read out the first draft of every chapter. It will amuse readers to know that having heard various drafts read out to her, she has never read the final version of any of my books!

1

Introduction

In AD 731, the prosperous Pallava kingdom in southern India faced an existential crisis. The Pallava king, Parameswara Varman II, had died suddenly without a direct heir. He had been on the throne for barely three years and it is likely that he had been killed in a raid by the Chalukya crown price, Vikramaditya.[1] There was a grave danger that neighbouring kingdoms would support rival claimants to the throne and then gobble up territory in the ensuing civil war.

The Pallava dynasty had carved out a sizeable kingdom in AD sixth and seventh centuries covering much of what are now the states of Tamil Nadu, Andhra Pradesh and southern Karnataka. Although it was not as large as some of the great empires of Indian history, what the kingdom lacked in size, it made up with its commercial and cultural vigour. The capital at Kanchipuram, 70 kms west of modern Chennai, was adorned with awe-inspiring temples. Its main port at Mahabalipuram (also called Mammalapuram, 60 kms south of modern Chennai) was busy with merchant fleets from across India and South East Asia, and even from as far as China and Arabia. However, in AD 731, it looked like the kingdom was about to collapse.

A grand assembly of leading scholars, chieftains and other prominent citizens deliberated the matter in Kanchipuram. The discussions went on for days. In the end, it was decided that the best option was to reach out to a collateral branch of the dynasty that had survived in a distant land. Five generations earlier, a young prince called Bhima, younger brother of the great Pallava king Simha-Vishnu, had gone to a distant kingdom, married a local princess and become its ruler. The grand assembly now hoped that they would be able to persuade one of Bhima's descendants to come and wear the Pallava crown.

A delegation of Brahmin scholars was prepared and must have hurried to Mahabalipuram in time to catch the turning monsoon winds. We are told that the delegation then undertook a long and arduous journey crossing rivers, jungles, mountains and deep seas to reach the court of Bhima's descendant, Hiranya Varman. There the envoys put forward their proposal. It so happened that Hiranya Varman had four sons and each of them was asked in turn if he was interested in taking the crown. The first three refused, daunted perhaps by the idea of a perilous journey and an uncertain future in a far-off kingdom. The youngest prince, however, took up the offer. He was barely twelve years old.

The delegation now hurried back to Kanchipuram where a rival claimant called Skanda was trying to establish himself. The usurper was defeated and the young prince was crowned as Nandi Varman Pallavamalla (or Nandi Varman II). There were probably many people who doubted his claim to the throne, which may explain why his later inscriptions would emphasize his 'pure' Pallava lineage. He also faced constant threats from rival claimants and external enemies, particularly the Chalukyas, and may even have spent some time in exile. Nevertheless, Nandi Varman II would eventually claw back the kingdom and become one of the greatest monarchs in the history of southern India. In this he was helped by a talented general Udayachandra, possibly a childhood friend who may have accompanied him from his country of birth. Nandi Varman II would rule his kingdom until AD 796 and preside over an economic and cultural boom.

We know about the remarkable tale of how a foreign prince was invited to rule over a kingdom in southern India because Nandi

Varman II himself tells us the story in inscriptions and bas-relief panels on the walls of the Vaikuntha Perumal temple in Kanchipuram. The temple is a little away from the main thoroughfare of the town and I found myself there on a windy January afternoon. The temple was closed for the afternoon but two friendly priests kindly let me in when I explained that I had come a long way to see the sculpted panels. So I spent a couple of hours alone 'reading' the story narrated by the panels.

What struck me were the unmistakably oriental facial features of many of the depicted individuals. For instance, there is a prominent figure of a Chinese traveller. The temple priests were convinced that it showed the famous Chinese pilgrim Xuan Zang (also spelled Hiuen Tsang). It is quite possible that they are right since we know from Xuan Zang's diaries that he had visited Kanchipuram a few decades before the temple was built but, given the volume of international trade and exchange that passed through Pallava ports, it could well be another Chinese visitor. However, what I found even more interesting about these panels were the obvious parallels with Khmer art. Anyone who has also visited Angkor and other sites in Cambodia would not fail to notice the similarities.

The close link between the Pallavas and the Cambodians is well known; even the Khmer script is derived directly from the Pallavas. There is also plenty of evidence of Pallava links with other parts of South East Asia. For instance, an inscription by Nandi Varman II has been found near the Thai-Malaysian border. This was once part of the Hindu–Buddhist kingdom of Kadaram in what is now Kedah, Malaysia. Usually historians assume that these connections were limited to trade and culture, but is it possible that Nandi Varman II was from South East Asia? It turns out that there is some reason to believe that not just Nandi Varman II but the Pallava dynasty itself may have had its roots in the region!

Scholars have long debated the origins of the Pallavas—some claiming local roots while others have speculated on north Indian or Parthian ancestry. There are several founding myths but all of them agree that the dynasty began with a marriage to a princess from a Naga or Serpent clan from across the seas. A Pallava inscription clearly suggests that the dynasty derived its royal legitimacy from this alliance.[2] While scholars have spent a lot of effort trying to speculate on the patrilineal origins of the dynasty, the Pallavas themselves seem to have placed greater emphasis on this matrilineal link to Naga royals.

So, where did this Naga princess come from? Most historians give little thought to female lineages and simply assume that she must have come from some small kingdom in nearby Sri Lanka.[3] But, what if she was from South East Asia? As we shall see, the term 'Naga', meaning serpent, is often associated with the people of this region. More specifically, the multi-headed cobra was the symbol of Cambodian royalty from ancient times and is still used to this day. It is also significant that the earlier mentioned Nandi Varman II inscription is very close to the archaeological remains of Kadaram in Malaysia. The site is located in the Bujang Valley.[4] The word *bhujang* is a Sanskrit synonym for *naga*, which means the area is literally called the Valley of the Serpents.

Whether Cambodian or Malay, it suggests that the Pallavas had been repeatedly marrying into the Naga royal clan. Nandi Varman's ancestor Bhima, in other words, had not sailed off to an unfamiliar land but to a country with which the Pallavas already had close family ties. This may explain why Nandi Varman II was able to make the claim that he was a 'pure' Pallava from both his father's and mother's lines. Not only was he a descendant of the Pallava prince Bhima, he was also the son of a Naga princess, the original source of the dynasty's royal legitimacy.

Within the compound of the Vaikuntha Perumal temple, under a large tree, the visitor will come across a colourful shrine dedicated to the snake spirits. These are not uncommon in parts of India but it takes on a special meaning when seen in the context of a temple built by Nandi Varman II.

The story of Nandi Varman II is intriguing in many ways. At one level, it is about the extraordinary life of a twelve-year-old prince who is unexpectedly invited to rule a faraway kingdom and somehow succeeds against the odds. At another level, it is about the Indian Ocean—the churn of people, goods and ideas along its shores that have defined human history from the very beginning.

The influence of Indian civilization on South East Asia is obvious to anyone who has travelled around the region and it is increasingly well documented. The impact that South East Asia had on cultural and historical events in India is less appreciated. The evidence, however, suggests that the influence flowed both ways. There are many examples, including the famed university of Nalanda in Bihar, that attracted students from around the Indian Ocean rim as well as from China and Central Asia. Few people realize that the university was partly funded by the Sri Vijaya kings of Sumatra.

A similar world of exchange and interaction also defined the western Indian Ocean for thousands of years. Over the centuries, Indian ports welcomed Arab, Persian, Roman, Greek and Jewish merchants even as Indian merchants found their way across the Middle East and down the African coast. Thus, the large Indian communities one encounters in the Persian Gulf countries, in East Africa and in South East Asia have a very long history. Conversely, the oldest living Jewish community in the world is to be found in the Indian state of Kerala, although its numbers have dwindled recently due to migration to Israel. Thus the churn of people continues.

India's geographical location and its cultural and economic weight made it the pivot of the Indian Ocean world, but readers should note that interaction and exchange between the eastern and western Indian Ocean did not always involve India or Indians. For instance, the Indonesians sailed right across the ocean in their outrigger boats and were the first humans to colonize Madagascar between AD sixth and ninth centuries. Their descendants still live there and continue to speak Malagasy, Madagascar's national language, which is derived from the dialects of Borneo.

Thus, when Vasco da Gama led the Portuguese fleet into the Indian Ocean in 1497–98, it had already been a highly interconnected ecosystem for a very long time. Its economic importance can be gauged from how both the Chinese and the Europeans, who were not directly a part of this ecosystem, made great efforts to gain access to it. Indeed, the discovery of the Americas by Columbus was an unintended consequence of the desire to find a trading route to the Indian Ocean. History is full of such unintended consequences.

Between the sixteenth and eighteenth centuries, the Europeans gradually came to dominate the Indian Ocean. It was not smooth sailing. The locals often fought back with determination and, in many cases, the Europeans fought bitterly with each other. Meanwhile, the discovery of the Americas gave the Atlantic a new economic and strategic importance even as the Mediterranean became a backwater. The Indian Ocean, nonetheless, remained the key arena of world affairs. We can gauge this from how the Dutch considered it a victory when they forced the English in 1667 to hand over the tiny nutmeg-growing island of Run in the East Indies, now Indonesia, in exchange for a much larger island in North America's eastern seaboard. That island was Manhattan.

By the early nineteenth century, the Atlantic was clearly beginning to rival the Indian Ocean. The latter was still a very important theatre of activity and, under British control, the period witnessed unprecedented movement of goods and people. The opening of the Suez Canal in 1869 and the deployment of steam-powered ships heralded a period of rapid globalization. Nevertheless, it is fair to say that by the end of the nineteenth century it was the Atlantic that held centre stage.

Then, in the second half of the twentieth century, the Pacific rim rose in importance due to the growing economic clout of California, Japan, and eventually, China. A great deal of shipping continued to flow between the Suez and the Straits of Malacca but, unlike in the past, they were mostly passing through to other places. For the only time in history, the ecosystem of the Indian Ocean was more a spectator than a participant.

A number of well-known writers like Robert Kaplan, however, feel that the pendulum is now gradually swinging back. In his influential book, *Monsoon: The Indian Ocean and the Future of American Power*, Kaplan argues that the geopolitics of the twenty-first century will be decided by events in the Indian Ocean rim.[5] This is not far-fetched given the demographic weight of countries like India and Indonesia, the natural resources of the Middle East, East Africa and Western Australia (yes, Australia is also an Indian Ocean country; people forget that), and the complex political–cultural mix of the region.

This book, of course, is not directly concerned with the future but more with how we got here. It is a brief and eclectic history of the Indian Ocean rim and the many forces—political, economic, sociocultural, technological and, not to forget, natural—that have shaped the world we see around us. Given this wide scope, I have not attempted to be comprehensive as it would have made the book both unreadable and unwritable. Instead, I have tried to give the reader a feel of a colourful and ever-changing Indian Ocean world and its impact on human history.

Readers should also note that this book does not strictly adhere to the exact geographical definition of the term 'Indian Ocean' as defined by the International Hydrographic Organization, Monaco. Such a definition is necessarily arbitrary and does not impact the flow of history. Therefore, I have included inlets like the Arabian Sea, the Red Sea, the Bay of Bengal and the Straits of Malacca, and places like Cambodia and Iran as required in the story although they may not be labelled on a conventional map as part of the Indian Ocean world. These places were part of the broader economic, cultural and political ecosystem of the Indian Ocean and need to be included in the narrative.

Looking in from the Sea

One of the things that this book hopes to show is the extent to which history looks different when witnessed from the coastlines rather than from an inland point of view. Most histories of Asia tend to tell the narrative from the perspective of continental empires—the Mauryan and Mughal empires in India, the Mongols in Central Asia, the Tang dynasty in China and so on. Maritime history only attracts some attention with the arrival of the Europeans. However, this completely ignores the rich maritime history that predated Vasco da Gama's famous voyage. Thus, the Cholas of India, the Majapahit of Indonesia and the Omanis are mentioned almost as footnotes. This is the equivalent of telling European history with little reference to Athens, Venice or the Vikings.

One of the interesting outcomes of the shift in viewpoint is how it changes our perceptions of both events and individuals. Take, for example, the Mauryan emperor Ashoka who is often portrayed in conventional histories as a great monarch and a pacifist. However, when seen from the perspective of the coastal state of Odisha, he appears much less benign. The same can be said of Tipu Sultan, the ruler of Mysore in the late eighteenth century, who is often lionized in India for his opposition to British colonial expansion. When seen from the perspective of the Kerala coast, he looks like a ruthless marauder.

With the shift of perspectives, one discovers instead the importance of remarkable individuals such as Odisha's Kharavela who probably ended the Mauryan empire, and Marthanda Varma of Travancore who decisively defeated the Dutch and ended their dreams of colonizing India. Moreover, compared to terrestrial history, maritime history is driven less by monarchs and dynasties and much more by a varied cast of characters including explorers, adventurers, merchants and even pirates. One comes across characters like Nathaniel Courthope of the English East India Company who heroically held out against the Dutch, under impossible circumstances, at his post on the remote Indonesian island of Run.

As mentioned earlier, one thing that particularly struck me when researching for this book was the extent to which previous histories of the Indian Ocean or the maritime Spice Route were written almost exclusively from a Western point of view—a view that tends to focus largely on developments after Europeans entered the scene. Even when earlier history is mentioned, it is treated either as background material or in terms of the medieval European yearning for Asian spices, as if the people of the Indian Ocean were sitting around lazily growing spices for export until the Europeans turned up and made things exciting. By the same token, such histories end when the Europeans leave in the mid-twentieth century, as if history subsequently stopped for the locals.

Even when dealing with the colonial period, we find there is almost exclusive focus on what the colonial powers were doing. The locals are mentioned only when they threaten colonial expansion in any way. In reality, the people of the region were reacting to the evolving situation in multiple ways. There were individuals like the Parsi opium merchant Jamsetjee Jeejeebhoy and the African slave trader Tippu Tip who became very wealthy by taking advantage of new opportunities. There were the large numbers of desperately poor Indian and Chinese labourers who used colonial-era networks and braved their way to far-off islands like Mauritius and Singapore. There were the Bugis pirates who became notorious in the waters of South East Asia. And then there was the heroic last stand of the Balinese against Dutch aggression in the early twentieth century.

Another systematic bias that I found in the existing literature is the preference given to writers and sources from outside the Indian Ocean world. Local texts, inscriptions and oral histories are routinely discounted as being somehow inferior sources than the testimonies of foreign visitors and travellers who are assumed to have greater credibility. I am not suggesting that we should not use the writings of foreign travellers—I have used them extensively in this book—but want to point out that such sources should not be blindly accepted as they too contain their own biases and prejudices. These not only pertain to colonial-era biases but are also evident in highly regarded precolonial sources. Take, for instance, Ibn Battuta, the famous fourteenth-century Moroccan traveller, who proudly recounts how he threw out an elderly Jewish physician from a dinner party hosted by the Sultan of Birgi for no apparent reason other than his religion. He had not behaved unusually badly and merely reflected a common prejudice of his times, but modern historians who use Ibn Battuta need to consciously adjust for this.[6] We see a similar slant in the writings of Chinese pilgrim-scholars like Xuan Zang who viewed the world exclusively from a Buddhist perspective. Thus, we are told of an incident where Xuan Zang is robbed of all his belongings and is helped by a group of Brahmins in Kashmir who give him new clothes and provisions. Far from being grateful after accepting all the gifts, Xuan Zang proceeds to lecture them on their 'erroneous doctrine'![7]

In later centuries, several European visitors would also leave us with narratives that are useful windows into their times. Again, we need to be careful when using their writings as they are, with a few notable exceptions, often systematically biased against the Hindu and Islamic cultures that they encounter. By the end of the eighteenth century, these narratives also contain an additional layer of racism. Thus, when European colonists came across the ruins of Great Zimbabwe in southern Africa in the nineteenth century, they simply assumed that the Africans were incapable of building it. The ruins, therefore, were interpreted as a sign that light-skinned colonists must have conquered southern Africa in ancient times, and there were even attempts to connect it to King Solomon and Queen Sheba.

As historian John Reader puts it, 'This view of African history compounded a prevailing belief that whatever was commendable in black Africa must have been introduced from somewhere else by lighter-skinned and (by implication) more intelligent people. . . . The idea was reinforced by colonial regimes and since independence the elites themselves have seized every opportunity to perpetuate it.'[8]

The Indian reader will probably have recognized the parallels with the Aryan Invasion Theory pushed by colonial-era historians to suggest that Indian civilization was a gift from light-skinned outsiders. It is then a small step to paint British colonial rulers as latter-day Aryans with a (noble) mission to civilize the natives. What is extraordinary is that this story about invading Aryans continues to survive, especially among the elite, despite the lack of any textual or archaeological support, and a plethora of genetic and other evidence against it.

Let it be clear, nonetheless, that local sources too should not be accepted uncritically. As we shall see, even the famous edicts of

Ashoka are partly political propaganda and should be taken with a pinch of salt. Acrimonious debates in newspaper columns, television shows and social media show that it is often not easy to interpret current affairs. So it shouldn't be surprising that it is difficult to disentangle history from the random fragments that have survived the ravages of time. This is why all narratives of history are based on some philosophical framework about the flow of events that allows the historian to make sense of it all.

The Philosophy of History

Since this book is not meant to be an academic tome, I was hesitant to write a section on the philosophy of history as I feared that the general reader would find it tedious. In the end, I decided to include a few lines on this as it would help explain the world view that flows through many of my writings.

The flow of historical events, the causes and effects, have been explained in numerous ways over time. In premodern times, the divine intervention of gods or of a monotheistic God was seen as a key driver of events, especially of sudden changes in direction. Those with a deterministic world view would blame Fate or their stars. Another popular way to explain history was to focus on heroic (or demonic) individuals whose thoughts and actions disproportionately influenced the course of history. This Great Man Theory may have been formalized in the early nineteenth century by writers like Thomas Carlyle, but the idea is embedded in most premodern histories and remains an important influence to this day. This should not be surprising since most history writing was financed directly or indirectly by 'great men' who liked to highlight their own importance.

Perhaps as a reaction to the Great Man Theory, by the late nineteenth century we see the rise of philosophies that emphasize grand social and economic forces. This approach de-emphasized the role of individuals and presented them as part of a larger machinery. Marxist history is a product of this line of thinking where events are driven by grand, inevitable socio-economic forces. In the Marxist version, the narrative of history flows along a predetermined track like some Victorian steam engine driven by the inescapable laws of Newton. Having thus framed history, Marxism could claim to foretell the end of history. As Eric Hobsbawm puts it, 'Marx wanted to prove *a priori* that a certain historical result, communism, was the inevitable result of historical development. But it is by no means clear that this can be shown by scientific historical analysis.' [9]

Marxist history was very influential through much of the twentieth century in academia, including in non-communist countries. However, the collapse of communism and the obvious failure of the framework to explain most events has led to its sharp decline in the twenty-first century. This has opened up the field to other philosophical frameworks.

My own writing, on subjects ranging from economics to urbanism, is strongly influenced by the fact that I view the world as a Complex Adaptive System—a chaotic place where the flow of events is influenced by the constant and often unpredictable interactions between a host of factors and independent agents. Examples of complex adaptive systems include ecological systems, financial markets, economies, the English language, cities, weather systems, common-law systems and arguably the Hindu religion. Contrast the fluid messiness of these with the neat but rigid architecture of mechanical systems that follow the laws of Newton. Thus viewed from the complex-adaptive perspective, history flows from the constant interaction of factors including technological innovation, geography and nature, grand social and economic forces, the actions of great individuals but also of not-so-great individuals, culture and ideology, pure chance and, who knows, perhaps even the occasional divine intervention.

In other words, history is not a predetermined path but the outcome of complex interactions that, at every point in time, can lead down many paths. This does not mean that history is completely random. Some outcomes are more likely than others and some patterns do emerge even if the flow of history does not quite repeat itself. As Mark Twain is said to have remarked, 'History does not repeat itself, but it rhymes.'[10]

A number of other thinkers have also used this general framework to analyse history. An interesting derivative put forward by historians like Niall Ferguson is to explore the counterfactuals or 'What ifs' of history. What if there had been no American War of Independence? What if Kennedy had survived the assassination attempt? While counterfactual histories can be useful to highlight the contingent nature of history and are often very entertaining, I am personally sceptical of them because the alternative scenario cannot be meaningfully recreated in a world where even the fluttering wings of a butterfly can influence the future state of the world. If Kennedy had not been assassinated, many other things would have also not happened—who knows then the path that history would have taken?

One of the implications of the complex-adaptive system framework is to recognize that once a particular path has been taken, all later events are influenced by it (this is called path dependence). It does not matter if this particular path was highly improbable to start with—once the turn is taken, it is hardwired into history and all subsequent events derive from it. All other paths, no matter how probable beforehand, are now dead. A corollary of such thinking is the Law of Unintended Consequences. History is full of them and one hopes that this realization will make 'great men' a little less certain of their impact on the course of history. By the same token, history is influenced by the actions of many ordinary men and women. This is why I have taken care to include a few of their stories in this book: the merchant Naruttam who helped the Omanis capture Muscat from the Portuguese in order to save his daughter; and Odakkal Mohammad who participated in the naval revolt in Bombay in 1946.

The Indian Soldier

For all the many twists and turns, there are several continuities in the long history of the Indian Ocean ranging from the constant migration of people to the stories people have been telling each other over hundreds of years. One such continuity is the presence of Indian soldiers and mercenaries serving in faraway lands since ancient times.

The global importance of Indian soldiering is not widely explored by historians perhaps because Indian empires, with a few exceptions, have rarely carried out military operations outside the subcontinent. In contrast, Indian soldiers and mercenaries have often fought wars from Europe to China. Once one begins to notice them, they seem to pop up everywhere in the historical record. In ancient times, one finds them fighting for the Persians against the Greeks and a little later, driving war elephants for the Macedonian general Seleucus against his rivals in the Middle East. During the medieval period, one finds Indian mercenaries fighting for Sinhalese rulers in Sri Lanka, dying for the Shiite cause in Karbala and protecting commercial interests of Tamil corporatized guilds in South East Asia. Later still they would serve the British in the Opium Wars in China, the Boer Wars in South Africa and across the globe during the World Wars.

This tradition remains alive in the subcontinent. Gurkhas from Nepal are widely considered the world's best infantry soldiers and continue to serve in the armies of many countries from Britain to Brunei. Similarly, India has been the single largest contributor to United Nations peacekeeping missions around the world since 1950.[11] Other countries in the subcontinent too have made major contributions. This is just one of the many continuities of history that we will encounter through the book.

The Female Line

A secondary theme that runs through this book will be the role played by matrilineal customs in the history of the Indian Ocean rim. Let me clarify at the outset that 'matrilineal' is not the same as 'matriarchal'. The latter relates to societies where women are the rulers/leaders as a matter of custom, but in reality, there are very few genuinely matriarchal societies in the world. Matrilineal societies, in contrast, are those that mark lineage through the mother and female ancestors. In such societies, men still run the show, although, in general, the status of women tends to be higher than in societies that are purely patriarchal and/or patrilineal. Note that matrilineal customs come in many forms and can coexist with forms of patrilineal systems—one cannot blindly paint all such societies with the same brush.

There are several instances of matrilineal societies along the Indian Ocean rim. Along the south-western coast of India we have the Nairs of Kerala and the Bunts of Karnataka. To the north-east of the country there are the Garo, Khasi and Jaintia tribes of Meghalaya. Then there are the Karen of Myanmar, the Minangkabau of West Sumatra and the Cham of Vietnam. As we shall see, the existence of various shades of matrilineal customs had an important influence on the history of the Indian Ocean and sometimes allowed powerful female leaders to emerge.

Notice how, excluding the groups along India's western coast, all the other matrilineal groups are concentrated in and around South East Asia. It is likely that they have all inherited their matrilineal customs from common Neolithic roots. Moreover, the tradition can be so deeply engrained that it often survives major sociocultural changes. Thus, the Minangkabau of Sumatra have mostly retained their matrilineal family structure to this day, despite having adopted Islam and the constant pressures from orthodox clerics.[12]

Matrilineal systems are not just a cultural oddity but had a real impact on the political history of the Indian Ocean. Royal legitimacy, for instance, was derived from the female lineage in many places. The effective founder of the Angkor empire in Cambodia, Jayavarman II, was from Java, Indonesia, and most likely acquired the throne through marriage. In AD 877, the throne passed to Indravarman I who was Jayavarman's queen's nephew.[13] The offices of Brahmin priests in ancient Cambodia, similarly, passed from uncle to nephew down the maternal line.[14] Given the importance of the female line, it is not surprising that royal inscriptions in this part of the world put a special emphasis on matrilineal genealogies.

It is quite interesting to compare how some societies opted for a matrilineal system and others did not. Along the south-western coast of India, for example, the custom probably evolved as a result of long-distance maritime trade which meant that the male population was constantly churning while the women were more rooted. This is why the Muslim community of the Kerala coast is still called Mappila or 'son-in-law' in memory of the Arab traders who came here from pre-Islamic times. Interestingly, the eastern coast of India did not develop similar customs despite being just as actively engaged in maritime trade with the matrilineal societies of South East Asia. This difference is perhaps just another example of how history does not evolve along predetermined paths and the same set of circumstances can lead to different outcomes.

This brings us back to why I decided to start this book with Nandi Varman II. His story draws together many of the elements that are explored in this book: the deep links of trade and culture across the Indian Ocean, the back-and-forth movement of people, the importance of the female lineage, but also the difficulty of piecing together history from random scraps of evidence. Moreover, it illustrates the contingent nature of history. The flow of events in southern India took a certain turn because a twelve-year-old boy in a faraway land decided to take a leap into the unknown. Who knows what would have happened to the Pallava kingdom if he had decided to stay back with his brothers?

2

Genetics and Ice

At 7.58 a.m. local time, on 26 December 2004, an undersea earthquake shook the ocean floor north-west of the island of Sumatra. The earthquake of 9.1 magnitude unleashed a tsunami that killed an estimated 228,000 people and caused tens of billions of dollars' worth of damage. The devastation was not limited to nearby Sumatra or Thailand but was spread across the Indian Ocean—India, Sri Lanka and even as far away as East Africa. It was a reminder that the Indian Ocean is not merely a geographic term but an ecosystem interconnected by both human and natural forces.

It appears that such tsunamis have taken place many times in the past and are remembered in the oral traditions of aboriginal tribes in the region. When rescue parties arrived to look for survivors among the Onge and Jarawa people of the Andaman and Nicobar Islands, they found that the tribes had suffered almost no casualties despite being very close to the epicentre. Evidently, they had followed an old oral tradition that instructed them to move inland to higher ground whenever the ground shook.[1] These tribes are said to have arrived on these islands more than 30,000 years ago as part of early human migrations and must have experienced such deadly tsunamis many times in their history. In contrast, the neighbouring Nicobarese tribes, who arrived in the islands less than 600 years ago, did not have this traditional memory and suffered hundreds of casualties. An Indian military base on Car Nicobar Island was also badly damaged. Thus, in order to understand the Indian Ocean, it is necessary to go back right to the beginning.

The Making of the Indian Ocean

The purpose of this chapter is to give the reader a broad overview of how the geographic and human landscape of the Indian Ocean rim took shape in prehistoric times. Those who have read my previous book, *Land of the Seven Rivers*, will be familiar with some of the material presented here, especially that pertaining to India, but I hope they will indulge me as I narrate the story of the broader region.

Till a hundred years ago, it was assumed that the relative positions of the continents and oceans were fixed. Geological change was seen in terms of vertical and not horizontal movement. This view was radically challenged by Alfred Wegener in 1912 and further elaborated in his book, *The Origin of Continents and Oceans*, published in 1915. Wegener argued that today's continents had once been part of a gigantic supercontinent and had later drifted apart like icebergs. The hypothesis explained an observation that had puzzled cartographers like Ortelius since the sixteenth century—the fact that the continents, especially those on opposite sides of the Atlantic, seemed to fit together like pieces of a jigsaw puzzle.

We now know that Wegener was right and that the planet's geological history has been defined by the periodic converging and drifting apart of its land masses. Around 270 million years ago, the continental land masses converged to form a gigantic supercontinent called Pangea. A map of Pangea would show India, Australia, Madagascar and Antarctica wedged together along what is now the eastern coast of Africa. In other words, the India Ocean simply did not exist.

THE BREAKUP OF PANGEA

PRESENT DAY

CRETACEOUS
90 million years ago

TRIASSIC
175 million years ago

LAURASIA

GONDWANA

PERMIAN
270 million years ago

Africa
Madagascar
India
Antarctica
Australia

It was on Pangea that the dinosaurs appeared around 230 million years ago. The supercontinent appears to have held together till around 175 million years ago when it began to split up due to a sequence of rifts. First, it broke up into two large land masses— the northern continent of Laurasia (which included North America, Europe and Asia) and the southern continent of Gondwana (which included South America, Africa, Australia, India and Antarctica). Incidentally, the name Gondwana is derived from the Gond tribe of central India.

Next, Gondwana itself began to break up. Geological studies suggest that India and Madagascar broke away together from Africa about 158–160 million years ago and then from Antarctica–Australia about 130 million years ago. Next, about 90 million years ago, India broke away from Madagascar and started drifting north. As it drifted north, the Indian craton passed over the Reunion hotspot, an area of long-term eruption, and experienced a period of intense volcanic activity that created the Deccan Traps in peninsular India. Scientists speculate that this volcanic activity may have contributed to the extinction of the dinosaurs (with the exception of those dinosaurs that evolved into birds).

There is some dispute about the exact trajectory of the northward movement, but around 55 million years ago India collided with the Eurasian plate. The collision pushed up and created the Himalayas. As a result, the seabed that had existed between India and Asia was thrust into the sky. This explains why fossils of marine animals can be found high up in the mountain range.[2] The Indian plate continues to push into Asia and the Himalayas are still rising by about 5 mm every year. This is why the Himalayan range is seismically very active and experiences frequent earthquakes.

Meanwhile, Australia and Antarctica began to tear apart like a zipper between 85 and 45 million years ago. Once separated, the Australian plate shifted north and became fused with the Indian plate, thus creating the Indo-Australian plate. This is a very simplified version of the sequence of tectonic events that created the Indian Ocean, and the process is still not complete. The Red Sea is the result of a growing rift between the Arabian and African plates, while East Africa is breaking away from the rest of the continent thereby creating the East African Rift Valley—the landscape where our species evolved.

We may even be witnessing the creation of new rifts. The western coast of Sumatra, Indonesia, runs along the boundary between the Indo-Australian plate and the Sunda plate (which covers much of South East Asia). This is why the area is prone to frequent earthquakes and tsunamis; this is what caused the deadly tsunami of 26 December 2004. Lesser known are a pair of strong undersea earthquakes that took place off the Sumatra coast in April 2012. These two quakes took place away from the main fault line and seismologists see it as a sign that the Indian and Australian plates are separating. The reason for this new rift is that the collision of the Indian plate into Asia has slowed it down whereas Australia is still moving quickly.[3] The resulting pressures will now cause the Indo-Australian plate to break into its constituents—a process that will probably cause frequent earthquakes in this area and could produce deadly tsunamis in the future.

In addition to tectonic movements, the Indian Ocean landscape is constantly being moulded by many other natural and environmental factors. The coastlines, for instance, have moved as the sea level has changed due to the periodic warming/cooling of our planet. Since the peak of the last Ice Age 18–20,000 years ago, the sea level has risen by 120 metres as the ice sheets have melted. This process flooded the coasts and, as we shall see, had a major impact on early human history. The sea level began to stabilize about 7000 years ago (i.e. 5000 BC) and remained broadly unchanged between AD 0 and AD 1800, but it has again begun to gradually rise since the nineteenth century.[4]

Numerous other factors also affect the Indian Ocean landscape—the shifting of sand and silt by ocean currents and rivers and, of course, human intervention. The complex interaction between all these factors means that the landscape is alive and constantly changing. Till very recently, histories were written as if the terrain was static but a growing number of researchers have begun to incorporate the impact of an evolving landscape into their writings.

Of Humans Big and Small

Modern humans appeared in the East African Rift Valley about 200,000 years ago. Being an exceedingly modest lot, and despite plenty of evidence to the contrary, we would come to name ourselves Homo Sapien, that is, 'wise man'. Note that there were several other hominids around at that time and it would not have been obvious at this stage that *Homo sapiens* would one day be the sole surviving human species. The Neanderthals were well established in Europe and the Middle East. The closely related Denisovans roamed across many parts of Asia. We have only discovered the existence of the Denisovans by chance in 2010 due to the genetic sequencing of an ancient finger bone.

There were also isolated remnants of earlier human groups. On the small island of Flores, Indonesia, one such group went through a process of dwarfing. It is unclear how archaic humans reached this island but it is likely that this happened at a time when sea levels were low and the island was easily accessible from the mainland. When sea levels rose, the group became trapped on an island with limited resources. In response to scarcity, the survivors reduced in size and evolved into a species named *Homo floresiensis* that reached a maximum height of one metre and a weight of 25 kgs. Nonetheless, they continued to produce stone tools and seemed to have hunted the island's dwarf elephants. There is evidence to suggest that this dwarf species may have survived till as recently as 12,000 years ago.[5]

At some stage, early *Homo sapiens* began to expand out of their original habitat in the Rift Valley. Thus, the first human eyes to look upon the open sea would have seen the waves of the Indian Ocean crashing into the East African shore. We know that at least one group migrated north, and archaeological remains found at the Skhul and Qafzeh caves in Israel suggest that *Homo sapiens* reached the Levant around 120,000 years ago. However, this initial foray out of Africa appears to have been unsuccessful and this group either died out or withdrew back into the African continent. Perhaps the climate turned colder and the Neanderthals, better adapted to cold, reoccupied the area.

So who were these early *Homo sapiens*? Genetic surveys suggest that the Khoi-San people of south-western Africa are the oldest surviving human population as they have the greatest genetic variation.[6] Note that Khoi-San is a composite term derived from the hunter–gatherer San people, also known as Kalahari 'bushmen', and the closely related Khoi people who engage in herding. Right at the onset, let me clarify that the Khoi-San are not a relic population of 'living fossils'. They are modern *Homo sapiens* who happen to carry the wider genetic mix from which the rest of us derive our ancestry.

The Long Walk to Australia

Most of the evidence now suggests that a small number of people, perhaps a single band, crossed over from Africa to the Arabian peninsula near what is now Yemen about 65–70,000 years ago. All non-Africans, despite their superficial differences, are said to be descendants of this tiny tribe.[7] We do not know why they left Africa but major droughts may have played a role as studies suggest that the water in Lake Malawi dropped by 95 per cent.[8] The landscape these humans were traversing would have looked very different from what we see now. The planet was a lot cooler, sea levels were far lower and shorelines extended 50–100 kms further out from today's contours. Thus, the hop over from what is now Djibouti to Yemen, across the Bab-el-Mandeb, would probably have been a short journey. Unless they crossed during the brief periods that the strait was dry land, it does suggest that early *Homo sapiens* already had the capability to build some sort of raft.

The Yemen–Oman coast encountered by the migrants would have been somewhat wetter than it is now and the Indian Ocean monsoons probably watered this area. Even today, a small area of Oman gets monsoon rains. As our ancestors moved further north, they would have arrived at what is now the Persian Gulf. However, at that time the whole area was above water forming a well-watered plain. As pointed out by researchers like Jeffrey Rose, the Persian Gulf 'was once a low-lying floodplain beginning at the confluence of the Tigris and Euphrates Rivers in Mesopotamia, the Karun River draining off the Iranian Plateau, and the Wadi Batin River flowing across northern Arabia. Together, these systems joined together into the Ur-Schatt River Valley. Further downstream, the Ur-Schatt was fed by additional surface runoff from both eastern Arabia as well as the Zagros Mountains. The Ur-Schatt catchment zone terminates at a large lake basin (>100,000 km^2) positioned in the heart of the Gulf some 140 m below current sea level.'[9]

In other words, the 'Gulf Oasis' was a veritable Garden of Eden and there was probably a significant expansion in population. Soon, they began to spread out along the Makran coast into India.[10] Today, the dry, sparsely populated deserts of Baluchistan look like a barrier between the worlds of the Indian subcontinent and the Middle East, but 60,000 years ago the coast was much wetter and acted as an important grassland/scrubland corridor for early human migrations. The coastline was also much further out and what is now the Saurashtra peninsula of Gujarat was not a peninsula at all but a continuous coast. Thus, the stretch from the Persian Gulf to north-west India was a genetic and cultural continuum for most of prehistory.

There is an interesting twist in the human story at this stage. As already pointed out, there were other human species around when *Homo sapiens* made their way out of Africa. They would all go extinct over time—the Neanderthals, for instance, steadily withdrew into Western Europe till the last of them died out in Gibraltar about 24,000 years ago.[11] We do not know exactly why they died out. Changes in climate may have played a role but it is difficult to avoid the conclusion that the arrival of *Homo sapiens* was an important factor. Perhaps the Neanderthals lost their best hunting grounds to the new entrants or perhaps our ancestors brought deadly diseases with them from Africa. Nonetheless, scholars have often speculated that there may have been some interbreeding between *Homo sapiens* and other humans.

Svante Pääbo and his team at the Max Plank Institute, Liepzig, finally cracked the puzzle when they discovered that around 1–4 per cent of the DNA of all non-Africans is derived from Neanderthals. This interbreeding, moreover, appears to have happened soon after *Homo sapiens* arrived in the Middle East. Most of the offspring from such mating were probably infertile, like mules derived from the mating of horses and donkeys, but a small number were able to pass on their genes. This means that the Neanderthals did not entirely die out but live on within us. Of course, this finding merely confirms what has long been suspected by anyone who has attempted to drive on the roads of Delhi.

The journey of how Svante Pääbo made this discovery is itself a story worth reading. Interested readers should pick up a copy of his autobiographical book, *Neanderthal Man: In Search of Lost Genomes*, published by Basic Books in 2014.

A research paper published in 2014 further reveals that the Neanderthal DNA that survived relates mostly to hair and skin.[12] Although we do not yet know what this implies, it should be noted that Neanderthals lived in a cold climate and were light-skinned and may also have had light hair. In contrast, early *Homo sapiens* would have all been uniformly dark given their tropical origins. One possibility is that Neanderthals introduced a variation in skin tone that would later get exacerbated by natural selection as modern humans settled in different climate zones due to factors like vitamin D deficiency, melanin protection from sun and so on.

About 50–55,000 years ago, a small adventurous group seems to have left the Persian Gulf–India continuum and headed east. They probably made their way along the Indian coast on foot and kept going till they reached what is now South East Asia. Almost the whole tribe seems to have kept moving since they have left only the tiniest genetic traces of their passage through the Indian subcontinent. When the group arrived in South East Asia, the sea level was much lower than it is today, and many of the islands of the region would have been connected by land to the Asian mainland. Thus, the group would have been able to spread out quickly on foot.

Their descendants are the Melanesians who now live in Papua New Guinea, Fiji, and parts of eastern Indonesia.

The early Melanesians were initially traversing territories that were already inhabited by other human species. There is evidence that they interbred with at least one such group, the Denisovans. Genetic studies show that Denisovans contributed up to 6 per cent of the DNA of Melanesians. Given all this mixing, forget racial purity, it seems most of us are not even pure *Homo sapiens*!

Then, about 45,000 years ago, a branch of this Melanesian group hopped across to Australia. Even allowing for lower sea levels and extended coastlines, this would have required the ability to cross a significant body of water. We know this because the flora and fauna of Asia and Australia have remained separate despite being so close to each other. An imaginary line called the Wallace Line, that runs between the Indonesian islands of Bali and Lombok, separates the two ecosystems. Although the two islands are barely 35 kms apart, the channel between them seems to be deep enough for animals from mainland Asia (such as the tiger) to make it to Bali but not Lombok even when sea levels were at their lowest.

The ancestors of the Australian aborigines, therefore, must have acquired the ability to build rafts that could cross seas that other human species could not. The arrival of humans in Australia was a major event. So far, *Homo sapiens* had been traversing lands that had witnessed other hominid species but they were now entering virgin territory. Their entry into Australia had a dramatic impact on the flora and fauna of the continent.

As an island that had been long separated from other continents, Australia was home to plants and animals that had evolved in isolation for a long time. There was a 200-kg, 2-metre-tall kangaroo, a marsupial lion, giant koalas and flightless birds twice the size of an ostrich. The diprotodon, a giant wombat weighing 2-and-a-half tons roamed the forests.[13] Many of these mega-creatures were marsupials who gave birth to small, helpless offspring that they then nursed in an abdominal pouch. Even the smaller creatures were strange, such as the platypus which is an egg-laying mammal with webbed feet and a duck's bill.

Human entry into this ecosystem had a devastating effect. Within a few thousand years almost all of the mega-fauna vanished. Of twenty-four species weighing over 50 kgs, twenty-three became extinct. It is thought unlikely that natural cycles like climate change would have caused this mass extinction since these creatures had already survived several cycles. Hunting for food was probably only one of the ways in which humans caused extinction. The ancestors of the Australian aborigines probably upset the overall ecological balance in several other ways. For instance, they may have used fire to clear and manage their landscape in order to benefit some species at the expense of others (contrary to popular perception, many hunter–gatherers actively managed their territories). The eucalyptus, which is rare in fossil records till 45,000 years ago, suddenly became very common at the expense of other plant species. In turn, this would have upset the whole food chain. This fits a pattern that we witness repeatedly through history whenever humans entered a virgin ecosystem like Madagascar or New Zealand.

We know virtually nothing about the individuals who made up these groups of early human explorers—their names, their world view, their relationships with each other. However, they have left behind paintings and handprints in a cave in Sulawesi, Indonesia. Discovered in the 1950s, they were originally thought to be 10,000 years old but have recently been dated to almost 40,000 years ago, among the oldest in the world.[14] The handprints, which include those of both adults and children, are particularly intriguing as if they are reaching out to us through the mists of time. They were created by spitting out a mouthful of mineral ochre over an outstretched hand in order to leave a stencilled outline. The result is very similar to the handprints made on rock surfaces by Australian aborigines well into modern times.

Populating the Indian Ocean Rim

As narrated above, a small group of modern humans made it out of Africa about 65,000 years ago and around 45,000 years ago they reached Australia, on the other side of the Indian Ocean. A substantial population remained in the Persian Gulf–north India continuum and one by one other groups migrated out.

Some 40,000 years ago, another group made its way across India to South East Asia. We cannot be sure but 42,000-year-old stone tools found recently in Purulia, in the Indian state of West Bengal, may be the remains of this migration.[15] When these people finally arrived in South East Asia, they would have found a terrain quite different from what we see today. As already mentioned, the sea level was a lot lower and the coastlines much further out. Islands like Sumatra, Java and Borneo were joined to the Asian mainland as part of a land mass called Sundaland. The new group, however, seems to have taken a more northward route than the Melanesians and settled in what is now Laos, Thailand, Vietnam, parts of southern China and probably extended out to adjoining areas that are now under water.

A recent study by a consortium of geneticists argues that this group of hunter–gatherers, usually associated with Y-chromosome haplogroup O-M175, became the ancestors of most people who today live in East and South East Asia including the Chinese, Japanese, Vietnamese, Thai, Tibetan, Burmese, Malay, Filipino and most Indonesians.[16] The Polynesians scattered across the Pacific are also derived from this group, as are a number of tribes who live in eastern India. At this stage, however, we are still dealing with small bands of closely related people. We will later see how subgroups descended from this migration would colonize the eastern Indian Ocean rim and even make their way to Madagascar.

Meanwhile, new groups continued to be pumped out by the Persian Gulf–north India area. Some headed into Europe, some decided to brave the freezing Siberian cold and a few even headed back to Africa. One specific group headed out around 30–35,000 years ago and settled in southern India. Not only was the coastline further out but Sri Lanka was then attached to India and there was a large area of dry land off the coast of present-day Tamil Nadu. In fact, as the planet drifted into a new Ice Age, the new migrants would have witnessed a further expansion of land area as sea levels kept falling. This group would evolve into what geneticists call 'Ancestral South Indians', which is one of the two main founder populations from which most Indians derive their ancestry.[17] Another group would make its way to the Andaman and Nicobar Islands (the ancestors of the Onge).

One should not be under the impression that the population ranging from the Middle East to north-western India was static except for the occasional outward migration. This population too was undergoing constant mutations and churn. Just as an illustration, take the male lineage known by geneticists as R1. This lineage emerged somewhere in the Persian Gulf–north India continuum, possibly Iran, before the last Ice Age. At some point, around 25,000 years ago, it gave rise to a western branch, R1b, and an eastern branch, R1a.[18] The former would eventually find its way to Western Europe where R1b is today the most common lineage. In contrast, R1a (particularly a subgroup, R1a1a) would later become an important component of the genetic cocktail that scientists call the 'Ancestral North Indians' who are the second of the two major founder populations from whom most Indians have descended.

The Indian reader may be tempted here to think of the Ancestral South Indians (ASI) as the Dravidians and the Ancestral North Indians (ANI) as the Aryans. While I have nothing against the words themselves, one should be cautious about using the terms as they are often used in the context of bogus nineteenth-century racial theories. The ANI and ASI are just different genetic cocktails and not 'pure' races. Moreover, we are dealing here with Stone Age bands and not horse-drawn chariots, cities and iron weapons that were said to be part of the Aryan–Dravidian rivalry.

This is a very simplified and stylized account of how the Indian Ocean rim was populated by modern humans. In reality, there would have been back-and-forth movements, dead ends and near extinctions. Also note that the genetic and archaeological evidence is still flowing in and the narrative is not set in stone, but the new information fits together much better than unreliable theories based on linguistics.

A further word of caution is warranted here. We are still dealing with tiny bands of Stone Age hunter–gatherers. A number of factors decided who died out and who survived and flourished—availability of food, changing climate, disease, tribal wars, the decisions of leaders and pure chance. A small difference in circumstances at this stage would show up as a big difference in the population distributions of later times. This is why anyone using the genetic data on early humans to support grand theories of racial and cultural superiority is missing the point.

The Age of Ice

Most traditional accounts about the emergence of civilization roughly run along the following script. Farming is 'discovered' somewhere in the Middle East and then spreads quickly, often with the help of Neolithic migrants who awe the locals with this new technology. Overwhelmed by the awesomeness of agriculture, hunter–gatherers leave their traditional life in droves and take to cultivating wheat and barley. This switch to farming is seen to imply large improvements in the quality of life and consequently, steady increases in population. At some point, it gets crowded enough to allow the building of cities and the emergence of civilization. Wonderful story, but it is mostly untrue.

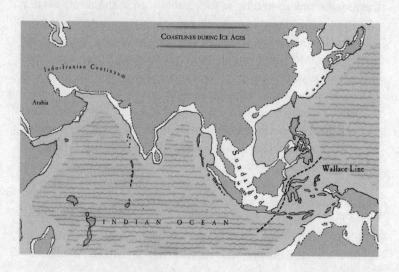

The last major Ice Age is key to understanding the sequence of events. The cycle of cooling started about 30,000 years ago and temperatures kept falling till the Ice Age peaked about 18–20,000 years ago. At the glacial maximum, one third of the Earth's land surface was covered in ice (compared to less than an eighth today) and half of the oceanic surface.[19] With so much water locked up in ice, sea levels dropped dramatically from 50 m below present-day levels 30,000 years ago to around 130 m below at the peak.

Falling sea levels, in turn, exposed large tracts of land. In South East Asia, Sundaland took over most of what is now the Gulf of Thailand and extended far into the South China Sea. The Ancestral South Indians would have witnessed very large tracts being opened up along the Indian coast, especially to the south-east. The Ancestral North Indians, who were newly coalescing into an identifiable group, would have been able to walk more than 150 kms out from today's Gujarat coast.

The retreat of the sea, however, did not make life easier for our ancestors. Many places had become just too cold but, even in warmer latitudes, climate became a lot drier and many rivers and lakes dried up. Central Asia became a very cold, dry desert that could support few animals or humans. Further south, the monsoons were still active but much weaker than today. The Himalayas were covered in glaciers and north-western areas of the Indian subcontinent may have been steppe-like temperate grasslands. We have evidence that even places like Bengal were relatively dry at the peak of the Ice Age. In Africa, the Sahara expanded by around 500 kms along its southern edge while Lake Victoria almost entirely dried up. At its peak, the sands of the Kalahari desert extended almost to the plains of the Zaire River in central Africa.

As one can imagine, the sharp increase in aridity caused a great deal of turmoil. In many places, people were forced to abandon old hunting grounds and move closer to the remaining rivers. The Sahara savannah had so far supported a significant population but desertification forced many to shift to the Nile. Note that the arid conditions meant that the Nile was not the broad river of earlier and later times but a modest tangle of braided channels that may not have even reached the Mediterranean.[20]

Surrounded by desert, the people settling along the Nile 'oasis' became increasingly sedentary. The 'oasis' ran from Sudan to Cairo, around 800 kms, but was no more than a few kilometres wide. We have evidence that human population steadily increased over time, probably through a combination of local births and further inward migration. This must have increased the pressures on the system and we even have the earliest evidence of a battle between two groups. Given the growing pressure, around 15,000 years ago, we can see signs of organized food production in the Nile floodplain—not quite farms but the active management of a semi-wild ecosystem, distinct from being a nomadic hunter-gatherer. The evidence suggests that Nile people harvested catfish and tubers of wild nutgrass.

People in other parts of the world would have gone through a very similar experience and may have also attempted some form of farming. Researchers have recently uncovered the remains of a 23,000-year-old farming settlement near the Sea of Galilee in Israel.[21] It appears that farming is a lot older than the traditional view that it was a Neolithic invention. It is more than likely that the Indian Ocean rim also had such pre-Neolithic farming communities.

One may be tempted to think that Egyptian civilization evolved directly from the Nile oasis people, but the actual course of events is much more complicated. After the glacial peak 18,000 years ago, the world began to warm up again. Rising sea levels began to inundate the coastlines while increased rainfall revived previously arid areas. By 12,500 years ago, Lake Victoria was full and the Sahara was again an inhabitable savannah. The combination of melting ice and increased rain also fed the rivers. On one hand, the return of a strongly flowing Nile may have washed away the carefully tended ecosystem of the 'oasis' phase but, on the other hand, the Sahara beckoned. Thus, the world's first 'farmers' drifted back to being hunter–gatherers! This is why we find cave paintings of savannah animals in the middle of the Sahara at locations that would appear uninhabitable today.

The Indian Ocean rim also went through a similar shift. The coasts of Sundaland and India were flooded and seawater began to encroach into the Persian Gulf by 12,500 years ago. However, at the same time, previously arid areas became much wetter and more habitable. As with the Sahara, the desert zone that extends across Arabia into western India also became much more humid and capable of supporting hunter–gatherers.[22] The northern latitudes also became much warmer as the glaciers retreated even as the monsoons became stronger in southern Asia. The combination of flooding coastlines and a warmer, wetter land mass led to a great deal of human migration into areas that had been previously uninhabitable.

From Cities to Farms

Then, in the midst of rising sea levels and all this migrating, the hunter–gatherers did something special—they built large monumental structures! In 1995, archaeologists digging a site called Göbekli Tepe in south-eastern Turkey made an astonishing discovery. As they dug, they found monumental pillared structures with elaborate carvings. The stone pillars were each 5–6 m high and weighed 7 tons. In a nearby quarry they even found a half-finished pillar weighing 50 tons. This would have been an important discovery by any standards, but what made it really special was the realization that it was 11,500 years old (i.e. 6000 years older than Stonehenge). In other words, these structures were built either by hunter–gatherers or by pre-Neolithic farming communities! We have no idea who these people were and why they built Göbekli Tepe. Possibly it was an important ceremonial or religious centre. Perhaps it also served as a trading hub.

The plot has thickened further as more such sites are being found around the world. A huge stepped pyramid has been discovered at Gunung Padang on Java, Indonesia. The layers were built at different times, but the oldest layers are at least as old as Göbekli Tepe. Yet again, we do not know what purpose it served and who built it.

Then, in 2001, a team from India's National Institute of Ocean
Technology found evidence of two large settlements while doing
undersea sonar surveys in the Gulf of Khambhat, off the coast of
Gujarat.[23] Although this site has not been fully researched due to its
depth, it is worth noting that it is at a location that would have been
flooded more than 7500 years ago; so the settlements would have
been built a lot earlier. It is likely there are several other such sites
that are still undiscovered or are now under the sea. Whatever the
reason for such constructions, there is no doubt that they required the
cooperation of large numbers of people, and hunter–gatherer societies
would have had to support those building and looking after these
projects. This has led researchers like Yuval Noah Hariri to wonder
if agriculture was invented to feed the workers and those who lived
in these settlements. In other words, did the need to feed urban hubs
lead to farming? Is it a coincidence that the wild varieties from which
wheat was domesticated grew just a few miles from Göbekli Tepe?

We do not know all the answers but these new discoveries
are challenging many well-established assumptions about the flow
of human history and the origins of civilization. At the very least,
we need to stop thinking of history as a smooth, linear transition
from Paleolithic to Neolithic, and then from the Bronze Age to the
Iron Age. The path of history is a lot more messy with different
people adopting different technologies at different times, sometimes
skipping a phase and occasionally retracing. Scholars may also need
to reconsider what we mean by terms like 'Neolithic'. Such terms
often come with assumptions about social and economic structures
that go beyond the use of a particular technology. I have continued
to use such terms for convenience in this book, but readers should
be aware that they have somewhat fluid meanings.

It was once thought that agriculture had a single point of origin
in the Middle East and that migrants carried the knowledge to other
places. We now know that both crops and animals were domesticated
at multiple locations around the world. Sugar cane was domesticated
by Melanesians in New Guinea. They may have also tamed banana
although a separate species may have been independently domesticated

in India or South East Asia. Rice and pigs were domesticated in China. Rice cultivation then spread quite quickly to South East Asia and to India. Sesame and cotton appear to have been first cultivated in India. West Africans learned to cultivate sorghum and African millet. Cows seem to have been domesticated in India and separately in the Middle East (the humped and non-humped varieties respectively). I am not even listing here the numerous crops that were domesticated entirely independently in the Americas.

It is no surprise that humans learned to farm since hunter–gatherers would have known quite a lot about plants and animals. The real question is, why did they bother to switch? By all accounts, agriculture did not improve the lives of people. It was risky business that required the upfront investment of a lot of effort while the returns were uncertain—the rains could fail, wild animals could destroy the crops and neighbouring tribes could steal the produce. Moreover, cultivation yielded a narrow variety of food compared to that available to hunter–gatherers. Most importantly, living in concentrated villages in close proximity to animals increased the likelihood of spreading disease. Analysis of human remains from Neolithic farming sites repeatedly shows that farmers were less healthy and had much shorter lifespans than their hunter–gatherer ancestors. This may explain why the Nile oasis people went back to hunting in the Sahara grasslands as soon as climate permitted them.

Whatever the original reason humans took to farming, it had one advantage—it produced more calories per unit area. A sedentary lifestyle may have also reduced the gap between births. This allowed for a big increase in human population even if the individual now had a lower quality of life. China's population today exceeds 1.3 billion but 40 per cent of its males derive their genes from just three Neolithic 'super-grandfathers'.[24]

After the Great Flood

Meanwhile, climate kept getting warmer and the coastlines kept getting inundated. In a last burst of flooding around 7000 years ago (i.e. 5000 BC), the Persian Gulf was completely inundated and came to look roughly like it does today. In India, the coastline shifted to turn Gujarat's Saurashtra region into a peninsula (and briefly an island). Sri Lanka separated from the Tamil coast and became an island. Sundaland, already much diminished, now witnessed the islands of Java, Sumatra and Borneo take shapes that would be familiar to us.

Most ancient civilizations have a myth about the Great Flood. There is the well-known biblical story of Noah and his Ark. The Sumerians mention the Great Flood in the epic of Gilgamesh. The Indians have the legend about Manu who was warned about the coming flood by the god Vishnu. So he built a large ship and filled it with wise sages, seeds and animals. Vishnu, in the form of a fish, then guided Manu's ship to safety. The survivors are said to have re-established civilization at the foothills of the Himalayas. Notice the similarity with the story of Noah. Indeed, many cultures around the world have a story about the Great Flood and one wonders if it is a memory of this period of climate change and coastal flooding.

All this flooding would have led to further migrations. Based on linguistic models, the current population of South East Asia was once thought to be descendants of migrants from Taiwan. However, genetic models now confirm that they already lived in northern parts of Sundaland and that they were probably dispersed by the floods. An interesting aspect of this group is the prevalence of a strong matrilineal streak. We do not know why this was the case but there may have been a phase during the transition to agriculture when the men were still mobile as hunters and herders while the women settled down to grow crops. This may have been especially true of rice-growing areas because rice requires greater investment in water management. The female line, being more stable, may have therefore become the social anchor. There is evidence that even Chinese clan names may have been matrilineal till the early Bronze Age.

Mind you, it was not just flooding but also shifting climate zones that affected the Neolithic people. After being habitable till 7500 years ago (i.e. 5500 BC), the Sahara steadily became more arid over the next thousand years. We see similar desertification across Arabia. As we shall see, the process of desertification would eventually spread east into western India.

Given these changes, we see migrations within and from the Indo-Iranian continuum. It appears that some groups, probably tired of all the flooding and desertification, took advantage of warmer conditions to push north. One such group carrying the R1a1a gene would make their way through Central Asia and eventually come to settle in Eastern Europe. This is why Iranians, Pakistanis and north Indians are more closely related to Eastern Europeans like Lithuanians and Poles than to R1b carrying Western Europeans who had separated much earlier.[25] It also explains some of the ancient cultural and linguistic links between Europe and India.

Note, however, that the links relate to the Neolithic or very early Bronze Age, and not the Iron Age—and the flow is from the south to the north and not the other way around.[26] In other words, this is not about some Iron Age 'invasion' of Iran and India from the steppes. To quote a paper by geneticist Peter Underhill and his colleagues: 'it would exclude any significant patrilineal gene flow from East Europe to Asia, at least since the mid-Holocene period'.[27] An independent study of Iranian genes also came to a similar conclusion: 'none of the identified sub-branches support a patrilineal gene flow from western Eurasia through southern Asia ascribable to the diffusion of the Indo-European languages'.[28]

Analysis of the genetic mix of Afghans similarly came to the conclusion that except for Uzbeks and Hazaras (who are known to have come during the medieval period), most Afghan groups have been living in the general area since Neolithic times. Moreover, they were found to be closely related to north Indians and their evolution into separate tribes coincided with the Bronze Age Harappan civilization in north-western India. Again, there is no evidence of an Iron Age invasion or migration from Central Asia. Indeed, the 2012 study by Marc Haber et al. specifically states, 'R1a1a-M17 does not support, as previously thought, expansion from Pontic Steppe bringing the Indo-European languages to Central Asia and India.'[29]

All these findings have been further confirmed by yet another study published in 2015. The study analysed the genes of 6600 men and found that the oldest strains of the R1a haplogroup are found in the Indian subcontinent (approximately 15,500 years old) compared to Eastern Europe (12,500 years old) and Northern Europe (6900 years old). This is again consistent with a post-Ice Age migration from the south to the north.[30]

So, if they are related, why do Lithuanians and Poles today look so different from modern Indians and Iranians? Firstly, remember that none of them is a 'pure race', and they have separately mixed with different streams of humanity over subsequent millennia. Secondly, the difference is mainly related to skin/hair tone which we know are very recent developments. The analysis of DNA extracted from the remains of European hunter–gatherers suggests that lighter skin may have spread among Europeans as recently as 5000 BC (i.e. after the migration) although I suspect some pre-existing north European populations may have become light-skinned much earlier.[31]

By 4500 BC, the flooding and desertification had pushed concentrations of people along the Nile in Egypt and the Euphrates and the Tigris in Mesopotamia. Although still relatively wet, the Indian subcontinent saw clusters emerge along the Indus and the Saraswati Rivers. The stage was set for the next big step in human history—civilization.

3

The Merchants of Meluhha

The traditional view locates the discovery of agriculture in the Middle East before it spread to other parts of the world. There is some evidence that this may have been generally true for Europe as it was repopulated after the Ice Age from the south and east. However, this unidirectional narrative is hardly applicable to the rest of the world and should be seen as a lingering vestige of the biblical world view that all civilization began in the Middle East. We now know that farming emerged independently in many parts of the world and that the Indian Ocean rim had multiple clusters. Thus, the story of the Indian Ocean rim is about the evolution of these clusters and their long-distance interactions from a very early stage.

India's Early Farmers

To be fair, archaeology had initially supported the traditional view since the earliest evidence of farming in the Indian subcontinent had been found in the extreme north-west. Early excavations in Baluchistan, now part of Pakistan, suggested that this was the first place in the subcontinent to witness agriculture-based settlements. Mehrgarh, in the Bolan valley, is the best documented site and may have been occupied before 6000 BC (i.e. 8000 years ago). The site provides a fascinating view of the transition from hunting to domestication of animals. The early layers are dominated by the bones of wild animals like gazelle, spotted deer, sambar, blackbuck, nilgai, wild ass, and even elephants. Notice that some of these animals would not thrive in the wild in the dry climatic conditions of present-day Baluchistan. In the later layers, the mix gradually switches to cattle, goat and sheep.[1]

Barley was the earliest crop at the site. Baluchistan would have been within the natural habitat zone of wild barley during that period. So, it is quite possible that at least one variety of barley was domesticated here.[2] A bit later we find that the inhabitants of Mehrgarh also began to grow wheat. Remember that Baluchistan is on the Indo-Iranian continuum, and people and trade were passing back and forth. Therefore, it is likely that wheat was acquired from the Middle East at an early stage.

More recent archaeological finds, however, suggest that farming appeared more or less simultaneously in a number of other clusters scattered across northern India. For instance, one concentration of Neolithic farm settlements have been found along the fringes of the Vindhya range in central India, just south of the modern city of Allahabad. As many as forty sites have been identified from the same period as the ones in Baluchistan. Interestingly, the central Indians were eating both wild and domesticated rice. It is currently believed that rice was domesticated in China and it is possible that the crop made its way to India via South East Asia. However, wild rice is still found in the general area, which could mean that it was independently domesticated in India.

We also find animal bones in the central Indian sites including cattle, deer, goats, wild boar and, hold your breath, horses.[3] This fits in with what we know of shifting climate zones and the discovery of horses painted on rocks at Bhimbetka, a Stone Age site further to the south in Madhya Pradesh. The point is that Indians appear to have been familiar with horses from a very early age which goes against the common view that the animal was domesticated in Central Asia and came to India in the Iron Age. New Neolithic sites are still being found and excavated, so our knowledge of this period is fluid. As pointed out in the previous chapter, there may have been even older settlements along the coast that are now under the sea, especially off the Gujarat coast.

Interestingly, agriculture appears to have spread to southern India much later. What was the reason behind this? As we have seen, hunter–gatherers were not always impressed by farming. It is possible that climatic conditions in the south allowed them to continue with their existing lifestyle. Equally interesting is the distribution of the farming communities when they did come up. We find them concentrated along the Krishna River and, its tributary, the Tungabhadra. In contrast, there is very little evidence of early farming settlements along the south-east (i.e. Tamil and Andhra) coast. This is puzzling as the area shows evidence of human activity from much earlier periods.[4] Perhaps the Neolithic sites were washed away by local rivers and covered with silt. Perhaps the settlements existed near the coast and were submerged by changing coastlines that ate into large tracts of land off the Tamil coast. My own guess is that faced with a choice between big game fishing and watching vegetables grow, the lads made the obvious choice.

The Rivers of Civilization

After a relatively benign period lasting several thousand years, the savannah grasslands that covered the Sahara and Arabia began to dry out again around 4500 BC. Populations that lived in the encroaching desert began to converge along the Nile in Egypt and the Euphrates and Tigris in Mesopotamia, both of which already had established farming communities. The influx led to a sharp increase in population but, unlike the arid period during the Ice Age, the major rivers continued to flow in full force. North-western parts of the Indian subcontinent also became drier while witnessing increased agricultural activity.

The need to manage increased pressure on the land was what possibly led to the emergence of complex political—alongside social and cultural—institutions in all these regions.[5] In other words, these hubs of riverine civilizations were born out of adversity and culminated in the creation of the first kingdoms/states. In Mesopotamia, we see the rise of Sumerian city states. By around 3100 BC, Upper and Lower Egypt are unified into a single kingdom with its capital in Memphis.

Meanwhile, the Indian subcontinent witnessed the growth of settlements along two major rivers and their tributaries. One of the rivers is the Indus and the other is now the dry riverbed of the Ghaggar. Satellite photos and ground surveys confirm that the Ghaggar was once a mighty river that emerged from the Himalayas near modern-day Chandigarh, then flowed through Haryana, Rajasthan and Sindh before entering the sea through the Rann of Kutchh in Gujarat. With the Sutlej and the Yamuna as its tributaries, the river initially would have had water flow comparable to that of the Indus.

After decades of debate, it is now accepted by most serious scholars that the Ghaggar is the same river that the earliest Hindu texts refer to as the Saraswati.[6] The importance of the river can be gauged from the fact that there are far more settlements clustered around the course of the Saraswati than along the Indus. This is why this civilization is now called the Indus–Saraswati civilization rather than the Indus Valley civilization. It is also known as the Harappan civilization after Harappa, one of its largest cities.

The Harappan civilization went through three phases. The earliest recognizable Harappan site at Bhirrana in Haryana, on the banks of the Saraswati–Ghaggar, has been carbon-dated to 7000 BC.[7] This makes it at least as old as the sites in Baluchistan which were once considered the oldest in the subcontinent. The early evolution of the settlements in the area is still being analysed and is not fully understood but the earliest level coincided with a period which enjoyed an increase in monsoon rains. However, from around 5000 BC, the monsoons begin to gradually weaken (although they were still much stronger than today).[8] As in Egypt and Mesopotamia, this coincided with densification of settlements along rivers. We know that by 3200 BC, at about the same time that Egypt was being unified, there are a large number of Harappan settlements on both the Saraswati and the Indus basins. This 'early' phase lasted till about 2600 BC.

The second phase, often dubbed the 'mature Harappan period', lasted from 2600 to 2000 BC. This is the period that saw the rise of major cities like Mohenjodaro, Harappa, Dholavira, Kalibangan and so on. Some of these settlements already existed in the previous phase but they now expanded by an order of magnitude. Recent excavations suggest that the largest of these cities was Rakhigarhi, Haryana, which is also in the Saraswati–Ghaggar basin. After 2000 BC, however, the archaeological evidence shows a steady decline— cities are abandoned, civic management deteriorates and there are signs of economic stress. Some of the settlements struggle on but the 'late' Harappan period peters out by 1400 BC. This is a simplified timeline and individual sites would have experienced somewhat different cycles.

The Harappans did not build great monuments like the pyramids but they outmatched their Egyptian and Sumerian peers in terms of population size, the sophistication of their cities and the sheer geographical reach of their civilization. At its height, there were Harappan settlements from Punjab in the north to Gujarat in the south, and from Baluchistan in the west to what is now western Uttar Pradesh in the east. We have even found outposts like Shortughai on the Afghanistan–Tajikistan border and Sutkagen-dor near Pakistan's border with Iran, not far from modern Gwadar.

The Maritime Hub of Dholavira

Given the maritime orientation of this book, we will focus here on the Harappan sites in the Indian state of Gujarat. To understand the context of the numerous archaeological discoveries in this area, let's begin with the landscape in which the Harappans built their settlements. First, western India was much wetter than it is today. Not only was monsoon rain stronger, the Rann of Kutchh received fresh water from both the Saraswati and the Indus. The estuary of the Indus was much further east than it is today and one of its major channels flowed into Kutchh. In fact, the Indus used to flow into Kutchh till as recently as the colonial period when a major earthquake in 1819 diverted the river. The fortress of the semi-abandoned town of Lakhpat still stands guard over the channel through which the Indus used to enter the Arabian Sea. Second, the relative sea level during Harappan times was several metres higher than it is today which meant that the Saurashtra peninsula was an island. Thus, ships could comfortably sail through what are now the salt flats and marshes of the Rann of Kutchh and then make their way out to the Gulf of Khambhat.[9]

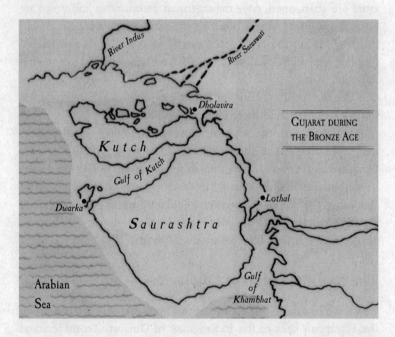

Dholavira may look today like it is too far inland to be an effective port but, as shown in the map, it was built on a strategically located island in the third millennium BC. It was accessible by boat from the Arabian Sea to the west as well as the Gulf of Khambhat to the south. Boats from Dholavira would have also been able to sail up the Indus and, at least initially, the Saraswati to the cities that were emerging along their banks. In other words, Dholavira would have served as a very important commercial, and possibly military, node.

There is evidence that by 2600 BC, the Saraswati began to dry up. We do not yet understand the exact factors that caused this, but tectonic shifts in northern India may have caused the Sutlej to shift to the Indus and the Yamuna to the Ganga. There is debate about exactly when the two tributaries shifted but it is reasonably certain that it happened well before the great cities of the mature period were built. This would have deprived the river of two important sources of perennial glacial water. Still, rainfall was quite heavy at first and a rain-fed but diminished Saraswati would have remained a significant river although, as time passed, it was no longer navigable all the way to Dholavira.

Interestingly, the mature period of the Harappan civilization seems to take off at a time that the Saraswati may have already started its decline. We see a sharp increase in villages and sophisticated urban settlements along both the Indus and the Saraswati during this time. It is unclear why the Harappans invested in building so many cities along a dying river. If we do not manage today's rivers sensibly, it is conceivable that future archaeologists will dig up the remains of twenty-first-century cities and wonder the same thing.

Meanwhile, the urban cluster at Dholavira expanded significantly. The site had a fortified acropolis and a 'lower town'. At some point the city was expanded to accommodate the growing population and the old lower town became the 'middle town' and the expanded area became the new lower town. A wooden signboard has been found near one of the gateways. We do not know what it says as the script has not been deciphered but my guess is that it's something mundane like: 'Keep Left for Bullock-Cart Parking'.

We see a proliferation of settlements in Gujarat during the mature period, in Kutchh as well as the island of Saurashtra. Of these sites, Lothal is one of the best known because of the discovery of a large dockyard which used sluice gates and a spill channel to regulate water levels. Next to the dockyard, there are remains of structures that may have been warehouses and a series of brick platforms where one can imagine stern customs officials inspecting the goods and unscrupulous merchants trying to bribe them.

Lothal is several kilometres away from the sea now and modern-day visitors will be surprised to know that it was once possible to sail from Dholavira to Lothal. In fact, it is quite possible that Lothal was a customs checkpoint for shipping headed north for Dholavira through the Gulf of Khambhat. There may have been a similar checkpoint for ships coming in from the west, perhaps at Bet Dwarka, where a number of Harappan-era anchors have been found.

In addition to internal trade, there is plenty of evidence that the Harappans had strong economic links with the Middle East. The merchant ships from Gujarat made their way along the Makran coast, trading along the way. They may have stopped near Gwadar to visit their outpost at Sutkagen-dor (near what is now the Pakistan–Iran border). A bit further west, they would have interacted with the people of the Jiroft civilization. This civilization has been recently discovered in south-eastern Iran. Although we know very little for sure about its people, archaeologists have found seals like those of the Harappans and signs of close cultural links.[10] In particular, several depictions of humped zebu cattle have been found in Bronze Age sites in southern Iran.[11] This is interesting because humped cattle have their origins in India and are common in Harappan iconography. In other words, the coastline from Gujarat to southern Iran was still a well-populated continuum with strong economic and cultural links. Were these links a result of Bronze Age trade or did the Jiroft people of southern Iran and the Harappans share a deeper ancestry going back to the Stone Age?

Some of the Harappans sailing to Iran would soon venture across the narrow strait to Oman. Archaeologists digging at Ras al-Junayz, on the eastern most tip of the Arabian peninsula, found that over 20 per cent of objects were of Harappan origin. There are a number of enigmatic beehive 'tombs' from this period scattered across Oman. Most of them are in areas that are too arid to sustain a population today but were much wetter in the Bronze Age. The builders of these structures would have almost certainly interacted with visiting Indian merchants. Many of these merchants would then have made their way further into the Persian Gulf and sailed to Bahrain where plenty of Harappan seals, pottery and beads have been found.[12]

Further west, Harappan-origin artefacts have also been found in ancient Mesopotamian cities like Kish, Nippur and Ur. The records of Akkadian king Sargon I (2334–2279 BC) refer to ships from Dilmun, Magan and Meluhha (i.e. Bahrain, Oman and the ports of Gujarat/ Sindh). However, note that the maritime route was not the only link between India and Mesopotamia. There were also land routes that made their way from the northern Harappan cities to Mesopotamia through Afghanistan and central Iran. There was also one that ran through Baluchistan and southern Iran along the Makran coast.

Trade with India had a big influence on the Persian Gulf area. For instance, Harappan weights and measures became the standard across the region. The locals also copied the Harappan seals. This was the beginning of a long commercial and cultural relationship that, despite booms and busts, continues to this day. Till as recently as the 1960s, the Indian rupee was used as legal tender in Oman, Qatar, Bahrain and the UAE! For a while, the Reserve Bank of India even issued a special Gulf rupee for use in these countries. It was only when the Indian rupee sharply devalued in June 1966 that these countries began to issue their own currencies (Bahrain had already made the shift a few years earlier).[13]

Today the most visible example of these links are the large numbers of Indians who live and work in the Gulf countries. This too has its origins in Harappan times. Mesopotamian inscriptions mention that the Meluhhans were numerous enough to have their own 'villages' or exclusive enclaves in and around Sumerian towns. We do not know for sure what these Indians were doing there— they could have been a mix of merchants, artisans and mercenaries—but they seem to have been an important part of the bustling economy of Bronze Age Mesopotamia. We also have a handful of references to individuals. For instance, there is a cylinder seal belonging to a

Meluhhan interpreter called Su-ilisu (of course, he may just have known a Harappan language and may not have been an Indian). Amusingly, we also know about a rowdy Meluhhan who was made to pay ten silver coins to someone called Urur as compensation for breaking his tooth in a brawl![14]

We have some idea of what the Harappans exported—carnelian beads, weights and measures, different types of wood, pots of ghee (clarified butter) and, most importantly, cotton textiles. The cotton plant was domesticated in India and cotton textiles would remain a major export throughout history. Oddly, we are not sure what the Harappans imported in exchange. Nothing of obvious Persian Gulf origin has ever been found in any Harappan site. Perhaps they imported perishables like dates and wine. Another possibility is that they imported copper from Oman as the remains of several ancient copper mines have been found there. The Harappans had their own copper sources such as Khetri near the Haryana–Rajasthan border, but the Gujarati Harappans may have preferred Omani copper.

Did the Harappans Compose the Vedas?

Despite the abundance of archaeological remains, we know little about the Harappans themselves. We are not sure what languages they spoke, what gods they worshipped, and their script remains stubbornly undecipherable. We do not even know if it was a unified empire or a network of independent city states that shared a civilization. These matters remain hot topics of acrimonious debate among academic historians.

The most obvious place to look for clues is the Rig Veda. It is the oldest and among the most sacred of Hindu scriptures. Composed in a very archaic form of Sanskrit, the Rig Veda was compiled over several generations by *rishis* and poet-philosophers, and remains in active use today. It contains ten 'books' of hymns and chants in praise of the gods. Although the text is mostly concerned with religious practice and philosophy, one can discern some things about the social and geographical context of those who composed the hymns.

The traditional view was that the Rig Veda was composed by so-called Aryans who came to India from Central Asia around 1500 BC. The problem is that the date is entirely arbitrary and there is no archaeological or genetic sign of a large-scale invasion/migration. The Rig Veda itself mentions no invasion/migration and suggests no knowledge of Central Asia. It is possible that its composers were aware of Central Asia and southern India, but the text does not mention it. Instead, its geographical horizons are mostly concerned with an area that it calls the Sapta Sindhu or Land of the Seven Rivers.

As discussed more fully in my previous book, *Land of the Seven Rivers: A Brief History of India's Geography*, the Sapta Sindhu was a relatively small area covering the modern-day state of Haryana and a few adjoining parts of Punjab and Rajasthan. This was the original homeland of the Bharata tribe that, according to the Rig Veda, defeated an alliance of ten tribes on the banks of the Ravi in Punjab. They then expanded their empire to the east by defeating a chieftain along the Yamuna. Thus, the Bharatas created the first known empire in the subcontinent and gave Indians the name by which they still call themselves. The text also suggests knowledge of a wider area including the Himalayas in the north, the Ganga on the east, the sea to the south and the rivers of what is now Pakistan's North-West Frontier Province. This roughly coincides with the geographical footprint of the Harappan civilization. So we have the remains of a large civilization and an extensive body of literature occupying the same geographical space during the Bronze Age. Surely it is not unreasonable to say that they belonged to the same people.

Given the genetic evidence discussed in the previous chapter, it would appear that most of the Harappan people were derived from the ANI gene pool who had coalesced in northern India around the end of the last Ice Age. However, given the large geographical spread and extensive trade links, it is likely that the civilization was multi-ethnic. The Rig Vedic people were part of the broader

Harappan milieu. The archaeological evidence suggests this as well. For instance, sacred fire altars have been identified at a number of places like Kalibangan whereas no large religious building has ever been found.[15] This is exactly what one should expect since we know that Vedic-era Hindus conducted elaborate fire sacrifices but did not build temples or worship idols.

There is an additional piece of evidence that one needs to consider. The Rig Veda repeatedly mentions the Saraswati River as the greatest of rivers.[16] It is clearly the most important geographical feature of the Vedic terrain. Forty-five hymns are dedicated to the river while the Ganga is barely mentioned twice. One of the hymns clearly places the river between the Yamuna and Sutlej—exactly where the dry riverbed of the Ghaggar is located. Importantly, the hymns describe a river in full flow and, unlike later texts, there is no mention of the river drying up. This would suggest that the text was certainly written before 2000 BC and most likely before 2600 BC— which would imply that we may be dealing with an early Harappan text. I am aware that some scholars will disagree but this is the simplest explanation from the available evidence. All other accounts inevitably require complicated explanations and implausible contortions. New information about this period is still flowing in and a clearer picture should emerge over the next decade.

The Churning of Genes

The great Harappan cities flourished till around 2000 BC when we see a sudden deterioration in economic and social conditions. It has now been confirmed by a series of studies that this was due to another shift in climate that also seems to have affected other Bronze Age civilizations. A study of an old lakebed in Haryana by scientists from Cambridge University found conclusive evidence that the summer monsoon abruptly became weaker 4100 years ago in north-west India.[17]

Note that this change in weather patterns in India was not an isolated incident as it coincides with similar shifts in Egypt and Mesopotamia where it caused great economic and political disruption. Iran's Jiroft civilization died out and was forgotten. Egypt's Old Kingdom collapsed and the country went back to being divided into Upper Egypt and Lower Egypt. In Mesopotamia, the Akkadian empire also collapsed around 2100 BC. A lamentation called 'The Curse of Akkad' describes what happened:[18]

> For the first time since cities were founded,
>> The great farmlands produced no grain,
>> The rivers produced no fish,
>> The irrigated orchards produced neither syrup nor wine,
>> The gathered clouds did not rain, the masgurum did not
> grow.
>> At that time, one shekel's worth of oil was only one-half
> quart,
>> One shekel's worth of grain was only one-half quart. . . .
>> These sold at such prices in the markets of all the cities!
>> He who slept on the roof, died on the roof,
>> He who slept in the house, had no burial,
>> People were flailing at themselves from hunger.

North-west India probably experienced something similar as monsoon rains failed. The Saraswati, already in decline, seems to have stopped flowing altogether. Post-Vedic texts tell us of how the river 'disappeared' underground. There is evidence that the Harappans tried to adapt to drier conditions by switching from high-yield wheat and barley to drought-resistant millets.[19] The problem was that the new crops had yields that could only support small rural communities but not large urban centres. The great Harappan cities were no longer tenable and were abandoned one by one as people migrated in search of water. Some groups would have shifted east into the Himalayan foothills and into the Gangetic plains. Those from Gujarat seem to have drifted south to the Narmada and Tapti valleys. Others would have drifted further afield.

These migrations show up clearly in the genetic records. The ANI and ASI populations suddenly go through a period of rapid mixing from around 2100 BC onward.[20] It is possible that this mixing was quickened by some ASI groups moving north at the same time that the ANI were moving south and east. The mixing of these two genetic pools is responsible for the bulk of India's present-day population. Of course, India is a large and diverse country and there are many groups that do not fit into this simple ANI–ASI framework but the coming together of these two populations is a very important event in the history of India and effectively triggers Indian civilization as we know it.

Genetic markers also suggest that this mixing went on for more than two thousand years, so much so that there are no 'pure' ANI and ASI any more. As a recent study put it: 'The most remarkable aspect of the ANI–ASI mixture is how pervasive it was, in the sense that it has left its mark in nearly every group in India. It has affected not just traditionally upper-caste groups, but also traditionally lower-caste and isolated tribes, all of whom are united in their history of mixture in the past few thousand years.'[21] In other words, after all this blending, the majority of Indians are most closely related to each other irrespective of their ancient origins. Sorry if this scientific finding offends any 'pure race' advocates!

Then, around AD 100 (a new study suggests AD 500[22]) the mixing abruptly stopped as different castes and tribes became strictly endogamous. The reasons for this are hazy, but castes do seem to be quite fluid in the oldest Indian texts and become much more rigid in later writings (although endogamous, the relative positions of most castes continued to be fluid into modern times). A fuller discussion on caste is beyond the scope of this book, but genetics has broadly confirmed the assertion by Dr Bhim Rao Ambedkar that the Indian caste system was a case of 'superimposition of endogamy on exogamy'.[23]

The migration of Harappans to the east and south would have spread their technologies and culture to these areas. Mainstream historians seem to assume that this implies a unidirectional flow of cultural and technological influence from the north-west of India to the east and south and then onward to South East Asia. This assumption is deep-rooted in Indian history writing but ends up giving a completely wrong impression. The reality is that there were already established populations and possibly even cities in the areas where the Harappans settled (a preliminary study hints that Varanasi may be as old as the Harappan cities).[24] Thus, plenty of influence flowed in reverse and Indian civilization is the result of a messy process where people, ideas and influences flowed in multiple directions—a bubbling mix and not a steam engine running on fixed rails. The people living in southern India may not have built sophisticated cities in the Bronze Age but it is they who initiated the Iron Age.

While northern Indians were building the great Harappan cities, southern Indians had continued to live in Neolithic settlements or as hunter–gatherer communities. The Bronze Age largely bypassed southern India, perhaps due to the paucity of copper ores in the region. Then, late in the third millennium BC, they did something amazing—they invented iron technology! The traditional view is that iron was introduced to India by invaders from Central Asia. Archaeological finds over the last two decades suggest instead that India was the likeliest place where iron was first mass produced.

Initially, the evidence pointed to the earliest use of the metal around the eighteenth century BC in the middle Gangetic plains but now it appears that it originated much further south and at a much earlier period. Students of the University of Hyderabad made a startling discovery in 2014–15 while doing excavations in their campus.[25] They found a number of iron artefacts, including weapons, that dated from around 2400–1800 BC. This is arguably the oldest systematic use of iron in the world. Far from being a military advantage exercised by Central Asian marauders, it appears that iron weaponry would have been an indigenous technological advantage.

The Indo-Iranians

So, if there was no 'invasion' from Central Asia, what explains the close cultural links between Vedic Indians and ancient Iranians? For instance, the oldest texts of Zoroastrianism, the religion of ancient Persia, are composed in a language very similar to Vedic Sanskrit. To this day, the Zoroastrians follow rituals and customs such as the fire sacrifice and the sacred thread that closely resemble Vedic tradition. As discussed in *Land of the Seven Rivers*, one possibility is that this similarity is derived from some Indian tribes that may have migrated west. Unlike the Vedic texts, ancient Iranians do refer to an 'original homeland'. They also seemed to have knowledge of the Saraswati River and of Sapta Sindhu. Perhaps the Persians are descendants of the Parsu tribe who were part of the ten-tribe alliance defeated by the Bharatas.

Another possibility is that the cultural links merely reflect the fact that the Iranians and north Indians were part of the same continuum until the Bronze Age. Given their geographical proximity, why does one need Central Asians to facilitate interaction? The location of the Jiroft civilization is particularly intriguing in this context because its sites are in south-east Iran and very close to the western most Harappan sites. Given the evidence of trade and use of zebu cattle, they may have been part of an ethnic continuum extending from north-west India. After 2000 BC, as eastern Iran and Baluchistan became increasingly hot and arid, the Jiroft people would have moved west towards Fars province. The ancient name of Fars is 'Parsa' and it is here that the Persians emerged as an identifiable people. Again notice that Fars is in southern Iran and not in the north as would be expected if they were migrants from Central Asia.

The Persians were not the only people with Vedic links in the Middle East. A military elite called the Mitanni migrated from the east into northern Iraq in the middle of the second millennium BC and came to dominate the region. In 1380 BC they entered into a treaty with the Hittites. The agreement was solemnized in the name of Vedic gods Indra, Varuna, Mitra and Nasatya. Perhaps it is no coincidence that the arrival of the Mitanni in the region also witnessed the introduction of a technology of Indian origin—iron. It is noteworthy that this is five centuries after the earliest mass production of iron took place in southern India.

Who were the Mitanni? Were they related to warrior tribes that, according to ancient Indian texts, migrated to the north-west and became 'mlechhas' or barbarians? Prior to the arrival of the Mitanni, iron was treated as a precious metal in the Middle East. Tiny quantities of meteorite iron were used to make prestige items in Anatolia (now Turkey) but large-scale extraction from ore was not known.[26] It is likely that the Mitanni used iron to carve out their empire in northern Iraq. However, their Hittite rivals soon mastered the technology and the two fought several wars for control of ore-rich areas.[27] The wars ended with the Hittites winning and, with the rise of the Assyrians, the Mitanni found themselves crushed between two powers in the thirteenth century BC. Nonetheless, the presence of a Vedic-related people using an Indian technology does suggest that some Indian tribes migrated out of India in the second millennium BC.

Let it be clear that I am not attempting to replace a unidirectional inward migration into India with a unidirectional outward migration. We are dealing with very long periods during which human and cultural movements would have gone in different directions for different reasons at different points of time. It appears that broadly the same genetic and/or cultural pool was sloshing back and forth between northern India and Iran since the Stone Age. At the end of the Ice Age, one branch colonized Central Asia from where a sub-branch migrated to Eastern Europe. Those who remained in Asia would have kept interacting. This sloshing may explain why the mixing of genes in India seems to happen in layers between the same groups.[28] Note that such non-linear movements are echoed in the later oral histories of many communities. The Gouda Saraswat Brahmins, for instance, claim to have migrated from the banks of the Saraswati River to Bengal and then later to the western coast of India. Long dismissed as myths, one wonders if these oral histories contain a memory of real population movements.

Interestingly, the Vedic–Mitanni god Mitra would remain a popular deity in the Middle East and, centuries later, would witness a major revival in the Roman empire (where he would be known as the solar god Mithras). The cult of Mithras would become very widespread in the late Roman period and, for a while, would provide serious competition to early Christianity. The pagan Romans used to celebrate a big festival called Saturnalia that went on for a week from 17 December. At the end of the festival, on the 25 December, the Mithras cult would celebrate the feast of Sol Invictus or Unconquered Sun. Many scholars believe that when the Christians came to dominate the Roman empire, they simply took over the popular pagan festival (after all, the actual birth date of Jesus Christ is not known).[29]

Mind you, not everyone agreed with this choice and the Orthodox Church still celebrates Christmas on 7 January. The Puritans would later disapprove of the unseemly heathen celebrations that clung to the festival and would try to ban Christmas in North America and Britain in the seventeenth and eighteenth centuries; they obviously thought that Merrie Olde England was a bit too merry.[30] Nevertheless, the 25 December holiday has survived as a day of festivity for most Christians and even non-Christians. Thus, one of the unintended consequences of early Iron Age migrations seems to be that the world has come to celebrate the birthday of an ancient god from Haryana!

The Ark of the Covenant

The collapse of the major Bronze Age cities around 2000 BC affected the thriving trade route between the Persian Gulf and India's western coast. By chance, the personal correspondence of a merchant in Ur, now Iraq, has survived in the ruins of his house and provides a direct view of how business networks may have begun to break down. The merchant, a certain Ea-Nasir, seems to have imported copper ingots from Magan (i.e. Oman) via Dilmun (i.e. Bahrain) around 1900 BC. Angry letters from his customers and creditors make for amusing reading after four thousand years although those who wrote the letters were clearly not amused. Here is one example from a business associate called Nanni:[31]

Now when you had come, you spoke saying this, 'I will give good ingots to Gimil-Sin.' This you said to me when you had

come. You have offered bad ingots to my messenger saying,
'If you will take it take it, if you will not take it go away.' Who
am I that you are treating me in this manner, treating me with
such contempt, and that between gentlemen such as we are.

Although new empires would later be re-established in Mesopotamia,
it would not resurrect the fortunes of Persian Gulf copper merchants
as Cyprus would replace Oman as the more important source. The
transition to the Iron Age would further reduce the importance of
Omani copper. Thus, Oman seems to have become a backwater.
Nonetheless, some trade must have continued to flow to the Indian
Ocean. We know this due to a most unusual artefact—the discovery
of black peppercorns stuffed up the nostrils of the mummy of Pharaoh
Ramses II. While we do not know if this condemned the pharaoh to
frequent sneezing in the afterlife, it shows that the Indian Ocean trade
networks of the thirteenth century BC were capable of transporting
pepper from its origin in south-western India to Egypt. Since it is
unlikely that sailors of this period could directly cross the Arabian Sea,
the spice was probably shipped up the coast from Kerala to Gujarat,
and then along the Makran coast to Oman. From here, there were
two possibilities. It could have continued along the old Persian Gulf
route to Mesopotamia and then overland to Egypt. However, it is just
as possible that pepper made its way south from Oman to Yemen and
Eritrea, a region that the ancient Egyptians called the Land of Punt.

We know that the ancient Egyptians sailed down the Red Sea
on frequent trading expeditions to the Land of Punt. One of the
expeditions is depicted on a panel at the memorial temple of Queen
Hatshepsut who ruled Egypt between 1473 and 1458 BC. Hatshepsut
is a fascinating character—a female pharaoh who dared to rule in her
own name. There are other female rulers in Egyptian history but she
overshadows them in terms of the scale of her building projects, her
military victories and, of course, her ambitious maritime expedition
to the Land of Punt.

The temple panels depict large galleys with sails, oars and stern-
side paddles for steering. They probably embarked from Wadi

Gawasis on Egypt's Red Sea coast where archaeologists have found coils of rope and cedar planks from that era.[32] From here they would have sailed down the Red Sea to what is now Yemen and Eritrea. The expedition would return with gold, ivory, different kinds of wood, exotic animals and, most importantly, frankincense (also perhaps Indian black pepper for stuffing up some mummy's nostrils).

Frankincense was a very valuable product of ancient Yemen and Oman. It is the dried resin of a thorny tree and gives off a pleasant smell when burned. It was widely used in religious ceremonies and is one of the gifts that the 'three wise men' are said to have brought for the baby Jesus. Even today, anyone visiting the Yemen–Oman coast will find it commonly sold in traditional markets and the smell of burning frankincense pervades shops, restaurants and homes.

So, who were the people who lived in the Land of Punt? Today we think of the Yemeni as being Arab but till the advent of Islam, south-eastern Arabia was home to a culture that was quite distinct from that of the rest of the peninsula. Its mountains and coasts were home to a number of related but constantly feuding tribes such as the Himyar, the Hadramawt and the Sabeans. Archaeologists have found as many as ten thousand inscriptions describing the lives, feuds, treaties and rulers of these tribes.

The Sabeans were one of the most powerful tribes. Around the eighth century BC, they created an empire that extended from Yemen into Eritrea and parts of Ethiopia. The Sabeans may have introduced wheat and barley to Ethiopia although a local cereal called 'teff' continues to be popular to this day. They also introduced their script which was originally written left-to-right and right-to-left on alternate lines; not such a silly idea if you think about it. The Sabean script would evolve into the Ge'ez script of the kingdom of Aksum and survives as the modern Ethiopian script (although it is now written exclusively left-to-right).

These early interactions between the Yemenis and the Egyptians would later extend to neighbouring lands and probably gave rise to the legend about King Solomon and Queen Sheba (i.e. Saba). According to the Ethiopian version of the legend, when

Queen Sheba returned after meeting Solomon in Jerusalem, she gave birth to a child named David. This child would grow up to be King Menelik I, founder of the Solomonic dynasty of Aksum. The legend also says that when David was a young man, he visited his father Solomon's court. At the time of departure, he stole the Ark of the Covenant and brought it back to Aksum. The Ark is supposed to be a wooden box covered in gold containing the two tablets received by Moses on which the Ten Commandments were inscribed by God himself.

Although there is no historical evidence supporting this story about Solomon, Sheba, Menelik and the stealing of the Ark, it has been part of the national founding myth of Ethiopia since the medieval 'Solomonic' dynasty came to power in AD 1262. The medieval dynasty promoted the story to give itself a biblical lineage and it would provide legitimacy to the royals till their rule ended in 1974 with Haile Selassie, the last emperor of Ethiopia. Nonetheless, the Ethiopian Orthodox Church claims that it is still in possession of the original Ark and replicas, known as *tabots*, continue to play an important role in religious festivals across the country.[33]

The Sundaland Diaspora

With all this migrating and churning going on in the western Indian Ocean rim, one adventurous band of Indians decided to be different and head east. They seem to have got into their boats somewhere on the country's eastern shore and sailed along the coast, past Sumatra and Java and eventually ended up in Australia! Recent genetic studies show that a bit more than 4000 years ago, a band of Indians turned up in Australia and contributed their DNA to the aborigines. This finding confounds the earlier belief that there were no new arrivals to the island continent between the initial migration of Melanesians 45,000 years ago and the arrival of the Europeans. Moreover, the new immigrants brought along their pets, the ancestors of the dingo dog.[34] This is possibly why the dingo looks suspiciously like the stray dogs one sees all over India.

The Indians were not the only people on the move in the region. As mentioned in the previous chapter, the coastlines of South East Asia witnessed major changes as Sundaland was inundated by the post-Ice Age floods. Recent genetic studies confirm that the region's current population landscape is heavily influenced by human migrations following the floods.[35] These South East Asian migrations involved two major ethnic groups—the Austronesians and the Austroasiatic. Someone with a dark sense of humour must have given them such similar names in order to purposely confuse future generations of researchers. To make it less confusing, let's call them AN and AA respectively. The AN included the ancestors of the Malays, Indonesians, Filipinos, Bruneians, Timorese and significant minorities in neighbouring countries. It also includes Taiwanese aborigines and the Polynesians spread across the Pacific. As one can see, they had a strong maritime culture.

It was once thought that this group originated in Taiwan but it now appears that they lived along the eastern coast of Sundaland and were forced by the floods to search for new homes. The outrigger canoe was an important part of their maritime culture. It is a simple design but clearly very effective as it allowed the AN to colonize most of the islands in South East Asia during the Neolithic period. Some of these islands may have had existing Melanesian populations who seem to have been squeezed into a smaller area in and around New Guinea and Fiji. A few centuries later, the eastern Polynesian branch of ANs would set out to colonize a swathe of islands across the Pacific—from New Zealand to Hawaii and Easter Island. Similarly, the western branch would sail across the Indian Ocean and settle in Madagascar. Thus the AN came to colonize a large swathe of the planet from Madagascar to Hawaii!

The speakers of AA languages were the other important ethnic group of South East Asia. They include the Vietnamese, Khmer (i.e. Cambodian) and the Mon in Myanmar and Thailand. Unlike their Malay and Polynesian cousins, however, this group seems to have preferred to migrate over the land rather than over sea. At some point, small groups of AAs drifted into north-east India. The descendants of these migrations are the Munda-speaking tribes, such as the Santhals, who are scattered all over eastern and central India. A somewhat later wave survives today as the Khasis of the state of Meghalaya. Thus it came to be that India's population mix includes people who speak languages related to Vietnamese and Khmer![36]

The folk tales and legends of South East Asia recall the Great Flood. For instance, the Laotian founding myth of Khun Borom tells us that the gods once became angry with the sinful and arrogant behaviour of humans and caused a flood that washed away all mortals. After the deluge they sent a buffalo that died and from its nostril grew a creeper that bore giant gourds. When the 'khun' (i.e. lords of heaven) cut open the gourds, a new generation of humans emerged from them with different gourds giving birth to different ethnic groups.[37]

The Laotian story is quite different from that of Noah or Manu, but it too remembers an earlier way of life that was destroyed by a huge flood and of how civilization had to be re-established. Similarly, the oral traditions of Australian aborigines also speak of swathes of coastline that were flooded. Till just a decade ago, it was common for scholars to dismiss indigenous oral histories as mere fantasy but latest research shows that they often contain folk memories of real events.[38]

The Daughters of Chitrangada

Matrilineal customs appear to have been an important feature of the AA-speaking groups migrating across South East Asia and into India's north-east. The Khasis of Meghalaya, for instance, remain matrilineal to this day. Traces of matrilineal customs seem to have been imbibed even by neighbouring communities that may never have been matrilineal. For instance, in Assamese Hindu weddings, the 'sindoor' (red vermilion) is applied to the forehead of the bride by the mother-in-law at the 'jurun' ceremony that precedes the wedding. The act of applying sindoor is a key part of Hindu marriage rituals and is usually the prerogative of the husband. The performance of this rite by the groom's mother symbolizes the women of the family accepting a new member—a very matrilineal view of a wedding.

So why were the AAs matrilineal? The answer to this riddle is found in the study of the genetics of the AA groups. It appears that the Indian branch is the result of almost exclusively male migrations.[39] At the risk of oversimplifying, one could say that groups like the Santhals and Khasis are the result of male migrants from South East Asia marrying local women. This fits in with the hypothesis offered in the previous chapter of matrilineal customs emerging in South East Asia due to a Neolithic male population that was relatively more mobile than the female population. We do not know exactly what drove these migrations but this movement was not quite one of conquest since the incoming males seem to have accepted the property rights of the local women.

It is fascinating that the Iron Age epic Mahabharata hints at the matrilineal streak in India's north-east. It tells us how the exiled prince Arjun visited the kingdom of Manipur. There he met the warrior princess Chitrangada and married her. However, note that the marriage took place on the explicit condition that Chitrangada would not have to follow Arjun back home as she and her children were heirs to the throne. Again notice the easy acceptance of a male outsider combined with the rootedness of the local female. The story does not end here. Ulupi, the queen of a neighbouring Naga tribe,[40] also falls in love with Arjun and kidnaps him. The epic then tells us of how Arjun is eventually restored to Chitrangada.

We are not concerned here about the historical veracity of this story. What is interesting for our purposes is the portrayal of two strong female characters and a social context that is different from that of the Gangetic heartland. It appears that the Iron Age composers of the Mahabharata, based in the north-west of India, were aware that the status of women was different in the north-east. Manipur remains home to formidable women including Mary Kom, five-time world boxing champion. The daughters of Chitrangada are alive and well.

4

Kharavela's Revenge

A number of sites in the central Gangetic plains have shown that iron implements were being used by 1700 BC but 'the quantity and types of iron artefacts, and the level of technical advancement indicate that the introduction of iron working took place even earlier'.[1] Recent discoveries near Hyderabad have confirmed that iron technology was indeed fairly well understood by the time it was adopted by northern India.

By 1300 BC, the use of iron had become commonplace across north and central India. This is also a time that India embarks on a new round of urbanization. The epics Ramayana and Mahabharata mention several of the cities that emerged during this period. One can debate whether or not the stories in the texts are loosely based on actual events, but there is adequate evidence that many of the places were real. Some of these Iron Age cities, such as Varanasi, have survived as urban centres till today.

It is during the Iron Age that two major highways came to connect the subcontinent. The first is an east–west road called Uttara Path (i.e. Northern Road) that ran from eastern Afghanistan, across the Gangetic plains to the ports of Bengal. This road would be repaired and rebuilt throughout Indian history and survives today as National Highway 1 between Amritsar and Delhi and as National Highway 2 between Delhi and Kolkata.

The second was a north–south highway called the Dakshina Path (i.e. Southern Road). This was more like a tangled network that started around the Allahabad–Varanasi section of the Gangetic plains and made its way in a south-westerly direction to Ujjain. Here it split into two with one branch going to the ports of Gujarat and the other branch making its way further south via Pratishthana (Paithan) to Kishkindha in Karnataka and beyond. People, goods and ideas would have made their way across India on these highways. It is no coincidence that many of the events described in the epics took place along them. Even if the narrative is fictional (or considerably embellished), many of the places are real enough.[2] In the sixth century BC, Gautam Buddha would preach his first sermon at Sarnath, the spot where the two ancient highways met. To this day, two of India's most important highways (NH2 and NH7) meet here.

Kingdoms of the Lion

The injection of Indian DNA into Australia around 2000 BC shows that people living on India's eastern seaboard were capable of sailing long distances even before the Iron Age. Archaeologists have found remains of a possible river port at a place called Golbai Sasan in Odisha that dates back to 2300 BC.[3] However, there is a distinct boom in coastal trade from around 800 BC. At the heart of this maritime boom was Kalinga (roughly modern Odisha) and the adjoining areas of West Bengal.

The remains of many ancient ports have been found all along the coast between the western most mouth of the Ganga and Chilika lake. The river connected the seaports to the kingdoms of the interior while the lake, which has an outlet to the sea, acted as a safe harbour. You will find bits of ancient pottery strewn everywhere if you walk along the banks of Chilika lake.

The Bengali–Odiya mariners were not capable of sailing directly across the Indian Ocean at this early stage. Instead, they would have hugged the shore and traded their way down the Andhra and Tamil coast. At some stage they seem to have sailed across to Sri Lanka and begun to settle there. Genetic studies have confirmed that the island was already inhabited by the ancestors of the Vedda, a small tribe that has long been suspected of being the original inhabitants.[4] They are probably descendants of people who had migrated here before the Great Flood separated them from the mainland. The new migrants from eastern India, however, would soon become the dominant population—the Sinhalese.

The *Mahavamsa*, an epic written in Pali, tells the founding myth of how the Sinhalese came to Sri Lanka.[5] It is said that at the beginning of the sixth century BC, the king of Vanga (i.e. Bengal) had a beautiful daughter who was kidnapped by a powerful lion. He kept the princess prisoner in a cave and had a son and daughter by her. The son Sinhabahu grew up to be a strong lad. One day, when the lion was away, he broke open the cave-prison and escaped with his mother and sister. The lion followed in hot pursuit. Eventually, after several adventures, Sinhabahu faced his father and killed him.

Sinhabahu then established a kingdom and built a capital city Sinhapura, which means Lion City (notice that this is derived from the same etymological roots as Singapore). Many years passed and Sinhabahu had a son called Vijaya who turned out to be a violent lout and a disgrace to the family. My guess is that he inherited that from the paternal grandfather. After hearing repeated complaints from his subjects, King Sinhabahu eventually decided to banish Vijaya and 700 of his supporters. So, Vijaya sailed south and landed in Sri Lanka. There he faced some resistance from the locals, presumably the Vedda, led by a woman called Kuveni. However, Vijaya prevailed and established his kingdom. The *Mahavamsa* tells us that King Vijaya now gave up his earlier erratic behaviour and ruled responsibly for thirty-eight years. He also married a Tamil princess from the Pandya clan.

The legend of Prince Vijaya should not be taken literally; I have always harboured some doubts about the bit related to the lion kidnapping the princess. Nevertheless, the epic makes it clear that the Sinhalese retained a memory of their Bengali–Odiya origins when the *Mahavamsa* was composed and compiled almost a thousand years later.

The Sinhalese link to eastern India matches genetic, linguistic and cultural evidence and survives in many little ways. For example, the lion is an important symbol of the Sinhalese people; they are literally the Lion People. One finds this echoed in Odisha which remains a major centre for the worship of Narasimha (the god Vishnu as half-lion and half-man). The town of Puri is famous for the temple of Jagannath, another form of Vishnu, but also has a very ancient temple to Narasimha and there are several rituals where the latter is given precedence to this day. Similarly, in Bengal, the goddess Durga is almost always depicted as riding a lion. In other words, the lion on the Sri Lankan flag and Durga's lion share the same cultural origins.

The clinching evidence on the origins of the Sinhalese, however, comes from another custom. Robert Knox, an Englishman who spent many years in Sri Lanka in the seventeenth century, made the following observation: 'In their infancy they have names whereby one may be called and distinguished from the other; but, when they come to years, it is an affront and shame to them, either men or women, to be called by those names.'[6] Bengali and Odiya readers will know exactly what this means.

Did the Phoenicians Circumnavigate Africa?

At the same time that settlers from Kalinga were colonizing Sri Lanka, a Greek historian called Herodotus was writing a remarkable book, *The Histories*, which is the first known attempt to systematically research and write down a historical narrative. Like a modern-day researcher, he weighed the evidence and often disbelieved what he was told. This does not mean that Herodotus is always right or unbiased (he seems to have a pro-Athenian tilt), but the approach is quite different from simply listing out the achievements of a powerful ruler or composing epics about heroic characters.

Herodotus is said to have been born around 484 BC near modern-day Bodrum, Turkey. In his book, he gives us a glimpse of what the people of the Mediterranean thought of the world of the Indian Ocean, which the ancient Greeks called the Erythraean Sea. The Persian Achaeminid empire of this period stretched from Egypt to the western bank of the Indus, and was constantly threatening the Greek city states. Since a large contingent of Indian soldiers was part of the Imperial army, Herodotus seems to have been familiar with Indians.

The Histories tells us that the Indian soldiers wore cotton clothes and carried bows and arrows made of cane and tipped with iron.[7] We are also told that the Indians had horses and chariots. While this description of Indian soldiers sounds true enough, Herodotus's knowledge of India itself is a garbled mix of fact and fiction that seems to have been picked up from different sources. He is aware that India is a large and populous country where numerous languages are spoken. He also recounts a Persian expedition that sailed down the Indus and made its way to Egypt through the Red Sea. This was probably an established trade route by this time. It seems to have been commercially important enough for Herodotus to have referred to a canal being built to connect the Red Sea to the Nile—an early Suez Canal!

Nevertheless, the Greeks seemed to believe that India was the eastern most inhabited country and that there were only oceans and deserts beyond it. The Persians probably fed them fabulous tales about the exotic East. Herodotus recounts the method by which the Indians were believed to mine gold. There was said to be a sandy desert in India inhabited by giant ants 'in size somewhat smaller than dogs, but bigger than foxes'. When these ants burrowed their nests into the ground, they dug out sand that was rich in gold. The Indians therefore made their way into the desert on camels to collect the sand in the mid day sun. However, the ants were dangerous and one had to collect the sand quickly and escape. We are categorically told that female camels were faster than the males, and should be preferred for the operation as there is a risk that the ants may come chasing after the gold diggers. Now, this is the kind of useful information one should always remember if one wants to avoid being eaten alive by rampaging giant ants.

Herodotus seems to have been told another tall tale by the Arabs about their sources of cinnamon. The cinnamon sticks were evidently collected by giant birds that used them to build nests high up on a sheer cliff. The Arabs claimed that they left large chunks of meat at the foot of the cliffs so that birds would pick them up and take them to their nests. However, the weight of the heavy meat pieces would often cause the nests to break and fall, and the Arabs would then collect the cinnamon. Various versions of this story would be used over the next fifteen hundred years by Indian Ocean merchants to conceal their sources. A version of it would make it into the Arabian Nights as the tale of Sindbad, the roc and the valley of diamonds.

While Herodotus thought that the descriptions of giant birds and ants were plausible, his book also includes stories that he finds implausible. One of these is about a Phoenician fleet said to have sailed around Africa. The fleet set out from the Red Sea and sailed down the coast of East Africa. At this stage they may not have been in entirely unfamiliar territory as Herodotus suggests that the Phoenicians had migrated to the Mediterranean from the Indian Ocean rim. In autumn they went ashore and sowed a tract of land with corn. Having replenished their food stocks with the harvest, they set sail again and in this way made it back after three years to the Mediterranean through the Straits of Gibraltar.

If true, this expedition would suggest that the ancients had gone around the Cape of Good Hope a good two thousand years before Vasco Da Gama! Herodotus, however, did not believe the story because of a minor detail—the Phoenicians insisted that when they made the turn at the bottom of Africa, the sun was to their right. Herodotus thought that this claim was just too absurd but we know that this is exactly what one should expect south of the Tropic of Capricorn. In other words, the ancient explorers may have been telling the truth!

The War Elephants

The history of ancient Greek city states is dominated by their conflicts with the Persian empire, the superpower of that time. The rivalry culminated in a large-scale Greek–Macedonian invasion led by Alexander III of Macedon, better known as Alexander the Great. After winning a series of battles in the Levant and conquering Egypt, Alexander's army decisively defeated the Persians led personally by Darius III in 331 BC at Gaugamela (near modern Mosul, northern Iraq). Roman-era historian Arrian mentions a contingent of Indian cavalry that fought for the Persian cause and continued to put up fierce resistance even after Darius had fled the battlefield. Not counting the Mitanni, this is the first explicit mention of Indian soldiers fighting in Iraq and it would not be the last. It is also interesting that the Indians were participating as cavalrymen because an early version of the stirrup was invented in India around this time.[8] One wonders if it was used by the Indian horsemen in this battle.

The victory at Gaugamela would have been enough to establish Alexander's control over the Persian empire, but he dreamed of conquering the whole known world. Thus, in the winter of 327–326 BC, he led his army through Afghanistan towards India. Along the way he subdued several small kingdoms including Massaga, probably in what is now eastern Afghanistan or Pakistan's North-West Frontier Province. The Massagan army had 7000 Indian mercenaries who put up a fierce resistance but the royal family finally agreed to Alexander's terms of surrender. The terms included a condition that the mercenaries would join the Macedonian invasion of India. Unfortunately, the Indians had not been consulted before the agreement and they refused to fight against their own countrymen. Alexander responded by massacring all of them.[9]

He next marched into the plains of Punjab where he and his local allies defeated Porus (probably relates to the Puru tribe who had lived in this area since Vedic times). Alexander wanted to keep pushing east but his troops were weary and wanted to go home. There were also rumours of a large army being mobilized by the Nandas of Magadh (roughly modern Bihar). The conqueror was forced by a near rebellion to change plans and decided to return home by sailing down the Indus on the mistaken belief that the river became the Nile in its lower reaches. In other words, the Macedonians thought that if they simply sailed down the Indus, they would end up in the Mediterranean. They seem to have reached this conclusion based on certain similarities between the flora and fauna of India and that of the upper reaches of the Nile. Arrian mentions crocodiles and a certain variety of beans, but it is quite likely that elephants added to the confusion. It is also likely that they misunderstood Herodotus's account of the Persian expedition that sailed down the Indus and then made its way to Egypt through the Red Sea.

Whatever the real reason for the decision, Alexander's army pillaged their way down the Indus till they arrived on the shores of the Arabian Sea in 325 BC. As already mentioned, the main channel of the river used to flow much further east of its current location and it is likely that the Macedonians reached the sea around Lakhpat in Kutchh. Having realized his mistake, Alexander sent back part of the army by sea following the old Harappan coastal route to the Persian Gulf. However, perhaps due to the lack of boats, he marched the bulk of his army through the deserts of Baluchistan and eastern Iran.

It was a very bad choice and thousands of soldiers died from hunger and thirst in the stark, barren landscape. Much of the plunder from years of campaigning had to be abandoned as most of the pack animals died. Alexander's army arrived in Mesopotamia undefeated but decimated. Recall that the same Persian Gulf–Gujarat stretch had been frequently crossed by early humans as they populated the world but climate change had now rendered it virtually uninhabitable. The Greeks found that the only people who survived in this dry, inhospitable Makran coast were the Ichthyophagi or 'fish-eaters'.

Alexander died soon after his return to Babylon, possibly poisoned by members of the Macedonian elite who had come to fear his increasingly erratic behaviour. His young son was later murdered and the generals divided up the empire among themselves. However, Alexander's brief incursion into the Indian subcontinent had an unintended consequence. A scholar called Chanakya and his protégé Chandragupta Maurya took advantage of the political confusion caused by the invasion to carve out a power base in India's north-west. After several attempts, they defeated the Nanda king of Magadh and created the foundations for the powerful Mauryan empire. In 305 BC, Chandragupta defeated Seleucus Nikator, the general who had taken over most of Alexander's Asian possessions.

The treaty between Seleucus and Chandragupta handed the Indians a large chunk of territory extending over Afghanistan and Baluchistan. One of Seleucus's daughters was also given in marriage to a Mauryan prince, perhaps Chandragupta himself or his son Bindusara. Seleucus, in return, received a gift of 500 Indian war elephants and their mahouts.

In the Battle of Ipsus, 301 BC, Seleucus used these elephants with devastating effect against rival generals and established himself as the most powerful of Alexander's successors. Thereafter, elephants became the symbol of the Seleucid empire and Seleucus was often depicted on coins seated on elephant-drawn chariots.[10] Given the importance of the animal in his war machine, he tried to ensure control over the supplies of war elephants from India. Ptolemy, the rival general who had taken control of Egypt, tried to circumvent the blockade by sourcing African elephants from the Kushites of Ethiopia. We have records of repeated expeditions sent to acquire the beasts from Ethiopia and of special boats being built to transport them. These elephants were not considered as good for combat as their Indian equivalents and the Kushites seem not to have been conversant in the art of training them for battle. Thus, the Ptolemies eventually smuggled in Indian mercenaries, probably by the Red Sea route, to train and man their war elephants.

Ashoka, the Not so Great

Chandragupta abdicated in 298 BC (or 303 BC according to another source) in favour of his son Bindusara who ruled till 273 BC. Bindusara had inherited an empire that was already very large—from Afghanistan to Bengal. He seems to have extended the realm further south till the empire covered all but the southern tip of the peninsula. For the most part, his rule seems to have been peaceful except for a few rebellions. He also seems to have maintained diplomatic and trade links with the kingdoms carved out from Alexander's empire.

In 274 BC, Bindusara suddenly fell ill and died. The crown prince Sushima was away fending off incursions on the north-western frontiers and rushed back to the imperial capital Pataliputra, present-day Patna. However, on arrival he found that Ashoka, one of his half-brothers, had taken control of the city with the help of Greek mercenaries.[11] It appears that Ashoka had Sushima killed at the eastern gates. The crown prince may have been roasted alive in the moat! This was followed by four years of a bloody civil war in which Ashoka seems to have killed all male rivals in his family. Buddhist texts mention that he killed ninety-nine half-brothers and only spared his full brother Tissa. Hundreds of loyalist officials were also killed; Ashoka is said to have personally decapitated 500 of them.[12] Having consolidated his power, he was finally crowned emperor in 270 BC.

All accounts agree that Ashoka's early rule was brutal and unpopular, and that he was known as 'Chandashoka' or Ashoka the Cruel. According to mainstream textbook narratives, however, Ashoka would invade Kalinga a few years later and, shocked by the death and destruction, would convert to Buddhism and become a pacifist. The reader will be surprised to discover that the popular narrative about this conversion is based on little evidence. Ashoka would invade Kalinga in 262 BC whereas we know from minor rock edicts that Ashoka had converted to Buddhism more than two years earlier. No Buddhist text links his conversion to the war and even Ashoka's eulogists like Charles Allen agree that his conversion predated the Kalinga war. Moreover, he seems to have had links with Buddhists for a decade before his conversion. The evidence suggests that his conversion to Buddhism was more to do with the politics of succession than with any regret he felt for sufferings of war.

The Mauryans were likely to have followed Vedic court rituals (certainly many of their top officials were Brahmins) but had eclectic religious affiliations in personal life. The founder of the line, Chandragupta, seems to have had links to the Jains in old age while his son Bindusara seems to have been partial to a heterodox sect called the Ajivikas. This is not an unusual arrangement in the Dharmic (i.e. Indic) family of religions. This eclectic approach remains alive to this day and lay followers of Dharmic religions think nothing of praying at each other's shrines. You will find many Hindus at the Golden Temple in Amritsar just as the streets of Bangkok are full of shrines dedicated to the Hindu god Brahma. The coronation of the king of Thailand is still carried out by Brahmin priests.

It is likely that when Ashoka usurped the throne, he was opposed by family members who had links to the Jains and the Ajivikas. He may have responded by reaching out to their rivals, the Buddhists, for support. The power struggle may even explain his invasion of Kalinga. The mainstream view is that Kalinga was an independent kingdom that was invaded by Ashoka but there is some reason to believe that it was either a rebellious province or a vassal that was no longer trusted.

We know that the Nandas, who preceded the Mauryas, had already conquered Kalinga and, therefore, it is likely that it became part of the Mauryan empire when Chandragupta took over the Nanda kingdom. In any case, it seems odd that a large and expansionist empire like that of the Mauryas would have tolerated an independent state so close to its capital Pataliputra and its main port at Tamralipti. In other words, Kalinga would not have been an entirely independent kingdom under Bindusara—it was either a province or a close vassal. Something obviously changed during the early years of Ashoka's reign and my guess is that it had either sided with Ashoka's rivals during the battle for succession or declared itself independent in the confusion.

Whatever the real reasons for attracting Ashoka's ire, a large Mauryan army marched into Kalinga around 262 BC. The traditional view is that the two armies met on the banks of the River Daya at Dhauli near modern Bhubaneswar. It is possible that Dhauli was the site of a skirmish but recent archaeological excavations point to a place called Yuddha Meruda being the site of the main battle followed by a desperate and bloody last stand at the Kalingan capital of Tosali.[13]

The remains of Tosali were discovered only recently by a team of archaeologists led by Debraj Pradhan, a humble and affable man who has made some extraordinary discoveries about Odisha's ancient past. The site is at a place called Radhanagar, a couple of hours' drive from Cuttack. It is situated in a broad fertile plain watered by the Brahmani River and surrounded by low hills. Surveying the beautiful valley from one of the hills, one is overwhelmed by a feeling of eternity— rice fields, fish ponds, coconut palms, mango trees, and thin wisps of woodsmoke rising from village huts. Other than a few power transmission towers, the scene is perhaps close to what it would have looked to Mauryan generals planning their final assault.

The remains of the city's earthwork defences suggest that Tosali was built in the middle of the plains; arguably a poor choice as the city's defences would have been better served if they were wedged more closely to one of the hills. Archaeologists have only excavated a small section of the walls but have found it riddled with arrowheads; a blizzard of arrows must have been unleashed by the Mauryan army. The Kalingans never stood a chance. Ashoka's own inscriptions tell us that 100,000 died in the war and an even larger number died from wounds and hunger. A further 150,000 were taken away as captives.

According to the official storyline, Ashoka was horrified by his own brutality and became a Buddhist and a pacifist. But, as we have seen, he was already a practising Buddhist by then, and from what we know of his early rule, he was hardly a man to be easily shocked by the sight of blood. The main evidence of his repentance comes from his own inscriptions. It is very curious, however, that this 'regret' is mentioned only in locations far away from Odisha (such as in Shahbazgarhi in north-western Pakistan). None of the inscriptions in Odisha express any remorse; any hint of regret is deliberately left out.

The Ashokan inscriptions at Dhauli are engraved on a rock at the base of a hill. Almost all tourists drive right past it to the white-coloured modern stupa at the top of the hill. So I found myself alone with the inscriptions and the translations put up by the Archaeological Survey of India. What will strike anyone reading them is how they specifically leave out any sign of regret. The silence is deafening.

If Ashoka was genuinely remorseful, he would have surely bothered to apologize to the people whom he had wronged. Far from it, he doesn't even offer to free the captives. Even the supposedly regretful inscriptions include a clear threat of further violence against other groups like the forest tribes who are unequivocally 'told of the power to punish them that Devanampriya possesses in spite of his repentance, in order that they may be ashamed of their crimes and may not be killed'.[14] This is no pacifist.

It is likely that Ashoka was using his inscriptions as a tool of political propaganda to counter his reputation for cruelty. As with the words of any politician, this does not mean he changed his behaviour. Moreover, many of the inscriptions are placed in locations where the average citizen or official of that time would not have been able to read them. Several historians including Nayanjot Lahiri have wondered about this. Is it possible that some of the inscriptions were really meant for later generations rather than his contemporaries?

The Buddhist text, Ashokavadana, tells us of more acts of genocide perpetrated by the emperor many years after he supposedly turned pacifist.[15] These were directed particularly at followers of the Jain and Ajivika sects; by all accounts he avoided conflicts with mainstream Hindus and was respectful towards Brahmins. The Ashokavadana recounts how Ashoka once had 18,000 Ajivikas in Bengal put to death in a single episode. If true, this would be the first known instance of large-scale religious persecution in Indian history (but, sadly not the last).

This is not the only incident mentioned in the text. A Jain devotee was found in Pataliputra drawing a picture showing Buddha bowing to a Jain tirthankara. Ashoka ordered him and his family to be locked inside their home and for the building to be set alight. He then ordered that he would pay a gold coin in exchange for every decapitated head of a Jain. The carnage only ended when someone mistakenly killed his only surviving brother, the Buddhist monk Vitashoka (also called Tissa). The story suggests frightening parallels with modern-day fundamentalists who kill cartoonists whom they accuse of insulting their religion.

Supporters of Ashoka may claim that these incidents are untrue and were inserted into the story by fundamentalist Buddhist writers in much later times. While this is entirely possible, let me remind readers that my alternative narrative is based on exactly the same texts and inscriptions used to praise Ashoka. Perhaps the same scepticism should be evenly applied to all the evidence and not just to portions of the text that do not suit the mainstream narrative.

In addition to the references of his continued cruelty, we also have reason to believe that Ashoka was not a successful administrator. In his later years, an increasingly unwell Ashoka watched his empire disintegrate from rebellion, internal family squabbles and fiscal stress. While he was still alive, the empire had probably lost all the north-western territories that had been acquired from Seleucus. Within a few years of Ashoka's death in 232 BC, the Satvahanas had taken over most of the territories in southern India and Kalinga too had seceded.

As one can see, Ashoka does not look like such a great king on closer inspection but a cruel and unpopular usurper who presided over the disintegration of a large and well-functioning empire built by his father and grandfather. At the very least, it must be accepted that evidence of Ashoka's greatness is thin and he was some shade of grey at best. Perhaps like many politicians, he made grand high-minded proclamations but acted entirely differently. This fits with the fact that he is not remembered as a great monarch in the Indian tradition but in hagiographic Buddhist texts written in countries that did not experience his reign. He was 'rediscovered' in the nineteenth century by colonial-era orientalists like James Prinsep. His elevation to being 'Ashoka the Great' is even more recent and is the result of political developments leading up to India's independence.[16]

After Independence, it appears academic historians were further encouraged to build up the legend of Ashoka the Great in order to provide a lineage to Jawaharlal Nehru's socialist project and inconvenient evidence was simply swept under the carpet.[17] This is not so different from how the medieval Ethiopians created a biblical lineage for the Solomonic dynasty. A few Western writers like Charles Allen have patronizingly written how ancient Indians were somehow foolish to have had little regard for a great king such as Ashoka. On a closer look, it appears that they knew what they were doing. What is more worrying is how easily modern Indians have come to accept a narrative based on such minimal evidence.

Mauryan Trade Routes

The establishment of a large united empire across the subcontinent would have led to a spurt in internal trade along both the northern and southern highways. In his treatise *Arthashastra*, Chanakya (also called Kautilya) has left us his opinion on the relative merits of trading along the Uttara Path and the Dakshina Path.[18] The text tells us that earlier scholars had a preference for the northern highway but Chanakya makes the case that the southern route was a much better source of all goods except horses and woollen cloth. Perhaps this reflects the changing economic dynamics of the subcontinent by the fourth century BC. Note that Chanakya specifically mentions diamonds, a gemstone that was at that time only found in peninsular India; a product of the volcanic processes that also created the Deccan plateau.

Meanwhile, maritime trade continued to do well. Ships would have sailed out of the ports of Gujarat and sailed along the Makran coast to the Persian Gulf while a branch would have made its way into the Red Sea. We know that Bindusara was in touch with Alexander's successors in the Middle East. He once asked Seleucus's successor Antiochus for figs, wine and a Greek philosopher. Antiochus sent the figs and the wine but politely refused to send the philosopher on the grounds that Greek law forbade the sale of scholars! So, what did Bindusara send in return? We know that Antiochus used Indian war elephants to fend off a major invasion by Gauls into Anatolia (modern-day Turkey). So it is quite likely that he was being supplied elephants and their mahouts by Bindusara. In other words, the Greeks had continued the Persian practice of using Indian soldiers although they had shifted from horsemen to mahouts for war elephants.

Ashoka too maintained the links with the Greek rulers of the Middle East. His thirteenth edict mentions that he sent missionaries to Antiyoka (Antiochus of Syria), Turamaya (Ptolemy of Egypt), Antikini (Antigonus of Macedonia), Maka (Magas of Cyrene) and Alikasundara (Alexander of Corinth). The Indian rendering of these ancient Greek names is interesting in itself.[19] Maritime trade was also active along the eastern coast and the same edict mentions the Cholas and Pandyas of Tamil country. The port of Tamralipti in Bengal was thriving during this period and it is probably from here that Ashoka's son Mahinda set sail for his mission to Sri Lanka.

Despite all these maritime linkages, let us not forget that sailing the seas was still dangerous business. The *Arthashastra* tells us that Chanakya preferred coastal and river routes over those crossing the high seas as he considered them too dangerous. The use of the monsoon winds had still not been mastered at this stage and it was considered foolhardy to sail too far from the coast. Or perhaps it was just a landlubber's suspicion of the deep ocean! Nonetheless, it is interesting that he mentions this at all as it suggests that there were some mariners in the fourth century BC who were confident enough to try transoceanic routes.

Kharavela's Revenge

Ashoka's successors tried hard to stabilize the empire after his death. It appears that they all distanced themselves from Ashoka's aggression and tried to mend relations across groups. Ashoka's immediate successor was Dasharatha who reached out to the Ajivikas and constructed the rock-cut Nagarjuni and Barabar caves for the sect.[20] These are located near Gaya, Bihar, and are the oldest rock-cut shrines in India. After Dasharatha, the empire seems to have broken up rapidly. One of Ashoka's sons or grandsons, Jalauka, carved out an independent kingdom in Kashmir where he promoted Shaivite Hinduism. In Pataliputra, the teenage Samprati took over the crown but was forced by intra-family feuds to shift to Ujjain.

Meanwhile, the Satvahanas began to take over the southern territories of the empire. They seem to have been from Andhra country and called themselves the 'Andhra-bhritya' or servants of the Andhras.[21] The modern Indian state of Andhra Pradesh is named after them although, ironically, the most likely location of their origin is now in the breakaway state of Telangana.

The Satvahanas would set up their capital at Pratishthana (modern Paithan), in present-day Maharashtra, a major node on the southern highway, and would take on the title 'Lords of Dakshina Path'. For some inexplicable reason, Indian's post-independence historians and archaeologists ignored the Satvahanas and it was only in 2015 that the government finally decided to re-examine sites that had been identified over a century ago by colonial-era researchers.[22]

As the Satvahanas expanded north, they came in conflict with the Indo-Greeks and Sakas (Scythians) who had taken over north-western India and were now trying to take control of the ports of Gujarat. An inscription in Nasik tells us of the Satvahana king Gautamiputra Satakarni who defeated and pushed back the Greeks and Scythians.

The invaders, however, seem to have met with less resistance from the later Mauryans and we see them making raids deeper and deeper into the Gangetic plains. Taking advantage of the situation, Kalinga rebelled and seceded under the leadership of the Chedi clan. Around 193 bc, a remarkable military leader called Kharavela came to the throne of Kalinga. We know about him because of a long inscription at Hathigumpha, or Elephant's Cave.[23]

We are told that in the early years of his reign, he led a large army against the Satvahanas and secured his western frontiers. Around 185 bc he seems to have marched north into Magadh where he defeated the invading Indo-Greek king Demetrius and forced him to retreat to Mathura. The irony is that the Kalingan army must have gone on this campaign on the invitation of the Mauryas who could no longer fend off the marauding foreign invaders who had reached their gates.

Kharavela realized that the old empire was on its last legs and four years later he returned with a large army and sacked the Mauryan capital. He tells us proudly that he brought back the Jain idols that had been taken away to Pataliputra at the time of the Nanda kings and that he made King Bahasatimita (probably the last Mauryan king Brihadhrata) bow to him. With the prestige of the Mauryas in tatters, the last emperor would be deposed by his general Pushyamitra Sunga who founded a new dynasty that would later re-establish control over most of north and central India.

Remember that Ashoka's brutal invasion has taken place only three generations earlier and would have still been fresh in Odiya memory. So, when Kharavela returned from his Magadh campaign, he had his exploits inscribed on a rock on Udayagiri hill, now effectively a suburb of Bhubaneswar. The hill has a number of beautifully carved caves cut into the hillside for the use of Jain monks. If one climbs up the hill and stands in front of Hathigumpha and looks out over Bhubaneswar, one can see Dhauli on a clear day (smog can often obscure the view). It is unmistakable how Kharavela had his inscriptions placed directly looking out at those of Ashoka at Dhauli. It is as if to tell Ashoka that he, Kharavela of Kalinga, had sacked Pataliputra and caused the end of Mauryan rule.

Archaeologists have recently uncovered a large fortified city from this period at Sishupalgarh, very close to modern Bhubaneswar. It is very likely the remains of Kharavela's capital, Kalinga-nagari. Although the expanding modern city is slowly encroaching into the site, the straight lines of the earthwork defences are still discernable and the moat now seems to function as a municipal drain. One of the city's main gateways has been excavated. Perhaps this is the very gate that Kharavela tells us he repaired after it had been damaged by a storm in the first year of his reign. India's eastern coastline remains prone to severe storms and I personally witnessed the damage wrought by Cyclone Phailin which had hit Odisha just a few weeks before I visited the archaeological site in 2013.

Kharavela's inscriptions suggest that he had defeated the Satvahanas, the Mauryas, the Indo-Greeks and even the Pandyas of Tamil country in the deep south. Having done all this, he declared that the 'wheel of conquest' had been turned—possibly meaning that he had conducted the Vedic ashwamedha-yagya and declared himself a Chakravarti (or World Conqueror).[24] This would have made him the most powerful Indian ruler of his time. Despite these achievements, Kharavela is almost never mentioned in Indian textbooks because history is written in a way that systematically emphasizes a continental viewpoint over the coastal perspective. It is as if political power was naturally centred in some inland city like Pataliputra or Delhi, and the rest of India must exist as mere provinces.

Kharavela's inscriptions are mostly about his military campaigns but there are a few references to economic concerns. The restoration of a number of reservoirs and the extension of an old Nanda-era canal are mentioned. The management of water supply was obviously an important activity expected of the state. There is also a fleeting mention of the king gifting Chinese silk to priests/monks. This would suggest that Indian merchants operating in South East Asia had connected to trade routes that extended all the way to China. We now turn to their exploits.

5

Kaundinya's Wedding

The period following the collapse of the Mauryan empire is somehow glossed over in history books as if the size of an empire is the only thing that matters. This is unfortunate as the period saw a boom in economic activity and mercantile trade. Merchant ships set sail from Satvahana and Kalinga ports, as well as those of the small kingdoms in the far south, to trade as far as Egypt in the west and Vietnam in the East.

As already discussed, Odiya–Bengali seafarers had been visiting and settling in Sri Lanka from the sixth century BC. At some point they also began to trade with South East Asia. However, in the initial phase, they did not have the confidence to sail directly across the Bay of Bengal. Instead, they hugged the coast till the Isthmus of Kra. This is the thin strip of land, now part of Thailand, from which the Malay peninsula hangs. Goods were then taken overland to the Gulf of Thailand from where they were loaded again on ships for ports in Cambodia and southern Vietnam. This explains why India's eastern coast established links with faraway Vietnam before the Indonesian islands of Java and Bali that may appear closer on a map. Óc Eo, in Vietnam's Mekong delta, seems to have become a major hub. From there, merchandise would be traded up the coast to China.

It is in the Mekong delta that we witness the establishment of the first Indianized kingdom of South East Asia around the first century BC. The Chinese called it the kingdom of Funan. There is an interesting legend about how this kingdom was founded. It is said that an Indian merchant ship was sailing through the region when it was attacked by pirates led by Soma, daughter of the chieftain of the local Naga clan. The Indians fought back and fended off the attackers led by a handsome young Brahmin called Kaundinya. Unfortunately, the ship had been damaged and had to be beached for repairs.

The merchants must have been worried about a second attack but luck turned in their favour. It appears Princess Soma had been impressed by Kaundinya's bravery and had fallen in love! She proposed marriage and the offer was accepted. This union is said to have founded a lineage that ruled Funan for many generations. We have no way of knowing if this legend is based on true events but slightly different versions of the story are repeated in inscriptions by both the Chams of Vietnam and the Khmers of Cambodia—the royal families of both claim descent from Soma and Kaundinya. It is also repeated in contemporary Chinese records.[1]

Notice how Kaundinya acquired his throne through marriage to a warrior princess. Moreover, it was the princess who made the proposal. Given that royal legitimacy had been acquired through the female line, we find that matrilineal genealogies would be given a great deal of importance over the fifteen hundred years that these Indianized kingdoms flourished in this part of the world.

This founding myth also explains why the serpent (naga) became such an important royal symbol in Khmer iconography. More than a thousand years later, the mystical union between the king and a 'serpent' princess remained an important part of the court ceremonials at Angkor.[2]

So, who was Kaundinya? We know nothing about him except that he was a Brahmin from India but his name provides a clue. While Kaundinya is not a common first name, it is the name of a gotra (i.e. male lineage) of Brahmins who still live along the Tamil–Andhra–Odisha coastline. Perhaps this is not a coincidence.

By the end of the second century BC, Indian mariners appear to have learned enough about the monsoon winds and ocean currents to attempt a more southern route across the Indian Ocean to the islands of Indonesia. Odisha's Lake Chilika was an important starting point for this voyage. It is a large brackish water lake with a small opening to the sea. The mariners of Kalinga, therefore, used the lake as a safe harbour. Even today, you are likely to find broken heaps of ancient pottery strewn along the lake's shores.

Note that the ships did not sail out directly for Indonesia. Instead they used the north-eastern monsoon winds that blow from mid-November to sail down the coast to Sri Lanka. This was already a well-known route and the merchants probably stopped along the way to trade as well. In Sri Lanka, the ships would have taken in fresh water and supplies before using ocean currents to cross the Indian Ocean to the northern tip of Sumatra (called Swarnadwipa, or Island of Gold in Sanskrit texts). From here, the ships could choose to sail down the Straits of Malacca towards Palembang and take the sea route to Borneo and Vietnam. Alternatively, they could head south hugging the western coast of Sumatra to Bali and Java (called Yavadwipa, or Island of Barley/Grain).

After finishing their purchases and sales, most ships would have used the countercurrent to return to Sri Lanka, and then Odisha. If the sailors started from Odisha in mid-November, it is estimated that they would reach the islands of Java/Bali by mid-January. They would now have two months to conduct their business before they started their return journey in mid-March. This would allow them to get back to Sri Lanka in time to catch the early South-West monsoon winds in May that would take them home.[3]

The merchants of Kalinga were not the only ones making the journey to Indonesia. There were merchants from the Tamil, Andhra and Bengal coasts too. There were even horse traders from India's north-west who made their way to the port of Tamralipti in Bengal and then sailed to Java and Sumatra. However, in the initial phase, it is the Sadhaba merchants of Kalinga who seem to have had a dominant influence. This is why Indians were known as 'keling' by the Malays and Javanese from ancient times although the term has acquired a somewhat derogatory connotation in recent times.

That era of maritime exploration and trade is still remembered in Odisha in folklore and festivals. The festival of Kartik Purnima takes place in mid-November when the winds shift and begin to blow from the north. This marks the time of year that ancient mariners would have set sail for Indonesia. Families, especially women and children, gather at the edge of a waterbody and place paper boats with oil lamps in the water. I witnessed the ritual on a beach near the temple town of Konark. Streams of people from nearby villages arrived before dawn to place their little boats in the water and watch them float away. A cool breeze blew from the north as promised and the full moon made the crashing waves glimmer. As per tradition, one must wait for the sun to rise. I watched my paper boat float away. This is how the families of the ancient mariners would have bid goodbye to their loved ones.

The maritime links to Kartik Purnima are remembered in many other ways. A fair is held every year in Cuttack called Bali Yatra which literally means 'The Journey to Bali'. It is also a tradition to perform songs and plays based on the old folk tale about Tapoi. The story goes that there was a wealthy merchant, a widower, who had seven sons and a daughter. The daughter, the youngest, was named Tapoi and her father and brothers doted on her. One year, the merchant decided to take all his sons on a long voyage to a distant land. He left Tapoi behind in the care of his seven daughters-in-law with clear instructions that they look after the young girl.

Unfortunately, Tapoi's sisters-in-law secretly hated her and mistreated her. She was made to cook, clean the cowshed and do all the washing. They even withheld food from her. After several months of tolerating all the physical and mental abuse, Tapoi eventually ran away into the forest. There she prayed to goddess Mangala, a form of Durga, who blessed her. A few days later, her father and brothers returned unexpectedly. They soon realized what had happened and brought Tapoi back from the forest. The evil sisters-in-law were punished. The folk tale not only hints at the tradition of long oceanic voyages but also expresses some of the inner anxieties of those who made these voyages—when will we get back home, what will happen to those left behind?

The most important Indian export was cotton textiles which would continue to be in much demand across the Indian Ocean rim till modern times. Excavations in South East Asia also show evidence of carnelian beads and a variety of metalware. By AD first century, we find that Indian merchants were also bringing along Mediterranean and West Asian products that they, in turn, had purchased from the Romans, Greeks and Arabs. Artefacts found in Sembiran in Bali clearly show that it was in close contact with Arikamedu, an Indo-Roman port, just outside Puducherry.[4]

Indian imports included Chinese silks, via ports in Vietnam, and camphor from Sumatra. The islands of Indonesia would have been a source of cloves, nutmeg and other spices. Many of the spices thought to be 'Indian' by medieval Europeans were actually from Indonesia except black pepper which grows along the south-western coast of India. Till the late eighteenth century, the world's entire supply of cloves came from the tiny islands of Ternate and Tidore in the Maluku group.

Trade links with South East Asia unsurprisingly led to cultural exchange. Within a few centuries we see the strong impact of Indic civilization on the region—the Buddhist and Hindu religions, the epics Mahabharata and Ramayana, the Sanskrit language, scripts, temple architecture and so on. Despite the later impact of Islam, European colonial rule and postcolonial modernity, the influence of ancient India remains alive in place and personal names, commonly used words, and in the arts and crafts. Buddhism is still the dominant religion across Myanmar to Vietnam, while Hinduism survives in pockets such as Bali.

There are some cultural artefacts that seem to have survived with little change from the very earliest phase of contact between the two regions. One cannot look at traditional masks from Bali, Sri Lanka and the Andhra–Odisha coast without being struck by the similarity. The same is true of Wayang Kulit, the Indonesian art of shadow puppetry, and its equivalent in Odisha and Andhra Pradesh. Imagine ancient mariners entertaining each other during the long nights of an ocean crossing by using their ship's sail to enact shadow-puppet plays, cultural roots anchoring them as they made a perilous journey to distant lands.

One should not be under the impression that influences always flowed unidirectionally from India to South East Asia. Far from it, Indian civilization was enriched in many ways by influences from the east. One commonplace example is the custom of chewing paan (betel leaves with areca nuts, usually with a bit of lime and other ingredients). While it is common across the Indian subcontinent, the areca nut, called 'supari' in Hindi, is originally from South East Asia and was chewed across the region and as far north as Taiwan.

Paan is still widely consumed in India but, in recent years, has become less popular in the urban areas of South East Asia. Still, the leaf and nut continue to play an important cultural role and are used in many ceremonies. I have eaten them at a wedding in Bali and found old villagers chewing them in the Philippines. The Vietnamese too use it for many marriage-related ceremonies. It is quite possible that they were used by the warrior princess Soma when she sent the marriage proposal to Kaundinya.

The supari that one chews today in most parts of India gives no more than a mild buzz. The Khasis of Meghalaya, however, have preserved a strain that can be surprisingly strong. Perhaps they brought it with them during their prehistoric migrations from Sundaland. Surprisingly, the strongest that I have eaten came from a wild variety that I accidentally discovered in Singapore of all places. Suffice to say, the tiny nut packed the punch of a bottle of rum!

Of Tamils and Sinhalese

Most of the early known history of the far south of the Indian peninsula, what are now the states of Kerala and Tamil Nadu, is about the rivalries between three clans—the Cholas, Cheras and Pandyas. The Cholas had their heartland in the Kaveri delta, the

Pandyas were further south near Madurai and the Cheras along the Kerala coast. Their relative strength waxed and waned over time but it is amazing how the same three clans battled each other over fifteen centuries (c. 300 BC to AD 1200)! Early Tamil poetry of the Sangam compilations provides vivid, if somewhat idealized, views of the times—prosperous cities, bustling bazaars and ports busy with merchant ships from foreign lands. The city of Madurai, the capital of the Pandyas, is described as follows in 'Maduraikkanchi', composed in the first century BC:[5]

> The city walls are sky high and contain strong sally-ports and gateways old and strong,
>> On whose doorposts is carved great Lakshmi's form.
>> Their strong built doors are blackened by the ghee poured
> as libation
>
> In the wide long streets that are broad as rivers,
>> Crowds of folk of various professions and speech create a
> noise in the morning market-place while buying things

Excavations in Tamil Nadu in recent years have unearthed remains of significant urban centres from this period such as one found under the hamlet of Keezhadi, near Madurai, in 2015.[6] The findings confirm that the cities mentioned in the Sangam literature are not imaginary even if the descriptions may have been embellished. Tamil nationalists of the twentieth century had attempted to use these texts to glorify some pristine Dravidian past but, ironically, Sangam literature is full of 'northern' influences. Far from being Dravidian purists, ancient Tamils credited the sage Agastya, a northerner, with formalizing Tamil grammar. The great Tamil kings similarly took great pride in building linkages with the epics. In other words, the very earliest Tamil texts suggest a people who were very proud of being part of a wider Indic civilization. As historian Nilakanta Sastri puts it, 'But none can miss the significance of the fact that early Tamil literature, the earliest to which we have access, is already full of charged words, conceptions and institutions of Sanskritic and northern origin.'[7]

Far from being concerned with a pristine civilization, Sangam literature celebrates interactions with the rest of the world with descriptions of bustling ports and foreign trade. One of the texts also makes the first definite reference to a naval battle where Chera king Udiyanjeral defeated an unspecified local adversary and took a number of Greek merchants captive. The captives were later freed upon providing a large ransom.[8]

By the fourth century BC, some Tamil groups began to settle in northern Sri Lanka. There was already a significant population of settlers from Odisha–Bengal, and the local Vedda population had been sidelined, as mentioned earlier. Several small kingdoms gradually emerged, scattered across the island, but one of them, Anuradhapura, seems to have gained prominence due to the backing of Emperor Ashoka. According to the *Mahavamsa*, Ashoka sent his son Mahinda to convert the ruler of Anuradhapura, Devanampiya Tissa, to Buddhism, in the third century BC.

In 177 BC, two Tamil adventurers captured the throne of Anuradhapura and ruled it for twenty-two years. They would be followed a decade later by another Tamil ruler, Ellara, who would rule for forty-four years and earn a reputation for ensuring justice and good governance. However, after the first three decades of peace, Ellara would be challenged by Dattagamani, the Sinhalese ruler of a southern kingdom. This would lead to fifteen years of war that is said to have culminated in a face-to-face duel unto death where the younger challenger killed Ellara (a bit unfair given that Ellara would have been over seventy by this time).

Later writings would present this moment as the victory of a Sinhala son-of-the-soil over a Tamil intruder as well as the consummation of the island's destiny as a Buddhist nation. However, as pointed out by K.M. de Silva, the island's pre-eminent historian, this is not how it would have seemed at the time that the events took place. Most of the Sinhalese were not Buddhist at this stage and many of them seem to have sided with Ellara.[9] Even the *Mahavamsa* agrees that Ellara was a good and popular king. Far from being so sure about who was the 'son-of-the-soil' in the second century BC, the Tamils and the Sinhalese would have seen themselves and each other as relatively recent immigrants.

We tend to think of the relations between the Sinhalese and Tamils of Sri Lanka (and by extension between Buddhists and Hindus) as being that of perpetual conflict, because we are influenced by the experience of the bloody Tamil separatist movement in the late twentieth century and its brutal suppression. The longer history, however, is much more complicated and involves both conflicts and alliances between kingdoms of the two ethnic groups at different points in time. If there is any pattern at all, there seems to have been a long-term alliance between the Sinhalese and the Tamil Pandyas of Madurai against other Tamil clans like the Cholas.

Moreover, the Sinhalese religion for most of its history was very eclectic and has always included strong Hindu elements. Upulvan, or Vishnu, is still worshipped by the Sinhalese as the guardian deity of Sri Lanka and virtually all major Buddhist temples have shrines to Hindu deities (called 'devalas'). This is even true of the holiest of holies, the Temple of the Tooth in Kandy. As any visitor will notice, pilgrims entering the temple must first pass a number of Hindu shrines before reaching the main building. Even the nearby souvenir stalls sell an eclectic mix of Hindu and Buddhist icons.

After Dattagamani defeated Ellara and united the island, he established himself in Anuradhapura. Except for a couple of brief interruptions, the city would remain the capital of the island's dominant kingdom for the next thousand years. Just like the political history of the southern tip of India was mostly about the rivalries between three clans, we find that this period of Lankan history would be dominated by the Moriya and Lamkanna clans. This was further complicated by intrigues within each clan. The politics of the times is best illustrated by the story of Sigiriya, one of the most spectacular historical sites in Asia.

Dhatusena, the king of Anuradhapura, was murdered by his son Kassapa in AD 477. Kassapa was the king's eldest son but by a junior concubine and consequently not in the line of succession. So, he captured power with the help of Migara, his cousin, who was the army commander. The crown prince Moggallana, however, escaped to southern India (probably finding shelter in the Pandya court).

Kassapa then decided to build a new capital for himself at Sigiriya. It is a site dominated by a gigantic rock. The new capital was laid out at the foot of the rock while the palace was built on the top. I strongly recommend visitors take the trouble to climb the rock; a moderately fit person will take about an hour and a quarter to make the round trip. The top is like a miniature Machu Picchu and provides amazing views of the surrounding countryside.

Sigiriya's moment in the sun, however, came to an abrupt end in AD 495 when Moggallana suddenly returned with an army of Indian mercenaries. He defeated Kassapa and killed him, and shifted the capital back to Anuradhapura. Sigiriya was gradually abandoned except for parts that were used as a Buddhist monastery. Nonetheless, medieval tourists would keep visiting the site for centuries, especially to admire the paintings of bare-breasted damsels that adorn a cave shelter halfway up the rock. These tourists expressed their admiration in graffiti love poems that can still be read. Here are some examples:[10]

> Lovely this lady
> Excellent the painter
> And when I look
> At hand and eye
> I do believe she lives

> We spoke
> But they did not answer
> Those lovely ladies of the mountain
> They did not give us
> Even the twitch of an eye-lid

It appears that some female visitors, seemingly irritated with their male companions, also left some graffiti:

> You fools!
> You come to Sihagiri and inscribe these verses
> Yet not one of you brings wine and molasses
> Remembering we are women.

Alexandria to Muzeris

Just as maritime trade boomed in the eastern Indian Ocean, there was a similar boom in trade between India's west coast and the Greco-Roman world. The trade routes are described in detail in *The Periplus of the Erythraean Sea*, a manual written by an Egyptian–Greek merchant in AD first century.[11] Some of the details suggest that the author had personally visited many of the places mentioned in the manuscript. Note that Erythraean Sea literally means Red Sea, but the term was used by the ancient Greeks more broadly to include the Indian Ocean.

The Periplus tells us that there were two routes from the Mediterranean to the Red Sea. One of the routes started from the ports of what are now Israel and Lebanon and made its way overland via Petra to the Gulf of Aqaba. The magnificent rock-cut remains of the city of Petra in Jordan, now a World Heritage Site, show us how the Nabataeans had grown rich from trade.

The alternative route for Roman merchants to the Red Sea ran through the great port of Alexandria in Egypt. The city was a cosmopolitan melting pot and we have evidence that it had a population of Indians. From Alexandria there were two options. One could make one's way directly from the Nile delta to Suez. This was not a new route and we know from Herodotus that the ancient pharaohs had attempted to build a canal from the Nile to the Red Sea, and that the project had been completed during the rule of Persian emperor Darius in the sixth century BC. However, the canal kept getting silted up, and despite being re-excavated by the Ptolemies in the third century BC, part of the journey had to be made on foot. At the time *The Periplus* was written, the more popular option was to sail up the Nile to Coptos (Qift) and then make the eleven-day crossing through the desert to the port of Berenice (Berenike) on Egypt's Red Sea coast.[12]

Archaeological excavations at Berenice have thrown up a variety of goods from India including peppercorns, seeds of the amla fruit (Indian gooseberry) from the lower Himalayas, cotton cloth, and even mung seeds from South East Asia. Pottery shards with Prakrit and Tamil markings have been found in a nearby settlement. Customs tokens, made of baked clay, have also been found in a rubbish pit. These tokens were given to merchants who had paid their taxes in Coptos and only the goods listed on the tokens were allowed to be loaded on outgoing ships by officials in Berenice. Customs receipts also mention carefully weighed pouches of coins—called marisippia. Many of these coins would make their way to the ports of India.

The first port down the coast from Berenice was a 'fair-sized village' called Adulis. This was a barren stretch of the coast, but Adulis served as the nearest access to the city of Aksum that had emerged as a major urban centre in the Ethiopian highlands. We are told that Aksum was eight days' journey inland and was the source of ivory and rhino horn. At this stage, the Ethiopians had not yet converted to Christianity and one can still see gigantic stone obelisks in Aksum, probably carved in memory of the pagan kings of that period. The monarchs of Ethiopia would be crowned in Aksum till the twentieth century.

As the merchant fleets made their way further down the Red Sea, they would have to pass the point where the Arabian peninsula comes nearest to the African coast. This is the most likely place where our early ancestors had crossed over from Africa before colonizing the rest of the world. The Periplus warns us that contrary winds and strong currents made this place dangerous for ships. The Arabs would later name it Bab-el-Mandeb or Gateway of Tears.

After the narrow strait, the sea widens out to the Gulf of Aden. By AD first century, the Sabeans had been pushed out by rival clans and the coast was controlled by the Himyarites and the Hadramawt. The Periplus tells us that this region was the source of frankincense. We are told that the gum was collected from the trees by the king's slaves and prisoners. Merchants, however, did not spend too much time here as it had a reputation for being unhealthy and 'pestilential even to those sailing along the coast'. Instead they headed for the island of Socotra.

Socotra is a fragment left over from the break-up of the supercontinent of Gondwana and its long isolation has left it with unique flora and fauna. The island's name is derived from Dwipa Sukhadhara, or 'the Island of Bliss' in Sanskrit. It is telling that an island so close to Arabia had a Sanskritic name and, *The Periplus* tells us that, in addition to Arabs and Greeks, it had a large population of Indians. One can still read graffiti left by these ancient mariners on the walls of Hoq cave on the island.

The traditional coastal route to India from Socotra was to head north to Oman. This coast was controlled by the Persians at that time and only 'fish-eaters' lived here. Indeed fishing still remains a very important source of food in this region. I have witnessed Omani fishermen selling their catch on the shore. The air is already heavy and hot by eight-thirty in the morning as the fishermen haul their catch to the market on the beach. The sea glistens a bright blue-green but the sun is relentless. In this treeless, barren landscape, man must live by the fruits of the sea.

Past the mouth of the Persian Gulf, the sailors would hit the Makran coast. From here, the ships would sail more directly east towards the Indus delta. *The Periplus* confirms that Sindh and parts of Gujarat were controlled by the Sakas (Scythians) and Parthians at that time. This fits with Satvahana inscriptions mentioned earlier that tell us of their wars with the Sakas.

Beyond the Indus, the text says that there was a large gulf that ran inland but was too shallow to be navigable. This is the Rann of Kutchh and one can see that, by AD first century, it was no longer possible to sail across it as in Harappan times. Next along the coast was the town of Baraca (probably Dwarka) after which the land gradually became more fertile and yielded a variety of crops—wheat, rice, sesame and, most importantly, cotton.

Having sailed past Saurashtra and the Gulf of Khambhat, the tired merchant ships would finally reach the estuary of the Narmada that led to the great port of Barygaza (Bharuch). *The Periplus* describes how shifting silt and sandbars made the entrance to the river perilous. Thus, the king of Barygaza appointed experienced fishermen as pilots to guide merchant ships. We are also warned of a wicked bore tide that could tear a ship from its moorings. The nautical details are so vivid that it is very likely that the author of *The Periplus* had personally visited the place.

The most important exports from Barygaza were different kinds of cotton textiles, which are still exported from this region. Iron and steel products would have also been exported as we know that these were coveted by communities living along the Red Sea. In exchange, one of the most important products ancient Indians imported was wine—and we are told that Italian wine was preferred over the Arabian and Syrian stuff; modern Indians would certainly agree with the verdict. The local kings also seem to have imported 'beautiful maidens for the harem'. With imported Italian wines and beautiful maidens, it is fair to say that the Saka and Indian nobility of that period knew how to lead the high life.

The Periplus shows that the Romans were aware that from Barygaza, India's western coast ran south in almost a straight line. The text lists a number of ports down the coast but arguably the most important was Muzeris (or Mucheripatanam as the Indians called it) which was the source of black pepper. We are told of how Arab and Greek ships flocked to the port. Excavations at the village of Pattanam, just north of modern Kochi, have recently allowed archaeologists to exactly identify the location of this ancient port. Many kinds of imported artefacts have been found here but some of the most common are wine and olive oil amphorae from as far away as France, Spain, Egypt and Turkey.[13]

The reason that the port of Muzeris was going through such a boom in international trade during the period *The Periplus* was written is that mariners had worked out in the previous century that they could use monsoon winds to sail directly between Socotra and southern India without hugging the coast. The author of *The Periplus* credits this discovery to a Greek pilot called Hippalus. It is curious that it took a Greek to work out how to harness the monsoon winds in the Arabian Sea when the Indians had been using them for generations in the Bay of Bengal to visit South East Asia. Perhaps ancient Arab and Indian mariners would have disputed Hippalus's claim.

The Periplus mentions Greeks and Arabs in Muzeris but not the Jews. However, a small Jewish trading community would have existed by the time the manual was written and, within a few decades, an influx of refugees would expand it significantly. After the Second Temple in Jerusalem was destroyed by the Romans in AD 70, many Jewish refugees came to settle around Muzeris. Thus, India became home to one of the oldest Jewish communities in the world. Their numbers have dwindled in recent decades due to emigration to Israel but their synagogues can still be visited in the Kochi–Kodungallur area.

Similarly, the Syrian Christian community claims descent from converts made by St Thomas who is said to have visited these parts in AD first century. Although the historical veracity of St Thomas' visit has been disputed by scholars, it is reasonably certain that Christians visited and settled along the Kerala coast at an early stage.[14] We know that a group of Christians fleeing persecution in the Persian empire came to India under the leadership of Thomas of Cana in AD 345. Seventy-two families settled near Muzeris and were given special trading privileges by the local Hindu king.[15] A few centuries later, early Muslims would build the Cheraman Masjid, the world's second oldest mosque, in the same general area. It is a testimony to the importance of ancient Muzeris that these early Jewish, Christian and Islamic sites are all located within a very short distance of each other. This is saying something at a time when the Christian community in Syria and Iraq is being systematically wiped out by the so-called Islamic State.

From The Periplus, we can gather that the Romans knew that the coast south of Muzeris ended in a cape—Kanyakumari—and that the island of Taprobane (i.e. Sri Lanka) lay beyond it. Given the repeated mention of the Pandyas, but not of the rival clans, it seems that The Periplus was composed at a time when the Pandyas were dominant.

We know from archaeological excavations that Roman traders made their way up the east coast as far as Arikamedu, close to modern

Puducherry. It is a beautiful turn in the river but the visitor will find little to reflect its ancient history except a large number of pottery shards that lie scattered about. *The Periplus* gets increasingly garbled as one goes further up the east coast. It shows an awareness of the Gangetic delta and mentions oriental tribes, but the details are quite blurred. The inland city of Thinae is mentioned as the source of silk (is this a reference to China?). So, it is fair to say that this was the limit of what the Romans knew about the Indian Ocean in AD first century.

Indo-Roman trade boomed in AD first and second centuries. Emperor Trajan had the Nile–Suez canal re-excavated; it began just south of modern Cairo and headed due east to the Red Sea.[16] About 120 ships made the round trip between India and the Red Sea ports every year. The availability of eastern luxuries transformed Roman tastes but the problem was that the empire ran a persistent trade deficit with India. This deficit had to be paid in gold and silver coins. Roman writer Pliny (AD 23–79) complained bitterly that, 'Not a year passed in which India did not take fifty million sesterces away from Rome.'

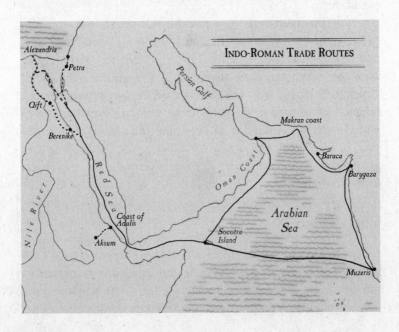

In a world where precious metals were used for minting coins, this was equivalent to severe monetary tightening. The Romans initially tried to solve the problem by curtailing trade but eventually they would resort to debasing their coins (i.e. reducing the content of gold and silver). This would eventually cause distortions and inflation in the Roman empire. Interestingly, the Indians continued to accept the debased coins although they recognized the higher quality of the older, high-content coins which continued to circulate in the Indian Ocean long after the reigns of emperors who had issued them.

Notice the similarity with the modern world where China runs a persistent surplus against the United States and accepts dollars in exchange. Everyone accuses the US of printing too many dollars but China keeps accumulating them as reserves. In this way a symbiotic imbalance keeps the world economy going despite the distortions it causes. Indeed, such imbalances have been at the heart of most periods of global economic expansion and can be surprisingly persistent.[17]

Note that merchants were not the only people who travelled between the Roman empire and India. We know, for instance, that it was fashionable for wealthy Roman women to consult Indian astrologers. We also have the story of Demetrius, a student of Greek philosophy, who was wrongly accused of stealing from a temple and arrested in Egypt. After he was exonerated and freed with compensation, he gifted all his property to a friend and sailed to India to study Vedic philosophy.[18] In other words, the shipping lines provided the infrastructure for all kinds of people to move back and forth across the seas.

The Waqwaq

Given the country's central location, it is not surprising that links between the eastern and western Indian Ocean were routed through India. However, as the knowledge of the winds and sea currents improved, seafarers became confident enough to cross the ocean directly. One of the most intriguing examples of this is the colonization of Madagascar by the Indonesians.

Madagascar is located close to Africa but, as discussed earlier, the two land masses had separated about 160 million years ago when Gondwana split up. Thus, the island's flora and fauna had evolved in isolation for a very long time and bore little resemblance to that of Africa next door. For instance, it was home to the elephant bird that stood three metres tall and weighed half a ton, the largest bird ever. Then there was the giant lemur that was larger than a gorilla and was the world's largest primate.

At some point in the fifth century, Indonesian sailors in their outrigger boats began to visit the island. In terms of seamanship, this matches the exploits of their Polynesian cousins in the Pacific. Thus, an island so close to the origin of our species in Africa was first colonized from the other side of the Indian Ocean. Recent genetic studies show that the first permanent settlement of the island was done by a tiny group from Indonesia around AD 800, and may have included just thirty women.[19] Similarly, the island's main language, Malagasy, has been traced back to south Borneo. Reflecting the spread of Indic influences in their homeland, the settlers also brought certain Hindu rituals and words from Sanskrit that survive in traces.

Predictably, humans were a shock to the isolated and fragile ecosystem of the island. The extinction of the elephant bird and the giant lemur coincided with the arrival of people and it is difficult to escape the conclusion that these events are somehow related. We saw how the arrival of humans in Australia had a very similar impact.

The settlers would come to be known as the Waqwaq, probably after their 'waqa' canoes, and would be feared as pirates by medieval Arab merchants sailing down the East African coast. The Waqwaq also made regular raids on the mainland to acquire slaves. We have records of how they even made an unsuccessful attempt to capture the fortified port of Qanbalu, on the island of Pemba (in present-day Tanzania) in AD 945.[20]

Despite their notoriety, the Indonesians also introduced new crops to Africa. It is believed that many staples like banana, yam, breadfruit and sugar cane were brought here by the Waqwaq (note that there is a rival theory that some of these were introduced by the Indians). These crops would spread into the continent's interior and would become a very important part of the local diet.

Over time, however, coastal Madagascar came to be dominated by the Arabs and Africans. Many of the Waqwaq then withdrew to the island's central highlands where they slowly forgot their maritime culture. As Richard Hall puts it in *Empires of the Monsoon*, 'Although they still buried their rulers in silver canoes, they could never go home again.'

Stitched Ships

One of the most common observations made by ancient and medieval travellers is that the ships of the Indian Ocean had hulls that were 'stitched' together with rope rather than nailed around a frame. This design most likely originated in India but seems to have been adopted by the Yemeni and Omani Arabs at an early stage. It is unclear why the Indians preferred to stitch together their ships when they were more than familiar with iron nails. Indeed, as demonstrated by Delhi's famous Iron Pillar, they even had the technology for rust-resistant iron.

One possibility is that the stitched technique gave the hull a degree of flexibility. This meant that the ship was less likely to break up if it ran into a shoal or sandbar. This was no small concern given that the Indian coastline has few natural harbours and most of the ports were either in an estuary or require sailing through a narrow passage like that of Lake Chilika. Moreover, using the monsoon winds implied that the sailing season coincided with rough surf. This meant that arriving ships were often beached rather than tied by the quayside.

The Indo-Arab stitched ships, however, were not the only ones plying the Indian Ocean. The South East Asians had their own design derived from the outrigger canoes that their prehistoric ancestors had used when they left the flooding coasts of Sundaland to settle in the islands. Perhaps the best depiction of eighth-century Indonesian outrigger ships is carved on the panels of Borobudur, Java. Using the panels as their guide, a group of enthusiasts recently recreated the 'Borobudur Ship'. Between August 2003 and February 2004, they further proved their point by sailing the reconstructed ship, named Samudra Raksha, from Java to Madagascar and then all the way to Ghana! The ship is now displayed at a museum in Borobudur.[21]

In addition to the local ship designs, the Indian Ocean also witnessed maritime technologies derived from outside the region. Greco-Roman ships were adapted from the designs that plied the Mediterranean. Later the Indian Ocean would see the entry of Chinese ships culminating in the voyages of Admiral Zheng He's 'Treasure Fleet' in the fifteenth century. In other words, the Indians and Arabs were quite familiar with different ship designs. The advantages of the stitched design must have been significant if it remained the preferred technique till the Europeans arrived at the end of the fifteenth century. There are still a few coastal villages in India that have preserved the skill of stitching together fishing boats but it is a dying art.

The Bantu Migrations

Even as the Indian Ocean world was witnessing a boom in maritime trade, the interiors of sub-Saharan Africa were experiencing profound demographic changes. Today sub-Saharan Africa is so dominated by Bantu-speaking people that we tend to assume that Africa was always like this. However, linguistic and, more recently, genetic data confirm that the Bantu people originated in what is now Nigeria and Cameroon around 5000 years ago, that is, the third millennium BC.[22]

Around the first millennium BC, they began to expand out of their original homeland. Roughly speaking, one branch pushed directly south into equatorial central Africa, through what is now the Democratic Republic of Congo. Another branch pushed east towards the East African Rift Valley before migrating south through what is now Kenya, Tanzania, Malawi and Zimbabwe.

As they pushed into these new areas, the Bantu replaced or assimilated with the people who already lived there. Till their arrival, hunter–gatherers related to the Khoi-San had inhabited eastern and southern Africa. Central Africa had similarly been inhabited by the Pygmies. This fits in with a story told by Herodotus about an ancient expedition that had crossed the Sahara and come upon a land with forests and Pygmies.

The Bantu, however, steadily replaced both groups. The success of the Bantu seems to have been driven initially by their skills at farming but from around 600 BC, it was strengthened by locally developed iron technology. In Gabon, for instance, archaeological evidence shows iron-using farmers replacing the stone-tool users around 300 BC.[23]

The process of migration still took many centuries and had not yet penetrated the southern tip of Africa when the Europeans arrived there. Thus, when Bartholomew Diaz and Vasco Da Gama arrived at the Cape of Good Hope at the end of the fifteenth century, they encountered Khoi-San pastoralists and hunter–gatherers. It is estimated that the Khoi-San population at that time was around 50,000 in the south-western Cape. However, they would steadily lose territory to the Bantu tribes and to the Europeans who contemptuously called them the 'Hottentots'.

6

Arabian Knights

The trade routes of the Indian Ocean became even more firmly established in AD fourth and fifth centuries. By this time, we find records of people from far outside the Indian Ocean rim, such as Chinese pilgrims and merchants, visiting India and criss-crossing the seas. Anchoring this period of prosperity and globalization was the remarkable empire of the Guptas.

The Gupta empire had its origins in the eastern Gangetic plains, in what is now Bihar and eastern Uttar Pradesh, where the dynasty's first emperor, Chandragupta I, established his power base. However, it was his son Samudragupta (AD 336–370) who dramatically expanded the empire. In a series of military campaigns he established direct or indirect control over nearly all of India. After establishing Gupta rule across the northern plains and central India, he led a campaign along the eastern coast into the deep south where he defeated in turn the rulers of Odisha and Andhra, and eventually Pallava king Vishnugopa of Kanchi. The northern conquests were directly ruled from the capital Pataliputra while the southern kings were allowed to rule their kingdoms as tribute-paying subordinates.

The empire was expended further by Samudragupta's son Chandragupta II (also called Vikramaditya), who reigned between

AD 375 and 413. From certain accounts it appears that he ascended the throne by removing his unpopular elder brother, Ramagupta.

According to a few surviving passages of a lost play called *Devi-Chandragupta*, the Gupta empire was invaded by the Sakas (Scythians) after Samudragupta's death. The new king Ramagupta found himself trapped and appealed for peace. One of the terms imposed by the Sakas was that Queen Dhruva-devi would have to be handed over to them. This insult to the family incensed the king's younger brother. Disguising himself as Dhruva-devi, he entered the Saka camp and killed their king before escaping. The invaders were forced to withdraw in disorder. This turned Chandragupta into a popular hero, but Ramagupta resented this and tried to assassinate his younger sibling. In the ensuing power struggle, Chandragupta finally killed his elder brother. He then crowned himself emperor and married Dhruva-devi.

This colourful story may not be an accurate rendition of real historical events, but Gupta-era inscriptions do show that Chandragupta II had a queen called Dhruva-devi and had children by her.[1] We also know that he led a number of successful military campaigns against the Saka and other Central Asian groups that had encroached into western India. The famous iron pillar in Delhi tells us that he crossed the estuary of the Indus and defeated the Bahlikas (Bactrians). This would have brought the ports of Gujarat and Sindh under Gupta control. We also have rock inscriptions mentioning Chandragupta Vikramaditya in the remote Hunza valley, in Gilgit–Baltistan to the far north, suggesting that Gupta armies had pushed beyond the Kashmir valley into the Pamirs.

The Guptas would enjoy direct and indirect control over most of the Indian subcontinent for several generations. North and central India was ruled directly from Pataliputra while peninsular India was managed through tributary kingdoms or close allies like the Vakatakas. Central Asian groups would continue to make occasional raids from the north-west but Chandragupta Vikramaditya's immediate successors Kumaragupta and Skandagupta were able to fend them off.

With peace established over such a large territory, the Gupta era witnessed an extraordinary economic and cultural boom, and is often referred to as the 'Golden Age' of classical India. The empire's ports in Gujarat and Bengal were busy with merchants, diplomats, scholars and pilgrims from China, Persia, Arabia, Ethiopia and the eastern Roman empire. Although the Guptas were staunch Hindus they followed a policy of religious tolerance. A Chinese text tells us that the Sri Lankan king Meghavarna sent a mission to Samudragupta to request permission to set up a monastery and rest house for Lankan pilgrims visiting Bodh Gaya. Permission was granted and a grand monastery was built; its magnificence was later described by the Chinese scholar–pilgrim Xuan Zang in the seventh century. The famous Nalanda University was also established under Gupta rule.

Fa Xian's Voyage Home

A Chinese scholar called Fa Xian (also spelled Fa Hien) visited India in the early fifth century and has left us a fascinating account of his journey. He came to India by land via Central Asia and spent several years in northern India studying Buddhist texts. Although his writings are heavily skewed towards places and matters of interest to a Buddhist pilgrim, Fa Xian leaves us with the impression that India was a prosperous and well-governed country under the Guptas. Most interestingly for the purposes of this book, he has left us a vivid account of his return journey by sea.[2]

Around AD 410, Fa Xian left the Gupta capital of Pataliputra and made his way down the Ganga. There were several ports in Bengal during this period. One of them was Chandraketugarh, the remains of which have been uncovered 30 kms north of modern-day Kolkata. Archaeologists excavating a mound near Kolkata airport have recently found the remains of another ancient settlement.[3] In other words, the city has a history that goes back much before the establishment of a colonial settlement in the seventeenth century.

Fa Xian would have sailed past all these settlements as he made his way to the most important port in Bengal—Tamralipti. The site of this famous port of antiquity is now called Tamluk, a couple of hours drive south-west of Kolkata, near where the Rupnarayan flows into the Gangetic delta. The old channel of the river that Fa Xian would have used, however, has dried up. Except for a 1200-year-old temple dedicated to goddess Kali, there is little there today to hint at its past glory.

Fa Xian remained here for two years copying sacred documents. He then boarded a big merchant ship that set sail with the first winds of the winter monsoons (probably around Kartik Purnima). We are told that it took just fourteen days for the ship to reach Sri Lanka. Fa Xian would spend another two years on the island studying and copying various scriptures. He tells us that Buddhism was flourishing and that the king, as the custodian of the sacred Tooth Relic, was a generous patron to the Buddhist sangha. Interestingly, he adds that the king lived his personal life strictly according to Hindu rules and rituals.

Next Fa Xian set sail for South East Asia on board a large merchant vessel. The ship must have been fairly large as it carried two hundred people and had a smaller vessel accompanying it with stores. Unfortunately, after two days of fair weather, the ships ran into a major storm and the larger ship sprang a leak. There was panic and some of the passengers tried to forcibly board the smaller boat. The crew of the smaller ship, fearing a stampede, cut the towing cable and sailed away. With little choice, the merchants began to throw their valuable cargo overboard to save their ship. Fa Xian also threw his water basin and pitcher. He feared he would be forced to throw away his beloved books too, but the weather soon cleared up.

After thirteen days they arrived at a small island. The ship was beached and the leak was repaired. No one was sure about the location of the island and there were fears that they would be attacked by pirates (it is likely that this was one of the islands off the north Sumatra coast or perhaps the Nicobar Islands). Eventually, the crew got its bearings and set on a new course. After ninety days at sea, they finally reached Java. Fa Xian spent five months there. All he tells us about Java is that it had an overwhelmingly Hindu population and very few Buddhists (this was not entirely true given the evidence of Borobudur).

He now boarded another merchant ship headed for China. This must have been a very big vessel because the crew alone numbered two hundred men. We are told, furthermore, that the ship carried adequate provisions for fifty days. Fa Xian was very comfortable on this ship and it is possible he even enjoyed a cabin. After a month at sea, however, they were hit by a major storm. Again, there was panic on board. Some of his co-passengers even blamed Fa Xian for bringing bad luck (perhaps they had heard of his previous voyage and thought this was too much of a coincidence)! Luckily an influential merchant intervened and calmed things down.

Meanwhile, the storm had blown the ship off course and they could not sight land even after seventy days at sea. Provisions and water were running desperately low and the crew members started blaming each other. Fed up with the bickering, some of the more experienced merchants took charge and set a new course to the north-west. Eventually, after another twelve days, they arrived on the Chinese coast.

This narrative is fascinating at many levels. It provides the earliest first-hand description of an actual voyage in the eastern Indian Ocean. It also tells us that by the fifth century, there was a well-established sea route from Bengal to Sri Lanka and onward to China via South East Asia. Despite all the dangers, there were large ships and experienced merchants that seemed to have routinely made the journey.

The Mystery of the Pallavas

As mentioned in the previous chapter, the early history of the southern tip of India is dominated by the rivalries of three clans—the Cheras, Pandyas and Cholas. The Sinhalese kings of Sri Lanka sometimes participated in this, usually as allies of the Pandyas. The exact territories and alliances waxed and waned but roughly speaking the core stronghold of the Cheras was the Kerala coast, for the Pandyas it was southern Tamil Nadu, around Madurai, and the Chola power base was the Kaveri delta. It is astonishing that this triangular contest continued for over fifteen centuries. Put in a European context, this would be equivalent to the War of the Roses still going on and having another thousand years to run!

Nevertheless, a few other dynasties did insert themselves into the story for significant periods of time. Perhaps the most important of these were the Pallavas of Kanchipuram (this is less than a two-hour drive from Chennai). A Pallava kingdom already existed when Samudragupta marched down on his southern campaign. However, there is a long-standing debate about the origins of this dynasty.[4] The texts and inscriptions variously hint at a Chola prince, an Andhra chieftain or a Brahmin scholar. Some scholars have even speculated about Parthian origins. Nevertheless, all the available evidence agrees that the dynasty gained its royal status from the marriage to a princess of the Naga clan. Clearly, this marriage alliance is an important part of the story.

As we know, the term 'Naga' was often used to refer to people with oriental features in North-East India or in South East Asia (i.e. the Sundaland diaspora). The Pallavas are known to have links with kingdoms in South East Asia that used the serpent as a symbol or called themselves the serpent people. As mentioned in Chapter 1, for instance, the remains of the Kadaram kingdom in Kedah, Malaysia, are concentrated in an area that is still called the Valley of the Serpents. Similarly, the multi-headed cobra was the symbol of royalty among the Khmer. It raises the possibility that the Naga princess who helped found the Pallava dynasty was from South East Asia—maybe a descendant of Princess Soma and Kaundinya! Perhaps this explains the especially close links between the Pallavas and the Indianized kingdoms of that part of the world.

In AD sixth century, the Pallavas began to expand their kingdom under king Simha-Vishnu who defeated the Cholas, the Pandyas and a mysterious tribe called the Kalabhras. Having secured themselves to the south, the Pallavas then turned their attention to the north where they came in conflict with the Chalukyas who had carved out a large kingdom in what are now the states of Karnataka and Maharashtra. The Pallava-Chalukya rivalry would last several generations with the pendulum of fortune swinging back and forth.

Simha-Vishnu had a younger brother Bhima who sailed to a distant land and became a ruler after marrying a local princess. Five generations later, when Simha-Vishnu's direct line died out, the Pallavas would bring back a twelve-year-old descendant of Bhima to sit on the throne. The boy would become Nandi Varman II whom readers will recall from the beginning of this book. It is interesting that his inscriptions emphasize that he was a 'pure' Pallava. One explanation would be that, being foreign-born, he needed to firmly emphasize his right to the throne. However, the oriental faces in the temple panels suggest he was not shy of his South East Asian links. Perhaps the term 'pure' has a somewhat different meaning. Remember that the Pallava dynasty began with a marriage to a Naga princess. So Nandi Varman II may have been making a different point—that he was the descendant of a Pallava prince—that is, Bhima—and a Naga queen and, consequently, a true Pallava.

At the height of their power, the Pallavas controlled Tamil Nadu, southern Karnataka, Andhra Pradesh and parts of Sri Lanka. Their capital of Kanchipuram and their main port in Mahabalipuram were impressive cities that the Pallava kings adorned with large Hindu temples. Several of them have survived in both locations and are well worth a visit. Modern-day tourists visiting Mahabalipuram usually see the rock-cut caves and the Shore Temple. They will often ignore a modern lighthouse on a hill behind the ancient monuments. However, maritime history buffs would be rewarded if they walked up to it because they will come across the remains of a Pallava-era lighthouse built around AD 630 where a fire was kept burning every night in order to guide ships to the port.

Although the archaeological remains in Mahabalipuram are impressive, most of the Pallava-era port city is now under the sea. There is an old legend that there were originally seven temples on the shore. It was said that the city's wealthy citizens grew so arrogant that the gods sent a great flood to punish them. The flood swept away all but one of the temples, the lonely Shore Temple that we see today. Historians had long discounted this oral history despite claims by local fishermen that their nets routinely got entangled in stone structures in the sea.

Then, in December 2004, a deadly tsunami hit coastlines across the Indian Ocean. Before the tsunami came in, the sea first withdrew and, for a few minutes, exposed several stone structures off the coast of Mahabalipuram. Later investigations by the Archaeological Survey of India have confirmed that there are indeed several temples and man-made structures that lie submerged off the coast.[5] Moreover, studies of the area have found evidence that this coastline has been hit by tsunamis repeatedly and it is possible that the flood mentioned in the legend relates to a tsunami.

With whom were the merchant fleets of Mahabalipuram trading? By the eighth century, there were already a number of well-developed Indianized kingdoms in South East Asia. The Sri Vijaya kingdom covered most of Sumatra and the Malay peninsula. It had two major urban hubs—Palembang on Sumatra and Kadaram on the peninsula. Java was another major political centre. Its kingdoms steadily extended their influence over islands such as Bali and Madura till it later grew into the great Majapahit empire that controlled a large swathe of what is now Indonesia. In Cambodia, the Khmers were welded into a kingdom that culminated in the Angkor empire. Further east, the kingdom of Champa stretched along the central and southern coast of Vietnam (some historians argue that it was more a confederacy than a centralized kingdom). These kingdoms traded with each other and with India and China. They also fought bitter wars, particularly the Khmers versus the Chams, and the Javans versus the Sri Vijaya.

Given the close political and commercial links between the Pallavas and these kingdoms, it is not surprising that the dominant source of Indian influence in South East Asia shifted from Odiya to Tamil during this period. For instance, the South East Asians adopted the Pallava version of the Brahmi script. This is why the scripts used to write Khmer, Thai, Lao, Burmese and Javanese-Kawi are derived from the Pallava script. Till the early nineteenth century, the Brahmi-derived Baybayin script was even used to write Tagalog in the Philippines.

As we saw from Fa Xian's account, the trade routes between India and China were well established by the fifth century. By the Pallava period, there were large Indian merchant communities living in Chinese ports. Since the 1930s, archaeologists have discovered evidence of a number of Hindu shrines and at least two large temples in and around the port city of Quanzhou.[6] These include stone carvings depicting mythological tales related to the gods Vishnu and Shiva that look identical to those found in southern India during the same period. In the nearby village of Chedian, locals still worship the image of a goddess who is clearly of Indian origin (the villagers see her as a form of the Chinese goddess Guanyin).

Arabia on the Eve of Islam

As we have seen, the history of ancient Yemen was about the rivalries between clans such as the Sabeans, Hadhramis and the Himyar. Their culture was quite distinct from that of the Arabs. However, from AD second century, the dynamics of the region began to change due to demographic, cultural and geopolitical shifts. Initially, the region witnessed the arrival of a large Jewish trader and refugee community from the west. The descendants of these Jewish settlers would survive in both Ethiopia and Yemen until the twentieth century.

Meanwhile, waves of Arabs from the area around modern Riyadh began to encroach into neighbouring territories. One branch pushed into Yemen and Oman. It is not clear why these large-scale migrations took place but Arab names suddenly start to appear in Yemeni inscriptions. The records suggest growing Arab assertiveness against the local clans as their numbers grew. One of them records the 'war against some of the Arabs on the borders of the tribe Hashid and in some of the lands of the Arabs, Arabs who had acted wrongfully against their lords, the kings of Saba'.[7] Note that as I type these words, a Saudi-led coalition pounds the Shiite Houthi rebels in Yemen.

Under demographic pressure, exacerbated by the breaching of an ancient Sabean dam, some Yemeni groups migrated north into Oman, which was witnessing its own Arab migration. Over time, these two migrations displaced or absorbed the existing Persianized population in Oman. To this day, most Omanis can trace their ancestry to the two migrations; the Yamani clans claim Yemeni origin and the Nizari clans claim central Arabian origin.

The Sabeans were, meanwhile, forced to accept an alliance with the Himyar who, for a while, imposed control over southern Arabia. However, the Himyar were themselves caught between the two great powers of the time—the Sassanian empire of Persia and their bitter rivals, the Byzantines. By this time the Byzantines (that is, the eastern Roman empire with its capital in Constantinople, modern Istanbul) had become enthusiastic and proselytizing Christians, and geopolitics took on a religious colour. The Byzantine emperor Constantius (337–361) dispatched ambassadors and the missionary Theophilus the Indian to the Himyarite court demanding permission to build churches and proselytize.

Ethiopia was one of the countries that was profoundly affected by this churn in geopolitics and religion during AD fourth century. Around the middle of AD fourth century, the Ethiopians captured two Christian teenagers, Frumentius and Edesius from a merchant ship on the Red Sea. They were taken to the capital Aksum where they served as slaves of the king. They soon came to be trusted and, shortly before his death, the king granted them their freedom and promoted them to high office. The widowed queen became dependent on them for running the kingdom and also entrusted the education of her infant son, the new king, to Frumentius.[8]

The former slaves now used their position to actively promote Christianity, and eventually, under the influence of his tutor, the young king Erazanes too converted to the faith. Thus, Ethiopia came to be a Christian country. This brought it into the cultural and geopolitical sphere of influence of the Byzantines. These changes were clearly noticed by the Indians of that period as they began to refer to the Ethiopians as 'Krishna Yavana' or dark Greeks.

In the early sixth century, the Aksum king Ella Asbeha attacked Yemen and placed a Christian king on the Himyar throne. Once the Ethiopians withdrew, there was a revolt against the Christians led by the Jews and the pro-Persian faction, and the country plunged into bloody civil war. A Jewish warlord called Yusuf captured the throne and attacked the chain of fortifications around the Straits of Bab-el-Mandeb. Contemporary accounts tell us that the raid left 12,500 dead and 11,000 captives (and yielded 290,000 sheep, oxen and camels as spoils of war).[9]

Ella Asbeha was not long in responding. He assembled a large army and a fleet to attack Yemen. Yusuf and his allies were killed and a Christian king was again placed on the throne. The Ethiopians also left behind a garrison and stipulated that the Yemeni had to pay a tribute to Aksum every year. However, soon after Ella Asbeha left, the garrison went rogue and replaced the king with their own candidate. In this way, a complicated civil war laid waste a prosperous country that had given rise to the legend about the Queen of Sheba.

Eventually some order was restored by the part-legendary hero Sayf Ibn Dhi-Yazan who used Persian help to evict the Ethiopians. Sayf became king under the understanding that he would pay tribute to the Sassanian monarch. However, Sayf was stabbed to death by a group of Ethiopian slaves and the Persian army was dispatched once again. This time the region was put under direct Persian rule.

These events need to be seen in the broader context of the prolonged wars between the Persians and Byzantines across the Middle East. The campaigns in Yemen were part of an attempt by the Byzantine–Ethiopian alliance to take control of the Red Sea trade route to India and bypass the rival Persian Gulf route. As a contemporary Byzantine put it, 'For it was impossible for the Ethiopians to buy silks from the Indians, since the Persian merchants always locate themselves in the very harbours where the Indians first put in, as they inhabit the adjoining country and are accustomed to buy the whole cargo.'[10]

As if the wars were not enough, the Middle East was also devastated by a deadly pandemic. Known as the Plague of Justinian, it was first reported in Egypt around AD 541. Egyptian grain ships then took it to the Byzantine capital Constantinople where it is said to have killed half the population. It soon spread across the Mediterranean and the Middle East where, over a few decades, it killed an estimated 25–50 million people. Thus, when the seventh century dawned, the Middle East was exhausted. These were the circumstances in which a completely new force emerged—Islam.

The Rise of Islam

The sudden rise of Islam radically changed the power dynamics of the western Indian Ocean in the seventh century. As is well known, Prophet Muhammad was initially not successful in convincing his own tribe, the Quraysh of Mecca, about his message. In AD 622, he and his followers slipped away to Medina. Their fortunes began to turn after they successfully defended Medina against an alliance of their enemies in AD 627. It is remembered as the Battle of the Trench as Muhammad used trenches to neutralize the enemy's superior cavalry. Within three years, he would capture Mecca and carve out a significant kingdom in the Arabian peninsula.

Having secured his base, the Prophet sent out messengers to the chieftains of neighbouring tribes asking them to join his cause. This included Yemeni and Omani groups that had tired of Persian rule and wanted to push them out. Muhammad's envoy is said to have arrived just as the Omanis led by King Julanda were contemplating a major offensive against the Persians. The Persians held the coast while the Omanis held the mountains in the interior. The Julanda princes received the envoy in Nizwa. It is an oasis surrounded by tall craggy mountains, and one can see why the Omanis would repeatedly fall back on it throughout history when threatened (although the picturesque fort and souk that one sees there today is of a much later period than being discussed here).[11] The contents of

Prophet Muhammad's letter to the Omanis are said to have survived and reads as follows:[12]

> In the name of Allah, the Beneficent, the Merciful,
>
> From Muhammad bin Abdullah to Gaifar and Abd, sons of Al-Julanda, peace is upon him who follows the guidance now and after,
>
> I am calling both of you in the name of Islam.
>
> You will be safe if you submit to Islam. I am the messenger of Allah to all of the people. I bring news of Islam to all the people, and will fight the infidels. I hope you accept Islam, but if you do not, then you will lose your country, and my horsemen will invade your territory, and my prophecy will dominate your country.

The Omanis were clearly impressed with the message for they accepted Islam. Thus, they are among the first people to have converted to the religion. Fortified by the new faith and the promise of Muhammad's support, the Omanis proceeded to oust the Persians from the settlements along the coast.

The Prophet died in AD 632, just two years after he had conquered Mecca. However, his immediate successors would rapidly expand the empire. The Arabs defeated the Persians at the Battle of Qadisiyyah in AD 637 which led to the fall of Ctesiphon, the capital of the Sassanians. Soon they would take over the whole of the Persian empire. The Byzantines put up a more spirited resistance in their heartlands of Anatolia but the Arabs captured Jerusalem by AD 638 and controlled the whole of Syria, Palestine and Egypt by AD 641.[13] Yemeni and Omani warriors played an important role in these early conquests.

In other words, within a decade of Muhammad's death, the Arabs came to control a vast empire. Their extraordinary success must have convinced them that God was really on their side. Unfortunately, such a rapid increase in wealth and power inevitably led to rivalries and tensions within the newly emerging elite. The power struggle culminated in the Battle of Karbala in AD 680 where Muhammad's grandson Husain ibn Ali and his followers were massacred by a much larger army sent by Umayyad Caliph Yazid. Husain is said to have died with his infant son in his arms. This incident created the Shia–Sunni sectarian divide that exists to this day.

Intriguingly, there is an oral tradition in India that Husain's party included a group of Hindu mercenaries who were also killed in the battle. This is why the Mohyal Brahmins of Punjab still join Shia Muslims in the annual ritual mourning of Muharram. Given the atmosphere of suspicion and intrigue within the Arab leadership, one should not be surprised that outsiders had been hired as personal guards. As we shall see, twelve centuries later, another group of Indian soldiers would find themselves under siege in Iraq.

The Umayyads next decided to impose direct control over the Omanis who, as early and willing converts to Islam, had come to expect a degree of autonomy. Two brothers, Sulaiman and Said, organized a heroic defence against a large army of 40,000 sent by land and sea. The Omanis were initially successful but the enemy kept getting reinforcements and eventually their resistance broke down. Around AD 700, the two brothers fled by ship with their families and followers to Africa. Thus began Oman's long relationship with the eastern seaboard of Africa, which the Arabs called the Land of Zunj.[14]

Umayyad rule came to a bloody end in AD 750 when the dynasty was overthrown by Abu-al-Abbas. It is said that after he defeated and killed his predecessor, he called a banquet of reconciliation for the surviving nobility of the former regime. After they had sat down to eat, they were all slaughtered to a man. A carpet then was laid out over the dead bodies and the new caliph and his followers then sat and ate upon the bed of corpses![15]

Given all this bloodshed, another wave of refugees fled to Africa. In this way, the east coast of Africa came to have a smattering of Arab settlements. Meanwhile, the remaining Omanis withdrew once more to the rough Al Hajar mountains around Nizwa. There they developed a distinct branch of Islam called Ibadhi. To this day, the majority of Omanis follow Ibadhi Islam.

The Arabian Nights

Despite disruptions caused by all the wars, merchants continued to sail between India and the Middle East. Few people realize that India is home to the second oldest mosque in the world—the Cheraman mosque in Kerala. If the claimed date is accurate, it was built by Arab merchants before the Prophet had conquered Mecca.[16] The mosque is located an hour's drive north of Kochi in the general area of Muzeris, highlighting yet again the importance of this ancient port. Old photographs show that the original structure of the mosque was based on local temple architecture but unfortunately, during renovations in 1984, the building was modified to add domes and minarets to conform to a more conventional view of Islamic architecture. There is talk now of reverting to the old design in order to attract tourists but it is never quite the same thing.

As we saw in the previous section, the initial years of the Abbasid caliphate were very bloody and rivals were mercilessly eliminated. Eventually, the Abbasids managed to establish order over the vast empire. They also shifted the capital from Damascus to Baghdad. Under the rule of Harun al-Rashid (AD 786–809), the empire enjoyed a period of peace and prosperity. However, at the same time, the relative simplicity of early Islam was replaced by a glittering court and the elaborate pomp reminiscent of the Sassanians. It was also a time that trade boomed in the western Indian Ocean.

The spirit of the times is echoed in the tales of the *Arabian Nights*. In the tale 'How Abu Hasan Broke Wind' we are told of a wealthy Yemeni merchant who had become very rich by trading with India.[17] Having loudly farted at his own wedding, he fled social embarrassment by sailing off to India where he settled in the port of Calicut (Kozhikode) in Kerala. We are informed that the local king, a Hindu, welcomed Arabs and that the port had a large community of Hadramawt Yemeni merchants. We are not concerned here with the storyline but the vivid description of medieval globalization.

The constant circulation of merchants and sailors meant that a significant part of the male population in Kerala was transitory while the female population was more rooted. Over time, it seems to have led to matrilineal social arrangements. The Nairs of Kerala and the Bunt of the Karnataka coast, both warrior clans, developed matrilineal customs. The Arab merchants also took on local wives and their descendants, the 'Mappila' Muslims, are now a quarter of Kerala's population. It is worth noting that the term 'Mappila' means son-in-law in the local Malayalam language.

The *Arabian Nights* contains many tales about merchants and voyages but arguably the most entertaining are those of Sindbad. The collection contains several of his voyages but his second voyage is especially interesting. It tells us that Sindbad's ship anchored near a beautiful island and he decided to go for a walk. Finding a nice spot, Sindbad fell asleep under a tree. Unfortunately, he slept for much longer than expected and, when he woke up, he discovered that his ship had left without him! Naturally he was very alarmed at being abandoned on what seemed an uninhabited island.

To cut a long story short, Sindbad soon found himself trapped in a valley with very steep sides. He was surprised to find that the valley floor was covered in valuable diamonds. However, he also discovered that there were huge serpents sleeping in nearby caves and that they would devour him as soon as they came out in the evening.

As he was thinking of ways to escape, a large chunk of meat landed near Sindbad and a giant eagle picked it up and flew off. Looking up, he saw that some people at the top of the ravine were throwing down large chunks of meat in the hope that some of the diamonds would stick to the flesh. The eagles would pick up the meat and take them to their nests. At this point, people would scare the birds off by making a lot of noise and collect their diamonds. Sindbad saw his opportunity and filled his pockets with diamonds before tying himself to a piece of meat. In due course, he was picked up by an eagle and made his escape from the valley. The diamonds made him a rich man.

Many readers will be familiar with this Sindbad adventure. What is remarkable is that a very similar tale was told by Herodotus when he wrote about how the Arabs acquired cinnamon. In other words, versions of this story had been circulating in the Indian Ocean for over a thousand years!

The Conquest of Sindh

By AD 711, Arab armies had reached Spain and within a few years they had won control over the Iberian peninsula. The Umayyads were simultaneously pushing east and, in AD 705, an Arab army invaded the Makran coast and took over Baluchistan. This brought them to the borders of Sindh and the first direct encounter with Indic civilization. The kingdom of Sindh was ruled at that time by Raja Dahir, who even Muslim sources accept was an able and popular ruler.

An initial exploratory expedition was repulsed but in AD 711, a more substantial military force was sent out from Iraq under the leadership of a young general called Muhammad bin Qasim. The campaign is recounted in the chronicles of Ferishta and in a text called *Chachnama*. According to Ferishta, the army first attacked Deval, a port in the Indus estuary, not far from modern Karachi. It seems that the town also had a large Hindu temple and was a place of pilgrimage. The town was defended by a fort garrisoned by four thousand Rajput soldiers. Muhammad bin Qasim directed a constant bombardment against the fort using catapults. Eventually the fort was stormed and all the defenders massacred. As a pilgrimage town, Deval also had a large Brahmin population. Ferishta tells us that every Brahmin male above the age of seventeen was decapitated and all their women and children were enslaved.[18]

After receiving reinforcements from Iraq, the Arabs moved north to meet Dahir's main army. Muhammad bin Qasim used a barrage of burning naphtha balls to disrupt the enemy's elephants before making a cavalry charge. Although surrounded and severely wounded, Raja Dahir fought till he was killed on the battlefield. The Sindhis now withdrew to the fort of Ajdur under the command of their queen where they remained under siege for several months.

Facing starvation, they eventually decided to commit 'jauhar'—the Hindu equivalent of the last stand. The gates were thrown open and the queen led the survivors out for a final charge and they were all massacred. Many of the remaining non-combatants committed suicide. In this way, the Arabs conquered Sindh.

The story does not end here. According to Ferishta, Muhammad bin Qasim captured two of Dahir's daughters and sent them to the caliph as a gift. They were added to the imperial harem; but when the caliph called the elder princess to his bed, she told him that she was no longer a virgin as Muhammad bin Qasim had already raped her. The caliph flew into a rage at this insult and had the general executed by having him sewn up in animal hide. When his corpse was presented to her, the brave princess confessed that she had lied in order to have her revenge. The veracity of this extraordinary tale of revenge is difficult to ascertain. Arab sources independently confirm that Muhammad bin Qasim was executed soon after his conquest of Sindh but they do not mention the princesses.

Despite the relative ease with which they had taken over Sindh, the Arabs found it difficult to expand beyond their foothold in the subcontinent. The Gurjara–Pratihara empire ruled over much of north India at that time and its armies easily fended off the Arabs. Indian inscriptions also record that the Arabs attempted to push into the Deccan through Gujarat and were repulsed by the Chalukya king Vikramaditya II. Indeed, Hindu rulers seem to have made counter-raids and continued to rule over Afghanistan till the end of the tenth century.

With eastward expansion blocked off, the Arabs turned their attention north towards Central Asia. The Turkic people of the region mostly worshipped the sky god Tengri or were Buddhist. There were also Hindu and Zoroastrian influences. In the middle of the eighth century, they found themselves caught between two great powers. The Chinese Tang dynasty was pushing in from the east while the Abbasid caliphate was pushing in from its base in Iran. The two faced each other at the Battle of Talas in AD 751 in which the Arabs decisively defeated the Tang army. Thus, Central Asia came into the Islamic sphere of influence rather than the Chinese.

Qissa-i-Sanjan[19]

When the Arabs conquered Persia in the seventh century, the majority of Iranians were Zoroastrian. After the conquest, however, more and more people converted to Islam. Faced with growing persecution, some of the remaining Zoroastrians fled to India where their descendants survive as the tiny Parsi community. The history of how this community settled in India is recounted in the *Qissa-i-Sanjan*, a text composed around 1600.

The text tells us that in the early tenth century, a small group of Zoroastrians left their homes in Khorasan, north-eastern Iran, and set out to look for a country where they could practise their religion in peace. They made their way south to the port of Hormuz from where these families sailed for India. It appears that they first landed on the island of Diu and spent a few years there. However, they still felt insecure and decided to head for a small Hindu kingdom on the Gujarati mainland around AD 936. The text says that the ruler of the kingdom was Jadi Rana (probably of the Jadeja Rajput clan) and describes him as 'liberal, sagacious and wise'.

Jadi Rana received the refugees warmly and listened patiently to their request for a place to settle. While he was sympathetic to their predicament, he was hesitant to let so many foreigners settle in his lands. There is a well-known legend, probably apocryphal, that the king asked one of his servants to bring a bowl filled with milk to the top. The message being that the bowl would overflow if any more milk was added. The leader of the Parsis, however, responded by adding some sugar to the milk. The dissolved sugar sweetened the milk but did not cause it to overflow. Thus, the account goes, the Parsis convinced the king.

The *Qissa* contains a somewhat different narrative that is likely to be more accurate. According to this version Jadi Rana asked the Parsis to explain their religion and rituals to him. He must have been struck by the obvious similarities between Zoroastrian and ancient Vedic rituals. The newcomers also composed sixteen Sanskrit slokas to explain their beliefs (these have been preserved). The king must have been satisfied by the explanations for he decided to give the Parsis refuge provided they accepted the following conditions in perpetuity: that they would give up arms; that they would adopt Gujarati as their language; that their women would wear the local dress; and finally, that all marriage ceremonies would be held in the evening (the last condition is particularly sensible, in my view, as morning weddings can be a real drag on the feasting).

The refugees accepted the conditions and the Parsis came to settle in Gujarat. A piece of forested land was identified and given to the newcomers who cleared it and set up a town that they named Sanjan after their city of origin in Khorasan. We are told that it was soon a prosperous settlement and that the Zoroastrians were given full freedom to practise their religion. A fire temple was built using a flame brought from Iran. It is also likely that news of this reached the remaining Zoroastrians in Iran and that Sanjan soon attracted new refugees.

The *Qissa* tells us that the settlement in Sanjan flourished till the fifteenth century when the town suffered an attack by a large Turkic army led by Alf Khan, general of Sultan Muhammad. The local prince, a descendant of Jadi Rana, rushed to defend Sanjan but was forced to request the Parsis to join his army, thereby lifting one of the original conditions. The text says that the defenders were able to repulse the first raid but, in 1464, Alf Khan returned with a larger army and occupied Sanjan. The surviving Parsis fled, taking with them a flame of the sacred fire. After a period of wandering, they would establish a new settlement at Navsari, close to Surat.

The Roaming Roma

Even as Arabs, Parsis and Jews were settling in India, at least one group of Indians migrated to the Middle East. It has long been suspected on cultural and linguistic grounds that the Roma (Gypsies) of Europe were of Indian origin. Genetic studies have confirmed that they are the descendants of medieval migrants from north-western India.[20] What were they doing in the Middle East?

One thing is certain, they were not there as slaves because they would not have been allowed to stay as a cohesive group and maintain their culture. Whatever they were doing, it was useful enough for Muslim kings who allowed them to maintain some sort of ethnic identity. Given the long history of Indian soldiers in the region, it is possible that the ancestors of the Roma were mercenaries. A more intriguing possibility is that they were imported as metal workers. India was famous in the ancient and medieval world for its metallurgy and we know that the famous 'Damascus sword' used by Muslim armies against the Crusades was made with Indian steel technology.

In the fifteenth century, the Roma accompanied the Turkish armies into the Balkans. Ottoman records mention Gypsies as blacksmiths, craftsmen and other service providers. They are also mentioned as musicians and dancers. Their attachment to military campaigns meant that they maintained their nomadic lifestyle. Over time they would leave Ottoman-controlled lands and wander far and wide across Europe. Their link to ironmongering, however, would survive into recent times.

7

Merchants, Temples and Rice

The Great City of Angkor

Even as the Arab conquests changed the political and cultural landscape of the western Indian Ocean, the eastern Indian Ocean continued largely as before. The Palas of Bengal and the Pallavas of Kanchi continued to trade with South East Asia and beyond. South East Asia remained a patchwork of Hindu–Buddhist kingdoms that were heavily influenced by the Indian civilization.

In the second half of the eighth century, the kingdoms in Java, Indonesia, began to flex their muscles and we have records of their raids on the Khmers of Cambodia and on Champa in southern Vietnam. A Javan inscription even claims that King Sanjaya ruled over the Khmers.[1] Not to be left out of the action, the Sri Vijaya king of Sumatra–Malaya also made a surprise raid on the hapless Khmers and killed the ruler of one of their kingdoms. It was amidst this turmoil that a new ruler, Jayavarman II, came to the Khmer throne. It was he who founded the Angkor empire, though not the city by which the empire is now known.

Very little is known about the origins of Jayavarman II but later inscriptions say that he came from Java to take the crown. What was he doing in Java? Was he a Khmer prince taken away by the Javanese as a hostage or was he Javanese? The only thing we know for sure is that he was very devoted to the Hindu god Shiva. It is also likely that his claim to the Khmer throne was acquired by marriage to a Khmer princess.

Having acquired power, he systematically subdued local rivals as well as fended off the raiders from both Java and Sri Vijaya. He next conducted the ancient Vedic ceremony that declared him as a Chakravarti Samrat or Universal Monarch. By doing this, he was signalling that the Khmers were no longer vassals of any external power.[2] A new capital called Indrapura was founded, the first of several new cities that Jayavarman II would establish. At the same time, the territories around the great lake of Tonle Sap were added to the growing kingdom and systematically settled. This would later lead to an economy based on hydraulics and intensive rice cultivation.

Jayavarman II died around AD 850. He was succeeded by his son who seems to have consolidated the fledgling empire till AD 877. The next king, Indravarman I, however, was Jayavarman II's queen's nephew.[3] Inscriptions also tell us that Indravarman I's wife traced her lineage back to the royal family of ancient Funan that had been established by Kaundinya and the Naga princess. As one can see, matrilineal descent was a very important component of royal legitimacy in Angkor. This is explicit in the inscriptions of the Angkor monarchs. For instance, when Indravarman built a grand Shiva temple at Bakong, he dedicated statues to Jayavarman II and his queen, his own parents and his maternal grandparents.

It was under Indravarman I that the Khmers began to build the complex hydraulic network of canals and lakes that allowed a major expansion in rice cultivation. By the time his son and successor Yashovarman I wore the crown, the Khmers ruled much of what is now Cambodia, Thailand and Laos. The empire now needed a grand capital and Yashovarman I laid out the first city in Angkor and named it after himself Yashodharapura. He also built a number of large Hindu temples. This includes the Preah Vihear temple, a UNESCO World Heritage Site, built on a mountaintop on the Thai-Cambodian border which is now the focus of a bitter dispute between the two countries. Despite the International Court of Justice in Hague ruling that it belonged to Cambodia, the conflict spiralled into an armed skirmish in 2011 and nearly escalated into a war.[4]

Angkor grew and prospered through most of the tenth century but there appears to have been instability and civil war at the beginning of the eleventh century. Yet again, power was captured by an outsider with a matrilineal claim to the throne. Suryavarman I was a prince of a vassal state but his mother came from the same maternal line as that of Jayavarman II's queen and Indravarman I's mother's family. Some Western historians have suggested that Suryavarman's claim to the throne was tenuous.[5] However, from a Khmer perspective, a matrilineal link to the royal Naga clan was an entirely legitimate claim to the crown.

Suryavarman I ruled over the empire for almost half a century (AD 1002–1050). He re-established control over territories that had broken away during the civil war as well as established temporary peace along the eastern border with Champa. He also expanded the capital and built a large palace complex that included a tiered pyramid called the Phimaen Akas or Sky Palace. A Chinese visitor, who visited Angkor a few generations later, reports that the stepped pyramid was topped with a golden pinnacle that no longer exists.

A modern-day visitor will almost certainly be told of the legend of how the ruling monarch was expected to spend the first watch of every night in the pyramid tower where he would sleep with a serpent princess in the form of a beautiful woman. While I am a little sceptical about the bit where snakes turn into women, it is a reminder of the importance of the Naga lineage in establishing the legitimacy of royal power. This is why the royal symbol of the Khmer kings was the seven-headed cobra which shows up frequently in their art.

THE INDIANIZED EMPIRES OF SOUTH EAST ASIA

BEFORE 13TH CENTURY JAVANESE EXPANSION

After Suryavarman I's death, the empire again suffered internal wars as well as renewed hostilities with the Chams. In 1113, order was restored by another powerful leader, Suryavarman II. It is he who built Angkor Wat, still the largest religious building in the world and a UNESCO World Heritage Site. Its sheer scale must be seen to be believed but, in order to imagine what it looked like in its heyday, one must remember that the towers were originally covered in gold leaf![6]

Note that Angkor Wat was originally a temple dedicated to the Hindu god Vishnu. When it was adapted to Buddhist use in later times, the main idol of Vishnu was moved out of the sanctum to a corridor near the main entrance. Visitors will find that it is still lovingly worshipped by the locals. This should not be surprising as Hinduism and Buddhism remain closely related and their adherents routinely visit each other's shrines. Just as Cambodian Buddhists worship Vishnu, Hindus venerate Buddha as an incarnation of Vishnu.

After a period of stability under Suryavarman II, the familiar pattern of war and disorder repeated itself. Suryavarman II's successors were particularly harassed by repeated raids made by the Chams. In 1177, the Chams made a naval attack that bypassed the usual land defences and took the Khmers completely by surprise. The invaders managed to reach the capital where the wooden palisades and moats of Yashodharapura proved inadequate. The Khmer king was killed and the city sacked. The empire descended into chaos. Once more, an energetic new leader, Jayavarman VII, came to the rescue of the empire. The maternal line was again important as he derived his legitimacy from the fact that his mother was Suryavarman I's granddaughter. The new king first dealt with the Chams and defeated them in a major naval battle that is vividly depicted on the wall of the Bayon temple. He then rebuilt the capital. Recognizing the limitations of the old defences, he built Angkor Thom to be more compact than Yashodharapura, but added laterite walls and a wide moat. Five stone causeways gave access to this royal city through monumental gates that were surmounted by gigantic human faces; this is the stuff of a million tourist photographs.

I apologize if the above narrative about Angkor's history seems like a long list of kings with very long names. It was unavoidable for two reasons. First, the idea was to illustrate the importance of matrilineal systems in the history of South East Asia. This was only possible by giving a taste of who succeeded whom. Second, I hoped to give the readers a sense of how Angkor evolved as an empire and a city.

At its height in the eleventh and twelfth centuries, Angkor was the largest urban agglomeration in the world. Analysis of satellite images have confirmed that the royal capital was surrounded by a densely populated, semi-rural 'suburbia' where non-agricultural activities were mixed in with intensive farming sustained by a complex water management system. Estimates vary, but it is reasonable to say that more than a million people lived in greater Angkor.

So what was Angkor like as a living city? In 1296, Chinese diplomat Zhou Daguan visited Angkor and stayed there for eleven months.[7] He has left us a detailed account of his visit which makes for fascinating reading. Enough of the city has survived that we can follow his footsteps and identify landmarks. But he also provides details that make the place come alive. For instance, he mentions the grand gateways of Angkor Thom topped with gigantic human heads, but he adds the detail that the middle face was covered in gold! This allows us to better understand what these monuments originally looked like.

Zhou Daguan has left a vivid description of a royal procession. The processions were led by a body of cavalry accompanied by standards and music. A few hundred beautifully attired palace women followed. Some carried gold and silver vessels, others burning tapers and still others were female warriors with swords and shields. Ministers and princes were next. Seated on elephants, they had gold and silver parasols according to their rank. After this came the queens and other women of the royal family—on palanquins and chariots. Finally, the king himself entered on a large elephant surrounded by an escort of palace guards, also on elephants. The king held in his hand the sacred sword, the symbol of royal power, and would be shaded by twenty parasols. It bears mentioning here that the last such procession took place in Cambodia as recently as 1901 during the ceremonial cutting of hair of Prince Chandralekha, son of King Norodom.

Zhou Daguan has also left us descriptions of more mundane everyday life. He tells us that the rich lived in houses with tiled roofs while the poor used thatch. The floors were covered in matting but there were no tables, chairs and beds. People both sat and slept on the mats. Moreover, the climate was so hot and humid that people sometimes got up at night to bathe. This would come as no surprise to anyone who has spent the day exploring the sites at Angkor—the still, steamy heat can wear down even those used to Singapore or Mumbai.

Interestingly, the Chinese diplomat wrote that commerce in the marketplace was mostly conducted by women. By paying rent to the local authority, they could set up a stall by displaying their goods on a mat laid out on the ground. Such scenes can still be seen across India and South East Asia. While women shopkeepers are not unusual, their dominance in the marketplace is particularly visible in the north east Indian states of Meghalaya and Manipur. Just wander around the local markets in Shillong or the Ima Keithel market in Imphal to understand what I mean. Readers will recall that the matrilineal Khasis are genetically and linguistically related to the Khmer. It is remarkable how certain cultural traits have survived from Neolithic times.

Geopolitics of the Chola-Era

The Cholas, as the reader will recall, were one of the three clans who dominated the southern tip of India in ancient times. During the period of Pallava rule, they had accepted the overlordship of Kanchi but still retained significant political clout. At the end of the ninth century, a Chola general called Aditya helped the Pallavas crush a revolt by the Pandyas, the other ancient Tamil clan. As a reward, he seems to have been given sizeable new territories. Aditya used the new resources to build up his military capability and in AD 873 he marched against his Pallava overlords. The Cholas defeated and killed the last Pallava king Aparajita (whose name ironically means 'he who cannot be defeated'). Aditya took care, however, to marry a Pallava princess and thereby absorb their lineage into his own.[8]

Over the next several decades, the Cholas steadily expanded their kingdom. They repeatedly defeated the combined armies of the Pandyas and their Sri Lankan allies. However, not all their military campaigns went well. When the Cholas attempted to expand northwards, they were beaten back by the Rashtrakutas who had replaced the Chalukyas in the Deccan plateau. In fact, the Rashtrakutas pushed back and occupied the old Pallava capital of Kanchi. It took several years for the Cholas to recover from the defeat but they seemed to have clawed back the lost territory by the time Rajaraja Chola came to the throne in AD 985.

Rajaraja is widely regarded by Tamils as their greatest king. He defeated the combined armies of the Pandyas, the Sinhalese and the ruler of Kerala. This gave him control over ports on both the eastern and western coasts. Next he decided to teach the Sri Lankans a lesson. A naval raid occupied the north of the island and sacked the Sinhalese capital of Anuradhapura. The Maldives was also added to the empire. As thanksgiving for his victories, Rajaraja then built the enormous Brihadeswara temple dedicated to Shiva. It is now a UNESCO World Heritage Site.

The next Chola ruler was Rajaraja's son Rajendra who assumed the throne in 1014. He initially had to put down revolts by the old rival clans and consolidate his control over Sri Lanka. He then led an extraordinary military expedition that made its way north to the banks of the Ganga. Although the Cholas did not attempt to maintain control over these northern lands, Rajendra was clearly very proud of having made his way to the holy river. Water from the Ganga was carried back in golden vessels and a new capital was built—'Gangaikonda Cholapuram' meaning, 'The City of the Chola who brought the Ganga'.

From the perspective of Indian Ocean history, however, the most significant event of Rajendra's rule was a major naval raid on the Sri Vijaya kingdom of Sumatra and Malaya. In order to appreciate the historical context of this event, one needs to step back and understand the geopolitical dynamics of the times. The maritime trade route between India and China had become very lucrative and there were two main routes. The first passed through the Straits of Malacca, between the Malay peninsula and Sumatra. The Sri Vijaya kingdom controlled this route. The second, more southerly route, passed through the Sunda Straits between Sumatra and Java. Although it was a bit of a detour for those going to China or Champa, it had better access to the spice growing Maluku and Banda islands. This route was usually controlled by the Javans. Not surprisingly, there was constant rivalry between the Sri Vijaya and the Javanese kingdoms.

The late tenth century was a period of prosperity in the Indian Ocean rim as trade boomed between the Song empire in China, the Cholas in southern India and the Shiite Fatimid caliphate that controlled Egypt and the Red Sea. The rivalries of South East Asia were proving to be a major threat to this economic pipeline. In AD 987, a Sri Vijaya diplomatic mission made its way to China.[9] During its stay in China, the diplomats were informed that their country was under attack from the Javan kingdom of Mataram. They decided to head home but the war escalated and the mission found itself stranded in Champa for a year. It is likely that they received new instructions from the capital for they headed back to China and pleaded with the Song emperor to place Sri Vijaya under its protection. Thus, China came to have influence in the region.

The Sri Vijaya would have been aware that the entry of the Chinese into the Indian Ocean could elicit a response from the Cholas. Thus, they simultaneously sent missions to the Chola kings and made generous grants to Hindu and Buddhist temples in Chola ports. Amusingly, Chinese records show that the Sri Vijaya were playing a double game because their diplomats were deliberately misrepresenting the situation by claiming that the Cholas paid tribute to them!

The Sri Vijaya seem to have used Chinese protection to build up their own strength. Not surprisingly, this caused their neighbours to become concerned. Around 1012, Suryavarman I, the king of Angkor, chose to send an unusual gift to Rajendra Chola—his personal war chariot with which he had defeated his enemies. In the Indic cultural context, such a gift has great symbolic importance and it is likely that Angkor was trying to woo the Cholas as a way to counterbalance the Sino-Sri Vijaya alliance. It is also possible, that Angkor was trying to reopen the old trade route through the Isthmus of Kra as a way to bypass the contested straits. Amidst all this hectic diplomacy, the Cholas sent a direct diplomatic mission to China in 1015.[10]

The ground situation, however, suddenly changed in 1016 when the Sri Vijaya and their allies defeated the Javanese and sacked the Mataram capital. This left the Sri Vijaya in control of both sea routes. We have evidence to suggest that it soon exploited this situation by exacting exorbitant tolls on merchant ships. Rajendra Chola probably sent a small naval expedition to Sumatra in 1017 as a warning but it was not taken seriously. Thus, the Chola returned in 1025 with a much larger fleet.

We do not know the exact sequence of events, but a study of the available information suggests the following: The fleet probably assembled near the main Chola port of Nagapattinam. Appropriately for a port that traded with South East Asia, the name means 'Port of the Nagas'. There is still a major port there but the medieval port was probably several kilometres to the south.[11] The Chola fleet would have first sailed south towards Sri Lanka before swinging east using ocean currents that would have taken them across to Sumatra. They probably then sailed down the west coast of the island towards the Strait of Sunda where they may have been resupplied by Javanese allies and picked up local guides.

The fleet now made its way north into the Straits of Malacca and systematically sacked Sri Vijaya ports along the way. Finally, we are told that the Cholas decisively defeated the main Sri Vijaya army in Kadaram (now Kedah province in Malaysia). The invading force then withdrew, stopping by at the Nicobar Islands on their way home.

The Chola raid significantly diminished Sri Vijaya power but it is remarkable that the Chinese did not do anything to support their supposed vassals. It is possible that the Chinese were just as annoyed at Sri Vijaya's rent extraction and had entered into an understanding with the Indians. The Sumatrans too seem to have accepted their reduced status as they continued to send ambassadors to the Chola court and even participated in a joint diplomatic mission to China. When a Chola naval fleet returned to Kadaram in 1068, it was in support of a Sri Vijaya king against his local rivals. Meanwhile, with external threats diminished, Java began to rebuild itself under a Balinese prince, Airlangga. The process of revival would culminate in the great Majapahit empire in the fourteenth century.

Merchant Guilds and Temple Banks

As one can see, maritime trade was not just a driver of the economy during the Chola era but was the key factor determining geopolitical developments. So, how did medieval Indian merchants organize themselves? The average reader may be under the impression that we are dealing with individual merchants functioning under the umbrella of royal protection. Individual merchants did exist and some of them became very wealthy and powerful. However, much of the trade was done by corporatized merchant guilds. Such organizations, created under contract, are called Samaya in inscriptions.[12] One of the largest guilds, called 'The Five Hundred', was established in Aihole, Karnataka and soon became a multinational corporation. Another guild, called Manigramam, was from Tamil country and is mentioned in Nandi Varman's inscriptions in Thailand!

A code of conduct called 'banaju-dharma' governed such organizations. Membership was based on economic interest and often cut across caste divisions—for instance, The Five Hundred was founded by Karnataka Brahmins but would later be dominated by Tamil Chettiars. Moreover, the supply chain depended on contracts between different guilds. Thus, the weavers' guild would contract with the merchants' guild to supply a certain amount of cloth for export. While these corporations had links to the ruling dynasties, they were capable of making independent arrangements for themselves. Thus, we find that business carried on irrespective of changing rulers, wars and geopolitical balance. Some of the larger guilds had companies of mercenaries that protected their interests from pirates, rivals and even avaricious rulers. In this way, the Manigramam guild survived several centuries till around AD 1300!

The network of temples played an important role in financing this economic model. Unlike their Sumerian and Egyptian contemporaries, Vedic Hindus had preferred simple fire altars to grand religious structures. This changed in later times as temples became the centre of social and cultural life. The early medieval period saw a sharp increase in temple building. Much of Indian classical music, dance, drama, sculpture, painting and other art forms evolved in the temples rather than at the royal court. What is less appreciated is that the temples were key to the financing of trade, industry and infrastructure building.

It is well known that medieval temples were very wealthy but the common impression is that this wealth was mostly due to royal grants. In reality, the network of large and small temples had a close relationship with merchant and artisan communities as well as the village/town councils; this is quite clear from an examination of various donations and contracts. Moreover, the reason that the temples accumulated so much wealth is that they acted as bankers and financiers!

For instance, a study of temple records by Kanakalatha Mukund shows that temple lending was mostly directed to corporatized bodies like guilds and village councils rather than individual merchants.[13] The temples lent money to village/town councils for infrastructure investment and to merchant and artisan guilds for business. Interest rates usually ranged from 12.5 to 15 per cent per annum. An eleventh-century inscription clearly shows that there was an active credit market. Thus, by the Chola period, Indian Ocean trade was no longer about individual merchants and small moneylenders, but was a sophisticated network of multinational guilds financed by large temple banks. Like globalized businesses of today, they too had to navigate between local political rivalries and those of major geopolitical powers.

The Odiya Candidate

The first shock to the Chola empire came in the 1060s. The Chalukyas had come back and retrieved their empire from the Rashtrakutas. This is another example of the persistence and cyclical revival of old dynasties in peninsular India. What makes them even more confusing is that it's often not entirely clear how the revivalists are related to the old dynasty. As the Chalukyas expanded south, they came in conflict with the Cholas. With the Cholas distracted by wars on their northern borders, the Sinhalese began to claw back their island under the leadership of Vijayabahu. Around 1070, the Cholas were finally pushed out. They would try to re-establish control over Sri Lanka but would not succeed.

There may be a temptation to see the wars between the Cholas and the Sinhalese kings in terms of ethnic conflict. However, one must realize that the Sri Lankans were part of an anti-Chola alliance led by another Tamil clan, the Pandyas. Indeed, Vijayabahu's army had several Tamil mercenary units. Having pushed the Cholas out, the Sinhalese would help the Pandyas recover their kingdom on the mainland. Thus, this is better seen as a struggle for supremacy between two geopolitical alliances rather than two ethnic groups. One can clearly see this in how events played out over the next two centuries.

After Vijayabahu, the Sinhalese kingdom was consumed by civil war and broke up into several kingdoms. These were reunited by a king called Parakramabahu.[14] Unfortunately he had no sons and after his death Sri Lanka appears to have slid back into chaos. At this moment in history, a complete outsider managed to capture the throne. His name was Nissanka Malla, an Odiya prince, who used the Sinhalese link to ancient Kalinga to claim descent from King Vijaya (recall the Kalingan prince who is said to have first settled the island in the sixth century BC). Given that his claim to the throne was always suspect, Nissanka converted to Buddhism and proclaimed that only a true Buddhist could be the king of Sri Lanka. Thus, it was an insecure Indian prince who cemented the link between Buddhism and the Sri Lankan throne!

The Cholas watched all this and decided to back their own Odiya candidate—Magha of Kalinga. According to the *Culavamsa*, sequel to the *Mahavamsa*, Magha landed in Sri Lanka with 24,000 soldiers and proceeded to carve out a kingdom in the north of the island. Although the Cholas were in severe decline by this time, they seem to have backed him as best they could. Magha also encouraged a lot of Tamils to settle in his kingdom. It is quite extraordinary that two adventurers from faraway Odisha were at the heart of a rivalry that would later come to be seen as Tamil–Sinhala conflict.

As if things were not complicated enough, Sri Lanka suffered a naval invasion from South East Asia in 1247. It was led by Chandrabhanu, a prince from a kingdom on the Malay peninsula. We do not know what prompted such a long-range expedition. It is possible that this was the last throw of the dice by the pro-Chola alliance in the Indian Ocean. The Sinhalese defeated the Malay prince with some difficulty and forced him to seek refuge in Magha's kingdom in the north. The prince from South East Asia then somehow managed to become the ruler of Magha's kingdom. It is possible that the Cholas gave him the throne after Magha's death. So here we have an impossible combination of a Malay prince ruling over a Tamil kingdom founded by an Odiya adventurer in the north of Sri Lanka!

It appears that Chandrabhanu still had ambitions of conquering the rest of the island and decided to make a second attempt. This time the Sinhalese asked for help from their traditional Pandya allies

who defeated and killed Chandrabhanu. However, in exchange for
their help, the Tamil clan took over the defeated king's territories.
When the Pandyas later collapsed during the Muslim invasions, this
territory would become an independent state. This is the origin of
the Tamil kingdom of Jaffna in northern Sri Lanka.

Memories of Fustat

I hope it is clear from the above narrative that the Bay of Bengal
and eastern Indian Ocean rim was a very interconnected region
linked over vast distances by maritime trade, cultural exchange, geopolitical rivalries, marriage alliances and military operations. The
same can be said of the Arabian Sea and western Indian Ocean rim.
The Yemeni port of Aden became a great hub for business with Arab
and Indian merchants flocking to it.

During this period, the Jews established an elaborate business
network that extended from the Mediterranean to the west coast of
India. The detailed records of how this group carried out business
are available to us due to a lucky combination of dry climate and
medieval superstition. The Jews of this period believed that they
could not destroy any document with the name of God written on
it. This included all business correspondence. So, when a merchant
died, his papers were sent to a repository in Fustat, Old Cairo. Tens
of thousands of manuscripts have survived and provide a very vivid
picture of the times.

For instance, we have a letter from Mahruz, a Jewish merchant
in Aden, to his cousin who had been attacked by pirates on the
western coast of India and had taken refuge in the Gujarati port
of Bharuch (the same port mentioned a thousand years earlier in
The Periplus). In the letter, Mahruz tells his cousin to get in touch
with his Indian contact Tinbu in case he needed money and help:
'If my lord, you need gold, please take it on my account from the
nakhoda Tinbu, for he is staying in Tana [on the Konkan coast],
and between him and me there are inseparable bonds of friendship
and brotherhood.'[15]

Great Zimbabwe and the Zunj

As we saw in the previous chapter, the east coast of Africa saw the establishment of a number of Arab and Persian settlements during the eighth and ninth centuries. The settlers were often dissident Muslims fleeing persecution—Ibadhi, Shia and Kharajite.[16] They created a string of ports down the coast—Mogadishu, Mombasa, Kilwa, Zanzibar and so on. The migrants soon married local women and absorbed local influences. The Swahili language is the outcome of the interaction between Arabic and Bantu languages. One could argue that more than just a language, it is an evolving culture that emerged from the churn of the Indian Ocean and would be further shaped by Portuguese, Indian, English and other influences.

Over time, the coastal settlements would grow from refugee outposts to prosperous ports. The key to their prosperity was their role in procuring two commodities from the African hinterlands—slaves and gold. So many African slaves would be transported to the Middle East that a revolt by them in AD 869 would take over much of southern Iraq, at the heart of the Abbasid empire. Known as the Zunj Revolt, the rebels would briefly run an independent state that included the port of Basra. It would take the Abbasids fifteen years of armed force, bribery and amnesties to quell the rebellion. Despite this shock, slavery would remain alive in the Middle East till 1962 when Saudi Arabia became the last country to abolish the practice.[17]

Meanwhile, the interiors of Africa began to witness political and economic changes due to the supply chains that needed to pump slaves and gold to the coast. By this time the Bantu migrants had largely replaced or absorbed the ancient Khoi-San hunter–gatherers. Since the 1930s, archaeologists have uncovered evidence of the small kingdom of Mapungubwe that existed in the eleventh and twelfth centuries in the Limpopo valley in Zimbabwe. The settlements have yielded beads from India and Egypt showing that goods from the Indian Ocean rim made it inland. The sites have also yielded the skeletons of a 'king' and a 'queen' who were buried along with gold ornaments and burial goods.[18]

Mapungubwe was soon superseded by a larger kingdom further north that has left behind the remains of hundreds of structures built in stone. The largest and most impressive of these structures are concentrated at Great Zimbabwe, the kingdom's capital. The term 'dzimba dzimabwe' means 'houses of stone' in the local Shona dialect. A related form—Zimbabwe—would become the name of the country when it became free in 1980. Excavations at Great Zimbabwe have yielded a glazed Persian bowl, Chinese dishes, Arab coins minted in Kilwa and so on. Recent genetic testing of a small local tribe has found DNA traces from Yemeni Jews! So, it is quite obvious that this kingdom had close trading relations with Indian Ocean ports like Kilwa.

The overwhelming evidence is that Great Zimbabwe was built and ruled by the local Shona people even if ideas and influences were exchanged with the Indian Ocean world. However, note that colonial-era historians would insist that native Africans were simply not capable of building such elaborate stone structures and that this was the work of colonizers from the north. Under the racist government of Rhodesia, any research suggesting a native origin was deliberately suppressed. Colonial-era histories would repeatedly stress that black Africans did not have a history till the Europeans arrived: 'They have stayed, for untold centuries, sunk in barbarism. . . . The heart of Africa was scarcely beating.'[19]

Indian readers will recognize the parallels with the colonial-era 'Aryan Invasion Theory' about how Indian civilization was a gift from white-skinned invaders from the north. It was commonly argued by colonial-era scholars that India was not even a country but merely a geographical term and that Hinduism was not a religion but a collective noun for a bunch of unconnected pagan cults. The subtext was that, therefore, there was nothing wrong in keeping India under colonial rule or denigrating Hinduism. It is amazing how many of these racist ideas have remained alive even after the end of the colonial era. Some of these ideas take forms that look benign but are startlingly insidious when examined. Take, for instance, popular fictional characters like Tarzan and Phantom who are white heroes 'protecting' the locals. The underlying message is that the natives are incapable of looking after themselves. A lingering justification for intervention—both overt and covert.

The Apocalypse

At the end of the twelfth century, the Indian Ocean rim could be divided into two zones of civilizational influence. There was an Islamic zone that ran from Central Asia to the Swahili coast, and an Indic zone that ran from eastern Afghanistan to southern Vietnam. Further east, there was the Chinese civilizational zone that ran from the Gobi desert to the Pacific Ocean, and included Japan, Korea and northern Vietnam. Although the exact borders of these zones shifted back and forth, it would have seemed to a casual observer of that time that a sort of equilibrium had been established. Unfortunately, this was about to unravel and all three civilizations would soon face a major shock. The source of their troubles was the same—the steppes of Central Asia.

India was the first to get a taste of what was to follow. Turkic invaders from Central Asia pushed out the Hindu Shahi rulers of Kabul and then began to make raids into India. Led by Mahmud of Ghazni, the Turks made as many as seventeen raids between AD 1000 and 1025 and destroyed and pillaged many of the prosperous cities and temple towns of north-western India. Perhaps the most infamous of these was an attack on the revered temple of Somnath in Gujarat. Fifty thousand of its defenders were put to the sword and some twenty million dirhams worth of gold, silver and gems were carried away. Somnath would be destroyed and rebuilt many times, but Mahmud's attack is still remembered most vividly. The temple that stands on the spot today was built in the 1950s. Its symbolic importance can be gauged from the fact that it was one of the first projects initiated by the Indian Republic.

Despite the death and destruction caused by Mahmud, the Turks were unable to hold territory beyond some parts of western Punjab and Sindh. Indeed, an alliance led by Raja Suheldeo Pasi defeated a large Turkic army led by Mahmud's nephew at the Battle of Bahraich in 1033 (one version of oral history suggests Suheldeo was himself killed in battle). For a century and a half after this defeat, the Turks seem to have kept out of the heartlands.

To an Indian of those times, the Turkic raids would have seemed like yet another round of incursions like those of the Macedonians, Huns, Bactrians and Scythians of the past. The invaders had been either pushed out or absorbed, and had not posed a civilizational threat. If anything, there seems to have been a sense of complacency. So when Prithviraj Chauhan, ruler of Delhi, fended off a raid by Muhammad Ghori in 1191, he allowed the invader to return home to Afghanistan! Ghori returned the following year to defeat and kill Prithviraj. This led to the establishment of the Delhi Sultanate and opened up the rest of India to conquest. Over the next two centuries, the Turks would lay waste ancient cities, temples and universities in one of the most bloody episodes in human history. It is difficult to estimate exact numbers, but millions would have perished.

Bands of Turkic adventurers poured into India to seek their fortune. Bakhtiyar Khilji was one of these adventurers.[20] He seems to have arrived in Ghazni from Central Asia around 1195 before moving to India as a soldier. He soon managed to get himself a small estate near Mirzapur (now in Uttar Pradesh) where he gathered a sizeable body of Central Asian soldiers of fortune like himself. Around 1200, Bakhtiyar attacked and destroyed the famous university of Nalanda. Most of the Brahmin scholars and Buddhist monks were put to death and its library was torched. Another famous university at Vikramshila was similarly destroyed soon thereafter.

The common practice of Buddhism in India had been in steady decline but it was still home to several institutions that attracted pilgrims and scholars from abroad. It now collapsed from the systematic destruction of these institutions. The Turks were unbelievably cruel towards Hindus and even fellow Muslims, but they seem to have reserved their worst for the Buddhists. One possible explanation for this is that they themselves had converted to Islam from Buddhism relatively recently and felt that they had to prove a point.

Encouraged by these successes, Bakhtiyar Khilji now decided to attempt the conquest of the wealthy kingdom of Bengal. Avoiding the usual routes, he led his army through the jungles of Jharkhand and made a surprise attack on Nabadwip, a pilgrimage town on the Ganga. It so happened that the aging ruler of Bengal, Lakshman Sen, was visiting the town when a scouting party of eighteen Turkic horsemen was seen approaching the city. Taken totally by surprise, Lakshman Sen and his retinue escaped by boat. The popular version of this story is often told as if Bakhtiyar Khilji conquered Bengal with eighteen horsemen. In reality, the Sen dynasty would keep up an active resistance in East Bengal for another half a century by using the riverine terrain against Turkic cavalry.

After pillaging Bengal for two years, Bakhtiyar, it would seem, got bored. Ever the thrill seeker, he now decided to cross the Himalayas and conquer Tibet. He marched north and crossed the Teesta River by a stone bridge. He also asked the king of Kamrup (modern Assam) for troops and supplies. The Assamese king delayed, so an impatient Bakhtiyar decided to carry on by himself. The Turks raped and looted their way through the mountains of Darjeeling and Sikkim before entering Tibet. Here he faced stiffer resistance. With supply lines stretched, Bakhtiyar decided to retreat but his army was relentlessly harassed by guerrilla attacks as it made its way back through the mountain passes. Supplies were so short that the Turks were forced to eat some of their horses.[21]

When the retreating army finally reached the Teesta, they found that the Assamese had destroyed the bridge and laid a trap. In the end, most of the Turks were killed by the Assamese or drowned in a desperate attempt to cross the fast-flowing river. Bakhtiyar escaped with only a hundred of his men. Unfortunately for him, he had now lost his authority and was soon assassinated by one of his followers. The death of Bakhtiyar Khilji, however, did not slow the Turks. In 1235, the great city of Ujjain, a major Hindu religious and cultural centre in Madhya Pradesh, was destroyed by the Delhi Sultanate.

If the Turks were feeling smug about their successes in India, they were about to get a taste of their own medicine. The Mongols led by Chengiz Khan attacked and devastated the Turkic homelands in Central Asia in 1220–22. They soon conquered Iran and went on to sack Baghdad in 1258. The region would be ruled by Chengiz Khan's descendants for the next century and, despite the fact that Mongols were generally tolerant of different religions, for a while there was genuine concern that Islam would not recover from this shock. Interestingly, till they converted to Islam towards the end of their rule, the Mongol rulers of Iran were Buddhists or shamanists. This Buddhist episode in Iranian history is now almost forgotten.

Even as the Mongols were marching into the Middle East, they were simultaneously making inroads into China. Chengiz Khan captured the Yanjing (modern Beijing) capital of the northern Jin kingdom in 1215. However, the conquest of the southern Song empire would be a long and bloody affair that would be completed by Chengiz's grandson, Kublai, in 1276. It is said that the last Song emperor, an eight-year-old boy, would die after jumping into the sea to avoid capture.

The rapid and simultaneous collapse of three established civilizations is difficult to explain merely on the basis of the tactical superiority of Turko-Mongol cavalry. All three civilizations had long experience of dealing with Central Asians. The popular perception in India is that the Hindus were unable to deal with a younger and more vigorous Islam. This too is inaccurate because Hindus had been dealing quite successfully with Islam for five centuries before Muhammad Ghori broke through. Moreover, the Turks did not conquer India during a period of glorious Muslim expansion but at a time when Islam itself was under severe stress in the Middle East and Central Asia. Were the established civilizations weakened by the equivalent of the Plague of Justinian in Asia? We know that the Black Death would devastate Europe and the Middle East in the following century, but did some such epidemic affect China and India in the thirteenth century? The available records are silent.

Whatever the reasons for the success of the Turks in India, the systematic destruction of temples did not just hurt intellectual and cultural life but also had a long-term paralysing impact on finance and risk-taking. As already discussed, temples acted as banks and their destruction meant that Indian merchant networks suddenly lost their financial muscle. Thus, we see a distinct decline in the importance of seafaring Indian merchants in the Indian Ocean rim from this point. The Indian merchant class became much more shore-based while the space they vacated was steadily taken over by Arabs and the Chinese. In other words, the Arabs and the Chinese recovered faster from the Turko-Mongol shock. In contrast, Indian Hindus imposed on themselves caste rules that discouraged the crossing of the seas. Why did a people with such a strong maritime tradition impose these restrictions on themselves? Was it a loss of civilizational self-confidence? I have long looked for a satisfactory answer but have not yet found one.

Nonetheless, I do not want to leave the reader with the impression that the Turks always had an easy time in India. Although they conquered the Gangetic plains with relative ease, they faced much stiffer resistance in other places. For instance, when they attempted to invade Odisha in 1247, the Turks were soundly defeated by Narasimha Deva I. It is said that the Odiya king pretended that he would embrace Islam and surrender the temple of Puri. However, while the Turks were celebrating their victory, the temple bells began to ring to signal a surprise attack by the Odiya army. The Odiya then chased the invaders back into Bengal. It is likely that the famous Sun Temple in Konark was built by Narasimha Deva I to celebrate this victory. At that time, Konark was a thriving port with links across the Indian Ocean. One of the temple's panels depicts the king, seated on an elephant, receiving the gift of a giraffe from a foreign ambassador!

The Travellers

Despite the destruction caused by the Turko-Mongol hordes on land, the maritime world of the Indian Ocean recovered soon enough. Perhaps the most vivid eyewitness account of the times has been left

behind by two travellers—Marco Polo and Ibn Battuta. The former
was born in 1254 to a Venetian merchant who made a journey to
China around 1260. A seventeen-year-old Marco Polo would join his
father when he decided to make a second journey in 1271. Over the
next twenty years, the Polos would travel extensively in the Mongol
empire before returning to Venice. Several years after his return,
Marco Polo would be captured in a war with Genoa and imprisoned.
It was in prison that he dictated his book, *The Travels*, to a cellmate.

The book is mostly remembered for its descriptions of the Silk
Route through Central Asia and of Kublai Khan's empire in China,
but it is often forgotten that Marco Polo returned home by the sea
route and has left us many interesting observations about the Indian
Ocean world. He set sail in 1290 from the port Zaiton (Quanzhou)
as part of a delegation accompanying a Mongol princess being sent
to get married to the Mongol ruler of Persia.

According to Marco Polo, the Chinese ships of the period were
the largest in the world:

> In most ships, are at least sixty cabins, each of which can easily
> accommodate one merchant. They have one steer oar and
> four masts. Often they add another two masts. . . . The crew
> needed to man a ship ranges from 150–300 according to her
> size. One ship can take five or six thousand baskets of pepper. [22]

Polo tells us that as they sailed south they stopped at the kingdom
of Champa. A few years earlier, the Mongols had sent a large army
to subdue the Chams who had stoutly defended their fortified cities.
However, the devastation in the countryside had been so great that
they had ultimately agreed to pay an annual tribute to Kublai Khan
of aloe wood and twenty elephants. From Champa, they sailed in a
south-westerly direction till they came to the island of Bintan (this
is probably the Indonesian island of the same name, just south of
Singapore). They then sailed up the Straits of Malacca along the
eastern coast of Sumatra. It appears that the Sri Vijaya kingdom had
disintegrated by this time as Polo tells us that it was divided into

eight independent kingdoms. He also tells us that most inhabitants of the island were Hindu–Buddhist but that the small kingdom of Ferlec had converted to Islam (this is probably Perlak in Aceh, in the northern tip of Sumatra).

As they made their way into the Bay of Bengal, the ships stopped by the Nicobar Islands. Polo is quite disapproving of the fact that 'the people live like beasts. I assure you that they go stark naked, men and women alike, without any covering of any sort'. This is an obvious reference to the native population of the Andaman and Nicobar Islands that, in some cases, have managed to maintain their hunter–gatherer lifestyles into modern times. However, note that this was a conscious preference rather than a lack of exposure to 'civilization'. Far from it, the heavy flow of mercantile trade past these islands meant that the Nicobarese were very familiar with things like cloth. Marco Polo tells us that the locals had acquired sashes of very high-quality silk that hung in their huts as a sign of wealth but steadfastly refused to wear them.

Marco Polo's ship now sailed across to Sri Lanka. Interestingly, he mentions that the island was once much larger and that part of it had been submerged in ancient times. One wonders if this medieval myth was a lingering memory of the Great Flood at the end of the last Ice Age. He next sailed north to India. Some of his accounts of the Indian coastline can be confusing at first glance as he mixes up the east and west coasts. Nevertheless, he relates some interesting anecdotes. For instance, he tells us that Indians were great believers in astrology and that business negotiations would often be suspended to avoid inauspicious times of the day. Polo also mentions that Indians had a peculiar way of drinking water—they poured the water into their mouths without the lips touching the cup. This way of drinking water still survives in parts of southern India!

Till Marco Polo's time, India was almost the only source of diamonds. *The Travels* relates how the Indians acquired these gems. Evidently the Indians claimed that there was a valley full of venomous snakes where the ground was covered in diamonds. The diamond merchants obtained the gems, you guessed it, by throwing large chunks of meat into the valley. The diamonds would stick to the meat that giant eagles picked up and carried to their nests. As one can see, the story mentioned by Herodotus and in the Arabian Nights was still circulating in the Indian Ocean. Perhaps one of the most successful cock and bull stories ever; one wonders who came up with it originally.

Marco Polo also mentions that the source of the diamonds was an inland kingdom ruled by a wise and popular queen. This is very likely a reference to Rudrama Devi, the queen of the Kakatiya dynasty who ruled over a kingdom that included the diamond mines of Golconda (just outside modern Hyderabad). She came to the throne in 1262 as her father did not have any sons.[23] Although she married a Chalukya prince, she remained the ruler and temple inscriptions tell us of how she personally led her armies to battle. She is depicted on a temple pillar riding a lion, like the goddess Durga, with a shield and sword.

Rudrama Devi ruled till around 1289, just a year before Marco Polo's visit. Since she too had no sons, the throne was passed to her daughter's son, Prataparudra. He would be the last Kakatiya king and would face the fury of repeated attacks by the armies of the Delhi Sultanate led by the notorious Malik Kafur. This is how Sultan Alauddin Khilji obtained the Koh-i-Noor diamond. An attack by the Turks on the city of Madurai further south ended the ancient Tamil dynasty of the Pandyas in 1311.

About half a century after Marco Polo, a Moroccan traveller called Ibn Battuta also visited India. He is arguably one of the greatest travel writers of all time and would eventually make his way to China before returning home to Tangier to write about his adventures. When Ibn Battuta visited India, the throne of Delhi was occupied by Muhammad bin Tughlaq. The Moroccan accepted a senior position in the Sultan's government and spent many years in Delhi, but eventually he grew to fear the cruel and erratic ruler. Therefore, he was very relieved when he got the opportunity to accompany a diplomatic mission to China.

Along with the rest of the embassy, Ibn Battuta made his way from Delhi to Gujarat and then to the port of Calicut (i.e. Kozhikode) in Kerala. In his writings, the Moroccan traveller casually mentions the chaos and devastation caused by the Turks across India—the destroyed cities and the lawless countryside. He also tells us of his brush with 'infidel bandits' who should be more properly seen as an indigenous resistance to the Turkish invaders. In Kerala, however, the old spice ports were still thriving and crowded with foreign merchant ships. Ibn Battuta confirms Marco Polo's testimony about the enormous size of Chinese ships. He describes a large junk that had a complement of a thousand men—six hundred soldiers and four hundred sailors:

> In the vessel they build four decks, and it has cabins, suites and salons for merchants; a set of several rooms and a latrine; it can be locked by the occupant, and he can take along with him slave girls and wives.[24]

Clearly, some merchants lived well on the cruise. However, this does not mean that these voyages were not dangerous, as Ibn Battuta soon found out.

When the Sultan's embassy arrived in Calicut, most of the space on the ships had already been taken. After some negotiations, the embassy and the Sultan's gifts were accommodated in a large junk but the Moroccan found that none of the bigger suites were available for him and his harem of slave girls. Now, Ibn Battuta was not a man who was willing to go on a long voyage without a private salon where he could enjoy his slave girls. So, he had his personal effects shifted to a smaller ship which could accommodate the ladies.

The evening before they were supposed to embark, a storm began to blow and the heavy surf meant that Ibn Battuta was unable to get on the ship. The next morning, it was found that the large junk carrying the main embassy had been dashed on the shore and many had been killed. Among the dead bodies that were washed up on the shore were several of his companions, including one whose head had been pierced by a large iron nail used to build

Chinese ships (the Indo-Arab stitching technique clearly had its advantages). Meanwhile, the smaller ship containing the Moroccan's personal effects decided to sail off without him! Thus, he suddenly found himself penniless and stranded in Calicut. He would try to desperately contact the surviving ship but later would find out that his personal goods and slaves had been seized by the authorities in Sumatra and sold off.

Ever the adventurer, Ibn Battuta was not to be held down by misfortune for long. He was afraid to return to Delhi as he did not know how the Sultan would react to the news of the failed embassy. So, he joined a Turkic warlord on his invasion of the Hindu kingdom of Goa. He would later visit the Maldives that had been converted from Buddhism to Islam only a few decades earlier. The islands were the source of cowry shells that were used as small change across the Indian Ocean till well into the modern era. Here he landed himself a job as a Qadi and married a local lass but found that, despite the religious conversion, the natives were continuing with pre-Islamic social mores. He writes disapprovingly:

> The womenfolk do not cover their heads, not even on one side. Most of them wear just one apron from the navel to the ground, the rest of their bodies being uncovered. It is thus that they walk abroad in the bazaars and elsewhere. When I was qadi there, I tried to put an end to the practice and ordered them to wear clothes, but I met with no success.[25]

Ibn Battuta ultimately would give up on the Maldivians and, leaving behind a pregnant wife, continue on his travels. He would eventually make his way through Sri Lanka and South East Asia to China. It is a testimony to the active trade routes of the times that in China he would meet a fellow Moroccan whom he had previously met several years earlier in Delhi. Marco Polo and Ibn Battuta may have written down their experiences but it is clear that they were using well-established networks used by many others.

8

Treasure and Spice

As the testimonies of Ibn Battuta and Marco Polo show, the world of Indian Ocean trade survived the Turko-Mongol shock even if the relative importance of Indian merchants declined thereafter. The Mongols managed to extend their influence over Champa but when they tried to extend it to Japan and Java, they were rebuffed. Meanwhile, the steady decline of the Sri Vijaya in Sumatra meant that Java became the centre of political power in the region. Under the vigorous leadership of Kertanagara, the Javans extended their control over nearby islands like Bali and Madura. This expansion was briefly interrupted by a civil war when Kertanagara was assassinated by a vassal who usurped the throne in 1292.

The murdered king's son-in-law, Kertarajasa, was organizing a revolt against the usurper when a Mongol fleet arrived from China with a large expeditionary force. Kertarajasa entered into an alliance with them and used them to recover the throne. If the Mongols were expecting the new king to become a grateful tributary, however, they were mistaken. Kertarajasa next turned on the foreigners and drove them away. He also established a new capital at Majapahit, the name by which his empire would be remembered.

Kertarajasa would be succeeded briefly by a son who died without issue, so the crown passed to his eldest daughter and her line. In medieval Java too, the matrilineal succession was important, but it was probably more like the Kakatiyas of south India, the female line being used when the direct patrilineal line did not produce a suitable male heir. Note how this is quite different from a purely patrilineal system where, in the absence of a son, the throne would pass to a nephew or male cousin even if distantly related.

Around 1350, Kertarajasa's grandson Rajasanagara (also known as Hayam Wuruk) came to the throne. His long rule is remembered as the 'golden age' of the Majapahit empire but it was really his prime minister Gaja Mada who was the driving force. Under Gaja Mada's guidance, the Majapahit established direct or indirect control over much of what is now Indonesia. It was perhaps inevitable that the Javans would come in conflict with the newly established Ming dynasty in China who had evicted the Mongols and were now actively expanding their zone of influence.

The Chinese initially tried to establish independent relations with the smaller kingdoms of Sumatra, perhaps justifying it as a continuation of the old relationship between the Song and Sri Vijaya. The Majapahit, however, became alarmed when the Chinese sent an embassy to crown the ruler of Malayu in 1377. This was clear interference in the Majapahit sphere of influence, and would have been seen as an attempt to create an alternative power centre. The Ming ambassadors were diverted to Java and killed. This resulted in a distinct cooling of diplomatic relations, and trade between China and South East Asia declined.[1] In fact, when the Ming emperor ordered his vassal, the Thai king of Ayutthaya, to inform the Majapahit about his displeasure at the decline in trade, the Javans responded by tightening their hold over the old Sri Vijaya capital of Palembang. This is the background to the great voyages of Admiral Zheng He.

The Treasure Fleet of the Dragon Throne

At the beginning of the fifteenth century, a new Ming emperor came to the throne and took the title Yongle (meaning Lasting Joy). At the very beginning of his rule, he decided to fund a series of grand voyages meant to project China's power in South East Asia and in the India Ocean rim. One cannot see them as voyages of exploration since Chinese ships had been visiting these parts for centuries. Rather, they were an attempt to display geopolitical reach and to establish a tributary system with the Ming at the apex.

Between 1405 and 1433, the Chinese fleet would make seven voyages that would visit Sumatra, India, Sri Lanka, Oman and the eastern coast of Africa. No one who saw the fleet would have been left unimpressed. Leading the expedition were large junks called 'treasure ships' that had nine masts and were 400 feet long (i.e. 122 metres). To put this in context, Columbus's flagship, Santa Maria, was only 85 feet long (i.e. 26 metres). They carried costly cargoes of porcelain, silk, lacquerware and other fine objects to be exchanged in trade or as gifts for local rulers. Accompanying the giant treasure ships were hundreds of smaller vessels including supply ships, water tankers, warships and so on. In total, as many as 27,000 sailors and soldiers would have been involved in each voyage.[2]

The admiral who helmed these voyages was the unlikeliest person to lead such an expedition—a Muslim eunuch of Mongol origin called Zheng He who began life in landlocked Yunnan! He had been captured as a young boy when the Ming were evicting Mongols from the province and was castrated before being presented as a servant to a prince. A bond of trust must have developed between the two boys because when the prince became Emperor Yongle, he put the young eunuch in charge of the Treasure Fleet.

The first fleet of 317 brightly painted ships set sail in the autumn of 1405 from Nanjing with a total crew of 27,000 men. It made its way through South East Asia and stopped at Java where Zheng He avoided any direct confrontation with the Majapahit. This was his first voyage and he probably wanted to gather information. The sheer size of his fleet was enough to awe the locals. He also avoided Palembang, the old capital of the Sri Vijaya, where a notorious Chinese pirate had established himself after evicting the Majapahit governor. The Treasure Fleet next made its way across to Sri

Lanka. Zheng He noted the internal politics of the island but did not linger long before heading for the Indian port of Calicut. It had emerged as the largest port on India's west coast after Muzeris had been destroyed by a flood in 1341. Here the Chinese spent several months trading their silks and porcelain for black pepper, pearls and other Indian goods. The fleet then headed back home. Off Sumatra, however, they engaged and destroyed the fleet of the Chinese pirate who had occupied Palembang. The survivors were taken back to China and executed.

Except for this skirmish, the first voyage had been one of information gathering. From now, the Chinese would use the Treasure Fleet to move the chess pieces on the geopolitical landscape of the Indian Ocean. The second voyage set sail after only a few months. Its purpose was to return various ambassadors to their home countries but also to install a new ruler in Calicut.[3] The ruler of Calicut, drawn from the matrilineal Nair warrior clan, was known as the Lord of the Seas or Samudrin (often misspelled as Zamorin). The Chinese records suggest that they succeeded in installing their candidate. Although Indian sources are less clear about Chinese involvement, we know that during this decade the Samudrins of Calicut expanded their power at the expense of rivals like Cochin (Kochi) and it is possible that Chinese support had something to do with it.

It was also on the second voyage that the Treasure Fleet visited Thailand. In the early fifteenth century, the Chinese were looking to strengthen the Thai as a way to further weaken the declining empire of Angkor.

The chronicler Ma Huan who accompanied the Treasure Fleet on its voyages has left us some amusing anecdotes about local social attitudes. He tells us that the Chinese envoys really enjoyed their Thai sojourn because the women, including married ones, were quite happy to eat, drink and sleep with them without restraint. In fact, the Chinese found that husbands were pleased when they slept with their wives as they took it as a compliment saying, 'My wife is beautiful and the man from the Middle Kingdom is delighted with her.' The mystery is how the ship captains managed to convince the sailors who went onshore to return to their ships.

Ma Huan also writes that the Chinese were initially puzzled when they heard a gentle tinkling sound whenever upper-class Thai men walked about. They learned that there was a custom of inserting hollow tin and gold beads into their foreskin and scrotum. The hollow beads had tiny grains of sand that made the tinkling sound. Ma Huan wrote that it looked 'liked a cluster of grapes' and was 'a most curious thing'. One can only be grateful that this custom died out and did not survive to become a modern fashion craze.

Over the next few voyages, we can see that Zheng He became increasingly confident as he gained experience. His fleet sailed widely from Bengal to the Swahili coast of Africa and then to the port of Hormuz at the mouth of the Persian Gulf. He also intervened systematically in local political rivalries where the opportunity presented itself in order to place compliant rulers on the throne. For instance, when the admiral visited Sri Lanka during the third voyage, he found that the island was in a state of civil war. The Chinese would capture at least one of the claimants to the throne and take him back to Nanjing to meet the Ming emperor. It appears that the sacred Tooth Relic was also taken to China. Both would be sent back to Sri Lanka as part of a plan to ensure Chinese influence over the island. The Chinese would similarly intervene in a war of succession in the kingdom of Samudra in Sumatra. However, the intervention with the most far-reaching historical implications was the support for the new kingdom of Melaka (also spelled Malacca) as a counterweight to the Majapahit of Java.[4]

The founder of Melaka was a prince called Parmeswara who claimed descent from the Sri Vijaya. He initially attempted to set up his base in Singapore but later decided to shift further north due to local rivalries and the continued fear of Javan attacks. The Chinese would provide him with systematic support from the very outset and we know that Parmeswara made at least one trip to China in order to personally pay obeisance to the Ming emperor. Interestingly, Melaka was now encouraged to convert to Islam. Although Zheng

He and many of his captains were Muslim, this should be seen mainly as a geostrategic move to create a permanent opposition to those troublesome Hindus of Java. It was probably also intended to create a permanent schism within Indic civilization and prevent a future anti-Chinese geopolitical alliance. Whatever the original motivations, Melaka prospered under Chinese protection while the Majapahit were steadily pushed back. This is the origin of the steady Islamization of South East Asia.

Meanwhile, back in China, the Treasure Fleets caused great excitement when they returned with ambassadors, goods and stories from faraway lands. The items that attracted the most curiosity, however, were giraffes that were seen as the 'qilin', mythical beasts that are considered sacred by the Chinese. The appearance of a qilin was seen to herald an age of prosperity and poems were written dedicated to the emperor and the giraffes. Problems were brewing, however, for Zheng He. The Confucian mandarins were increasingly suspicious of the power being accumulated by the eunuch lobby. So after Yongle died in 1424, the mandarins would steadily undermine the navy which was controlled by the eunuchs. After one last voyage in 1431–33, the treasure ships were allowed to rot and the records of the voyages were deliberately suppressed.

China would withdraw into an isolationism from which it would emerge only in the second half of the twentieth century. For a while it may have seemed that the Indian Ocean would revert to the Arabs but, as often happens in history, the flow of events took an unexpected turn due to the arrival of a completely new player—the Portuguese. Their arrival sped up the dissolution of an old order that was already crumbling.

The End of an Era

The voyages of the Treasure Fleet may have stopped after 1433, but they had set in motion a chain of events that would fundamentally change the dynamics of South East Asia. As already mentioned, the Chinese had helped Melaka emerge as a rival to the Majapahit empire. A Muslim alliance led by Melaka was soon encroaching into western Java and the empire would steadily lose control over its spice ports. Although the Majapahit would hold on to their heartlands in eastern Java till the end of the century, they were now clearly in decline. As the empire crumbled, many members of the Javan elite accepted Islam. Those who refused to convert, withdrew to the island of Bali in the early sixteenth century, where they have kept alive their culture to this day. Small Hindu communities have also survived in Java such as the Tenggerese who live in inaccessible villages in the volcanic highlands around Mount Bromo.[5]

The kingdom of Angkor, meanwhile, was under pressure from incursions by the Thai. The Thai were originally from southern China (Yunnan/Guangxi) but slowly encroached into the northern fringes of the Khmer empire. By the middle of the fourteenth century, they had established a new capital at Ayutthaya (named after Ayodhya in India), not far from modern Bangkok. It is well worth a day trip although overrun by tourists. When I first visited the place in the early nineties, it still had a rustic feel and one could cycle alone among the rice paddies looking at semi-abandoned sites.

With the tacit support of the Ming Treasure Fleet, the Thai would become increasingly aggressive and in 1431, they would sack Angkor. The great city would be abandoned although a much-reduced Khmer kingdom would survive. The Thai, however, would absorb many elements of the culture of Angkor. This is why much of what is now considered traditional Thai art and culture is of Khmer origin.

Even as the Khmers were getting pushed aside by the Thai, their traditional Cham rivals were facing an existential threat. For centuries, the kingdom of Champa had covered the southern half of Vietnam just as the kingdom of Dai Viet (literally Great Viet) had covered northern Vietnam. When Zheng He was embarking on his voyages, the Ming were simultaneously invading Dai Viet. Although initially defeated, the Vietnamese kept up a guerrilla war that the Ming soon found too expensive to sustain. The Chinese were eventually squeezed out in 1428. The Viet spent the next couple of decades rebuilding their economy but in 1446 they invaded Champa and briefly held its capital. In 1471, they returned in even greater force. Records suggest that 60,000 died in a last stand and that 30,000 captives were carried away (including the royal family).[6]

Thus ended the kingdom of Champa that had lasted for one and a half millennia. It has left behind many enigmatic temples strewn across southern Vietnam. Sadly the most important temple cluster in My Son was heavily damaged by American carpet bombing during the Vietnam War and, despite being designated as a UNESCO World Heritage Site, there is relatively little left to see. A small Cham community survives in Vietnam although many converted to Islam in the sixteenth century. Nonetheless, the tiny Balamon–Cham community (numbering around 30,000) still preserves a form of ancient Shaivite Hinduism in remote villages in southern Vietnam. As we sipped strong local coffee at a Ho Chi Minh City cafe, Prof. Sakaya, himself a Cham Hindu, told me that it is their belief that when they die, the sacred bull Nandi comes to take their soul to the holy land of India.[7]

Again, the question arises—why did these long-surviving Indianized kingdoms in South East Asia simultaneously collapse? Chinese intervention may have played a role but it is arguably not the full story. By studying tree rings, researchers have found evidence that severe droughts and floods may have caused the complex hydraulic networks of Angkor to collapse in the fifteenth century.[8] Java and Champa were also rice-based societies and it is likely that they too suffered from the same climatic fluctuations. Thus, it is possible that nature had a role to play in the collapse of these kingdoms.

Vasco's Cannons

One of the intriguing aspects of the medieval world is the success with which the Arabs blocked information about the Indian Ocean from reaching the Europeans. Despite the accounts of occasional European travellers like Marco Polo, there was so much misinformation around that it became easy for blatant charlatans like John Mandeville to thrive. Mandeville was an Englishman who left his country in 1322 and returned after thirty-four years claiming that he had been to China, India, Java and other places in the East. He then wrote a book of fantastical tales about one-eyed giants, women with dogs' heads and two-headed geese. He also embellished the widely held medieval European belief that there was a powerful Christian king called Prester John in India who would be a willing ally against the Muslims. The Europeans lapped up these stories and Mandeville's book was closely studied by scholars, explorers and kings.

In the fifteenth century, some Europeans began to look for ways to break the Muslim stranglehold on trade with Asia. One option was to find a sea route to the Indies by sailing around Africa. The Portuguese took the lead and began to systematically sail down the west coast of Africa. In 1487, a captain called Bartholomew Diaz finally reached the southern tip of Africa. Most history books give the impression that the Portuguese then waited for a full decade before sending a fleet under Vasco da Gama to further explore the route. Given the importance attached by the Portuguese throne to this project, it is hardly likely that the voyage was casually postponed. Far from it, there is evidence to suggest that the Portuguese followed up Diaz's discovery with a number of secret voyages to properly document the winds and currents.[9] After all, the Portuguese were quite suspicious of a certain Christopher Columbus who seemed to be sniffing around for information.

There was another reason why the Portuguese waited. King John II had dispatched two spies disguised as Moroccan merchants to make their way to the Indian Ocean through the Red Sea in order to gather information on what the Portuguese fleet should expect after they rounded Africa. The two spies—Pero da Covilha and Afonso de Paiva—made their way to Aden where they split. The former would criss-cross the Indian Ocean for two years collecting information on various ports and kingdoms. His Arabic must have been very convincing because he would face certain death if discovered. Paiva, meanwhile, made his way inland to Ethiopia in the hope of finding the mythical Christian king Prester John. He would have been disappointed by what he saw. The Ethiopians had been surrounded by the Arabs for centuries and had somehow survived in isolation by retreating into the highlands.

After exploring the Indian Ocean, Covilha made it back to Aden and then to Cairo where he hoped to meet his companion. However, he soon realized that Paiva had died. He was preparing to return to Lisbon when he was contacted by two Jewish merchants carrying a secret message from King John II. The letter specifically asked for details on Prester John's kingdom. Covilha, therefore, sent back a report on the Indian Ocean ports with the merchants and decided to explore Ethiopia himself. It appears that the spy was now addicted to his wandering life because he even made an unnecessary and risky detour to see Mecca for himself. When he finally reached Ethiopia, however, the dowager Queen Helena refused to let him leave as he had learned too much about the beleaguered kingdom's defences. Instead he was given a local wife and an estate (although he had a wife and estate back in Portugal) and asked to settle down. Thirty years later, a Portuguese emissary would find Covilha living the life of an Ethiopian nobleman!

After years of preparation, a Portuguese fleet under Vasco da Gama set sail in 1497 for India. Four years earlier, Columbus had returned from his voyage to the Americas but, thanks to all the intelligence gathering, the Portuguese seemed to have been quite confident that they were on the right track. Da Gama's fleet consisted of three ships—San Gabriel, San Rafael, and the small caravel, Berrio (an additional store ship accompanied them part of the way). They had a combined crew of 180 carefully selected men. The ships were also armed with cannons which were not widely known in the Indian Ocean.

The fleet set sail on 8 July and arrived at the Cape of Good Hope by early November. Although displaced from the rest of Africa by the Bantu, the Khoi-San were still the majority in the southern tip of the continent. They were not impressed by the newcomers and there was a skirmish in which Da Gama was slightly wounded by a spear. A very vindictive man, Da Gama would probably have wanted to exact revenge but there were more important things on his mind. After negotiating stormy waters off Natal, the ships continued north, past the delta of the Zambezi. Here the fleet began to come across Arab dhows and settlements—Vasco da Gama now knew he was in the Indian Ocean!

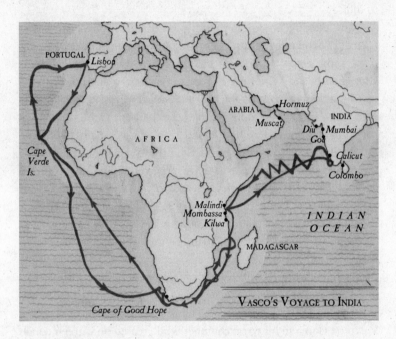

In order to keep their mission secret, the European interlopers initially pretended that they were Turks and fellow Muslims. The Iberian peninsula had been recently freed from Arab rule and there were several Arabic speakers in Da Gama's crew. However, the pretence soon broke down and the Portuguese narrowly escaped being ambushed by the Sultan of Mombasa.

The fleet now kept sailing up the Swahili coast but news of their arrival seemed to have travelled ahead of them. Da Gama desperately needed a friendly harbour to replenish supplies and, most importantly, a pilot who could guide them across the ocean to India. At last, he received a friendly welcome at Malindi—the source of one of the giraffes Zheng He had taken to China. The port was also a bitter rival of Mombasa and a Shia outpost in an increasingly Sunni coast.[10] Its ruler had no illusion about Da Gama's mission but he desperately needed allies. So, it was the Sultan of Malindi who provided Vasco da Gama with an experienced pilot for the crossing to India.

The crossing took less than a month and the fleet arrived at Calicut (Kozhikode, Kerala) on 14 May 1498. The open harbour was filled with vessels of all sizes and the beach was lined with shops and warehouses. When the Europeans arrived, many boats rowed up to sell them coconuts, chicken and other fresh produce. Families of curious sightseers, along with their children, came out to see the ships that looked quite different from those usually plying the Indian Ocean. A crowded street called the Avenue of Trees led to the palace. The ground was strewn with white blossoms from the trees. We are also told that the rich and powerful were carried about in palanquins and were preceded by men blowing a trumpet to clear the way. This may explain why modern Indians love to blow their car horns; it is an assertion of their self-importance. On his way to the palace, Vasco da Gama even stopped to pray at a Hindu temple under the mistaken belief that the Hindus were heretical Christians!

The opulent palace was spread over a square mile and surrounded by lacquered walls. The Samudrin of Calicut received Vasco da Gama in his royal chamber while seated on a green couch below a silk canopy. He was bare-bodied above the waist except for a string of pearls and a heart-shaped emerald surrounded by rubies, the insignia of royalty. Vasco da Gama knelt and presented a letter from King Manuel (John II's successor). He also laid out the gifts he had brought with him. The Samudrin was evidently not impressed with the gifts but agreed to trade in pepper and other spices in exchange for gold and silver.

The Arab merchants of Calicut were understandably unhappy to see their monopoly being broken. They even arranged to kidnap da Gama before he could return to his ship but the Samudrin intervened and had him freed. The prosperity of Calicut depended on free trade and he had to ensure that the principle was upheld even if he felt uneasy about the newcomers. The Portuguese fleet, however, did not wait for long. After purchasing pepper, they lifted their anchors and headed home. Da Gama wanted to get home as soon as possible to tell his king about his discoveries. He received a rapturous welcome and was showered with honours and 20,000 gold cruzados. However, the human cost of the expedition had been great—two-thirds of the crew had perished during the voyage, including Vasco da Gama's brother. This did not deter King Manuel from declaring himself 'Lord of Guinea, and of the Conquest, the Navigation and Commerce of Ethiopia, Arabia, Persia and India'.

Preparations now began for sending a much larger fleet to India. It would have thirteen ships armed with cannons and 1200 men under the overall command of Pedro Alvares Cabral. Despite the loss of some ships along the way, the fleet arrived in Calicut in September 1500 and demanded that the Samudrin expel all the Arabs and trade exclusively with Portugal. The Indians, understandably, were not keen on such an arrangement. While prolonged negotiations were continuing, a large Arab ship loaded with cargo and pilgrims decided to set sail for Aden. Cabral seized the ship and the Arabs retaliated by attacking a Portuguese contingent that was in the city. The Portuguese now seized ten more ships in the harbour and burned their crew alive in full view of the people ashore. Next they bombarded the city for two days and even forced the Samudrin to flee from his palace—a humiliation that the rulers of Calicut would never forget.

Thus began the European domination of the Indian Ocean. The fleet now headed south for Cochin (Kochi), a rival port that had lived in the shadow of Calicut since the time of Zheng He's visit. As had happened in the case of Malindi, the Portuguese would exploit a local rivalry in order to establish themselves. Cabral hurriedly loaded his ship with pepper and other spices, made payments in gold coins, and headed home. In order to gauge the potential profits, note that pepper that made its way to Venice by the traditional Rea Sea route would cost sixty to a hundred times its price on the Kerala coast. With the discovery of the new route, it was clear that Venice was ruined.[11]

Using the profits from these successful voyages, the Portuguese now rapidly scaled up the number of fleets operating in the Indian Ocean. Within a couple of decades they had sacked or occupied many of the important ports in the western Indian Ocean region— Muscat, Mombasa, Socotra, Hormuz, Malacca and so on. Even by the standards of that time, they established a well-deserved reputation for extreme cruelty. For example, when Vasco da Gama returned on a second voyage to Calicut, he refused to negotiate and simply bombarded the city for three days. He also seized all the ships he found in the harbour and their crews—800 men in all. They were paraded on ships' decks and then killed by having their arms, noses and ears amputated. The body parts were piled into a boat and sent ashore. When the Samudrin sent a Brahmin to negotiate for peace, he was gruesomely mutilated and sent back. His two sons and a nephew, who had accompanied him, were hanged from the mast. In other words, the maritime world of the Indian Ocean rim now experienced a shock similar to what had been experienced by the inland cities of Asia during the Turko-Mongol invasions.

The Islamic world clearly needed to respond and it fell on the Turks to provide a comeback. The Ottoman Turks were the most powerful Muslim empire of that time and had taken Constantinople (i.e. Istanbul) in 1453, thereby ending the last vestige of the Byzantines. Although their military tactics were derived from the Central Asian steppes, they had recently developed naval capability in the Mediterranean. However, they were aware that their galleys were not capable of dealing with the much more demanding conditions in the Indian Ocean. The traditional vessels of the Arabs were also deemed unsuitable as the stitched ships could not take the shock wave from firing cannons. Thus, twelve large warships were custom-built on the Red Sea and fitted out with cannons. Interestingly, Venice provided the Turks with inputs from their spies in Portugal and even put a team of gunners at the Sultan's disposal. Clearly, economic interests trumped all other differences.

The Turkish fleet sailed down the Red Sea in early 1507 under the command of Amir Husayn and headed for the Indian coast. Together with reinforcements sent by Calicut, the Turks won a battle against a small and unprepared Portuguese fleet anchored at Chaul (near modern Mumbai). The Portuguese were enraged and a large fleet was assembled. The two sides met near the island of Diu, just off the coast of Gujarat in February 1509. In the battle that followed, the superiority of European ship and cannon designs was fully displayed. Within hours, Husayn's defensive line had been shattered and the Turks were forced to flee. An additional factor that helped the Portuguese was the fact that forces sent by the Sultan of Gujarat remained neutral rather than help their fellow Muslims. The Turkish admiral would complain bitterly about this treachery when he faced the Ottoman Sultan in Istanbul.

Despite these victories, the Portuguese were still operating like nomadic pirates and did not have a permanent establishment in the Indian Ocean yet. After another unsuccessful raid on Calicut, it was decided that Goa would be a good place to build a base. Under the command of Afonso de Albuquerque, the Portuguese attacked and took Goa from the Sultan of Bijapur in 1510. Albuquerque would boast to King Manuel in a letter:

> Then I burned the city and put everyone to the sword and for
> four days your men shed blood continuously. No matter where
> we found them, we did not spare the life of a single Muslim; we
> filled the mosques with them and set them on fire. . . . [12]

Soon the Portuguese had built a network of fortifications around the Indian Ocean rim from where they controlled their maritime empire. Perhaps the best preserved of these forts can be seen today on the island of Diu. The ramparts offer fine views over the Arabian Sea and an excellent collection of early cannons still stand guard. The fort would fend off a second Turkish attempt against the

Europeans in 1538. The only reminder of this second failed attempt is an enormous Turkish cannon that can be seen in Junagarh fort museum on the mainland.

The Swashbucklers

Better technology may partly explain Portugal's success, but it was also driven by the fact that its expeditions attracted extraordinary adventurers. Often cruel and bloodthirsty, they were also willing to take enormous personal risks. Two such characters were Ferdinand Magellan and Francisco Serrao, close friends who would participate in the first Portuguese attempt to capture Malacca in 1509. Magellan would later become famous for having led the first successful circumnavigation of the globe (although he would be killed in the Philippines and would not complete the voyage himself). Serrao is now almost forgotten but his story is just as fascinating and closely linked to that of Magellan.

The first Portuguese attack on Malacca ended in defeat and Serrao narrowly escaped with his life thanks to a last-minute rescue by Magellan. Two years later, he returned as part of a large fleet under the personal command of Afonso de Albuquerque. The Malaccans put up a spirited defence but were eventually overcome. Albuquerque then ordered the construction of a new fort on a natural hill overlooking the town; the Dutch would later destroy most of it but the remains of one of its gates survive. Meanwhile, Serrao was made captain of one of three ships sent out to scout the Spice Islands further east.[13]

Although his ship was leaking badly, Serrao somehow made it to the Banda Islands, the world's only source of nutmegs. While the other ships loaded nutmegs, Serrao purchased a Chinese junk as replacement. It tells us something about the man's self-confidence that it was manned with a crew of just nine Portuguese and a dozen Malays. On the return journey, however, a storm separated the three ships. Serrao's junk was blown into a reef and he lost several of his men. The survivors were now marooned on a small uninhabited island with no water. Nonetheless, Serrao kept his cool and took care to retrieve his guns before hiding his men in the undergrowth in anticipation of local pirates who may come to investigate the wreck. Sure enough, a boatload of pirates arrived and, at a pre-decided signal, the Portuguese party rushed to the beach and captured the pirates and their boat.

The survivors now headed for the nearest inhabited island of Hitu. The chiefs of this island were at this time at war with a nearby island and Serrao decided to impress them by joining in a surprise attack. There were only a handful of Portuguese guns, but the defenders were totally unused to them and were routed. Serrao and his band of merry men retuned as heroes to Hitu and their fame spread to nearby islands. While they were celebrating their victory with women and arrack, a flotilla of war canoes arrived with an invitation from the Sultan of Ternate.

The twin volcanic islands of Tidore and Ternate were the world's only source of cloves but their rulers were bitter rivals. Serrao must have already heard of them and he accepted the invitation. News of Portuguese victories in the Indian Ocean had clearly reached these parts, for Serrao was received like royalty when he reached Ternate. He soon established himself as the Sultan's right-hand man. When a Portuguese fleet finally reached the island a couple of years later, the captain was amazed at the influential status held by Serrao and by his lavish lifestyle. They seethed in envy at a colleague who they saw as a renegade and deserter who had gone native. For the moment, however, they recognized that Serrao's unique position was an advantage and he was allowed to continue.

Serrao sent back letters to his superiors as well as to his friend Magellan, whom he urged to join him in the Spice Islands. These letters were what inspired Magellan with the idea that Ternate and Tidore were so far east that they could be accessed easily by sailing west from the Americas. The problem was that the Portuguese authorities were not keen on exploring an idea that could provide the Spanish with easy access to the Spice Islands. So, Magellan took his plans to the Spanish who agreed to fund his expedition.

In March 1521, after sailing around South America and enduring many hardships, Magellan's fleet managed to reach the Philippines. When the Spanish landed on the island of Cebu, the area was ruled by a Hindu dynasty of possibly Tamil origin. Magellan signed a treaty with Raja Humabon and converted him to Catholicism. This is the basis on which the Spanish would later claim the islands. One of Humabon's vassal chiefs Lapulapu, however, refused and the Spanish were obliged to demonstrate their military superiority. It is not known why Magellan decided to storm Lapulapu's island personally but it is possible that he was trying to live up to Serrao's exploits. In any event, he was surrounded and killed on the beach.

Magellan's remaining fleet, however, continued on its voyage and a few weeks later anchored at Tidore. Here they heard that Serrao had died a few weeks earlier, possibly poisoned by local rivals. It is amazing how close Serrao and Magellan had come to achieving their rendezvous on the other side of the world. Thus ended a story of friendship and swashbuckling adventure. Only one ship from Magellan's fleet with twenty-one survivors would make it back to Spain. Its cargo of cloves was valued at ten thousand times what it had cost in Tidore.

In the Name of the Cross

One of the enclaves acquired by the Portuguese during the sixteenth century was Mumbai, then a collection of marshy islands. The sculpted caves of Elephanta Island suggest that the area had been an important commercial hub in the seventh and eighth centuries, but it had since declined. The first Portuguese landing on the islands in 1509 was a brutal raid: 'Our men captured many cows and some blacks who were hiding among the bushes, and of whom the good were kept and the rest were killed.'[14] Over the next few decades the Portuguese managed to establish a small enclave here. One of its earliest European residents was Garcia da Orta, a physician and naturalist, who would spend decades quietly studying the medicinal properties of local herbs and their use by Indian and Arab doctors.

His best-known work is *Colloquies on the Simples and Drugs of India*, first published in Goa in 1561. The treatise would turn him into a national hero in Portugal. This is ironical as Garcia was living quietly in this remote outpost because he wanted to stay away from the authorities in Lisbon!

In order to understand why, we need to go back to 1492 when the Spanish ended Moorish rule in the Iberian peninsula and ordered the mass expulsion of Jews and Muslims. Those who remained behind were forced to become Christians known as New Christians. However, it was always suspected that these new converts continued to practise their old religion in secret. It was to ferret out these covert Jews and Muslims that the Spanish Inquisition was originally founded. Garcia da Orta's parents were Spanish Jews who fled to Portugal to escape persecution. Unfortunately, a few years later, the Portuguese too expelled the Jews. Indeed, Vasco da Gama's voyage had been partly funded by the wealth expropriated from the expelled Jews. The Orta family, however, remained in Portugal by ostensibly converting to Catholicism but they were always afraid of being investigated by the Inquisition.[15]

There is evidence that the Ortas continued to practise Judaism in secret and even had secret Hebrew names. Garcia's secret name was Abraham. This is the real reason that Garcia da Orta was living quietly in Mumbai (incidentally, he refers to the place both as *Bombaim* and *Mombaim* in his writings). Over time, he used his contacts in the colonial headquarters in Goa to bring over family members and other New Christians from Portugal. In this way, Goa and other Portuguese enclaves ended up with a sizeable New Christian population. Although there was always an air of uncertainty, things were tolerable till the arrival of Francis Xavier, a Jesuit missionary, in 1542.

Xavier, later to be canonized as a saint, is known today in India for the numerous Jesuit schools and colleges named after him. However, it was he who invited the Inquisition to Goa before leaving for Malacca. When the Inquisition arrived in Goa, the vast majority of the local population practised Hinduism and there were

numerous temples dedicated to goddess Shanta-Durga. Egged on
by the Jesuits, the Portuguese would destroy hundreds of temples.
Thousands of Hindus would be killed or forcibly converted to
Christianity. Many small children were forcibly taken away and
baptized.[16] The remains of destroyed temples can still be seen in
Goa, some with churches built over them. In recent years, a handful
of these temples have been rebuilt by local Hindus. One example
is the Mahalasa Narayani temple in the village of Verna, which was
destroyed in 1567 and was rebuilt in 2000–05 (incidentally the site
also has a large stone carving of a female figure that may date back
to the Neolithic age).[17]

The Inquisition soon turned on the communities of Syrian
Christians who had lived peacefully on India's west coast for
over a thousand years before the arrival of the Portuguese. Their
ancient rituals were condemned as heretical and they were forced
to accept Latin rites; many of their books and records composed in
Syriac were burned.[18] Not surprisingly, the Inquisition also began
to scrutinize the New Christians. Many would be tortured and
killed including Garcia da Orta's sister Catrina who was burned at
the stake as 'as an impertinent Jewess' in 1569, a year after Garcia's
death. Her husband confessed under torture that the famous
physician had kept 'the Sabbath on Saturday'. It is a reflection
of the vindictiveness of the Inquisition that Orta's remains were
dug out of his grave and burned, and the ashes thrown into the
Mandovi River.[19]

Vijayanagar—The City of Victory[20]

When the Portuguese first arrived in India, most of the northern
and central parts of the subcontinent were ruled by Muslim rulers of
Turkic, Afghan and Persian extract (although there remained several
pockets of resistance such as the kingdom of Mewar). The southern
half of the Indian peninsula, however, was home to a remarkable
Hindu empire remembered today by the name of its capital—
Vijayanagar. Built on the banks of the Tungabhadra River, it was

then the largest city in the world. Both Calicut and Cochin were nominally the vassals of the kings who ruled from this city.

The city had been established in 1336 by two brothers Hukka (also called Harihara) and Bukka in the aftermath of the Delhi Sultan's raids that destroyed the old kingdoms of southern India. It is said that Hukka and Bukka had been captured and forcibly converted to Islam but had later escaped and reverted to Hinduism. They now began to gather together and organize the shattered remains of the defeated armies. Very soon they were able to establish control over a sizeable kingdom.

According to the traditional founding myth of Vijayanagar, the two princes were out hunting near Hampi when their hunting dogs gave chase to a hare. Just when it seemed that the hare was cornered, it suddenly turned around and attacked the hounds who fled in disarray. When the brothers related this story to their spiritual guru, Vidyaranya, they were told that it was a sign that this was a favourable site for their capital city.[21] While this legend may not be literally true, there were other good reasons for choosing the site. As anyone who has visited Hampi will know, it is a strange landscape of rocky outcrops and low hills. Hukka and Bukka would have realized that this terrain was their best defence against Turkic cavalry. Moreover, the area had a special place in the Hindu imagination. Just across the river is Kishkindha, home of the monkey kingdom mentioned in the epic Ramayana.

Many foreign visitors have left us eyewitness accounts of how the city looked in the fifteenth and sixteenth centuries. Abdul Razzaq, an envoy from the Timurid ruler of Persia, wrote that the city had seven concentric walls that enclosed a vast area. The area between the first and third walls was semi-rural with cultivated fields and gardens. Between the third and the seventh were homes, grand temples, workshops and bustling bazaars. At the centre was the royal citadel that contained the palace and the grand assembly hall. Razzaq tells us that rock-cut aqueducts and canals brought water from the river to the palace complex. The remains of the city at Hampi are truly spectacular and are comparable to those at

Angkor, except that the dense Cambodian jungle is replaced here by gigantic rock outcrops littered across the landscape. A fair amount of agriculture continues to be practised within the UNESCO World Heritage Site, in many cases using the medieval canal system. The visitor will have little difficulty recognizing many of the features described by Abdul Razzaq and other travellers.

Once the Portuguese established themselves on the Indian coast, a number of Europeans also visited Vijayanagar and have left us detailed accounts. These include horse traders Domingo Paes and Fernao Nuniz who wrote about Vijayanagar under Krishnadeva Raya, arguably the greatest of its rulers. They describe the grand feasts, dancing and ceremonies that accompanied the Mahanavami festival. They also describe life in the court. Interestingly, Nuniz tells us that women ran the show within the palace complex including:

> women who wrestle, and others who are astrologers and soothsayers; and women who write all the accounts of expenses that occurred inside the gates, and others whose duty is to write all the affairs of the kingdom and compare their books with the writers outside; women also for music who play instruments and sing. Even the wives of the king are well versed in music.[22]

We also have a description of the larger-than-life personality of Krishnadeva Raya. Paes tells us that he was a fitness fanatic:

> he takes in his arms great weights made of earthware, and then, taking a sword, he exercises himself with it till he has sweated out all the oil, and then he wrestles with one of his wrestlers. After his labour, he mounts a horse and gallops about the plain in one direction and another till dawn, for he does all this before daybreak.

Krishnadeva Raya was also a vigorous military leader and personally led several campaigns against the Deccan Sultans. The Portuguese horse traders were awed by the sheer size of the Vijayanagar army. Interestingly, we are told that the armies both of Vijayanagar and of the Deccan Sultans included significant numbers of European mercenaries who were valued as gunners and musketeers. Although not explicitly mentioned, we know that these armies would also have included units of African slave-soldiers. Muslim rulers had long used slave-soldiers but it appears that Vijayanagar and the Portuguese also adopted the practice. A few of them like the Ethiopian-born general Malik Ambar would rise to hold high office. The descendants of these Africans survive today as the tiny Siddi community in Karnataka, Hyderabad and also in Gujarat. They usually adopted the culture of the rulers they served—so, in the former territories of the Vijayanagar empire they are now mostly Hindus while further north they are mostly Muslims or Christians. Recent genetic tests have confirmed that Siddis are mostly derived from the Bantu-speaking people of East Africa.[23]

Unfortunately, the great city was sacked and abandoned just a few decades after Krishnadeva Raya's death. In 1565, a grand alliance of all the Muslim sultans marched against Vijayanagar. After a closely fought battle at Talikota, 100 kms north of the city, the Vijayanagar army was forced to retreat. The generals decided to withdraw south rather than protect the capital and its formidable defences were not put to the test. The largest city in the world was savagely pillaged for six months and never recovered. A much-diminished kingdom survived for several decades after this catastrophe but the authority of the king steadily faded away.

In 1639, a later king called Sriranga Deva Raya would grant permission to Francis Day of the English East India Company to build a trading station on a small strip of land at a fishing village called Madraspatnam. The English would build a fort called Fort St George on this strip of land. The king ordered the new settlement to be named after himself as 'Srirangarayalapatanam' (or City of Sri Ranga Raya) but the local Nayak, chieftain, ignored declining royal authority and named it after his father as Chennapatanam or Chennai, the city that we know today.[24] Who knows, if Vijayanagar

had won the Battle of Talikota, we would be calling it Srirangarai!
Of course, the wheels of history may have rolled in a completely
different direction and the city may never have been built.

The Warrior Queens of Ullal

The Portuguese had had a hot-and-cold relationship with Vijayanagar
but the empire's decline opened up large sections of the Indian
coast for exploitation without restraint. Even before the battle of
Talikota, the Portuguese had been sniffing around for a base on the
Kanara coast (this is the stretch between Goa and Kerala). Their
efforts were thwarted, however, by the remarkable warrior queen
of the tiny kingdom of Ullal near Mangalore. She belonged to the
Chowtha dynasty that were of Gujarati Jain origin but had adopted
the matrilineal customs of the region. Tradition decreed that a king's
successor was his sister's son but Thirumala Raya did not have a
nephew. So, he decided instead to train his niece Abbakka to succeed
him. Although she married the ruler of nearby Mangalore, she stayed
back in Ullal as its ruler.[25]

In 1555, the Portuguese sent a fleet under Don Alvaro da Silviera
to subdue Mangalore and Ullal. Although Rani Abbakka and her
husband may have had strained relations, they seem to have jointly
fended off the attack. Both kingdoms were nominally feudatories
of Vijayanagar and the Portuguese decided not to press the issue
and agreed to a truce. However, they decided to try their luck
once again after Vijayanagar was defeated at Talikota. A large fleet
was dispatched from Goa in 1567 under the command of General
Joao Peixoto. The city of Ullal and the palace were captured, but
the queen managed to stay hidden in a mosque. She then gathered
200 of her men and organized a counter-attack in which scores of
Portuguese, including Peixoto, were killed. Abbakka now chased the
survivors back to their ships where Admiral Mascarenhas was also
killed.

Over the next fifteen years, Abbakka seems to have held the
Kanara coast with the help of an alliance with the Samudrin of

Kozhikode to the south and the Sultans of Bijapur to the north. It must have rankled the Portuguese that they had been beaten by a woman. They waited for their chance and returned in 1581 with the help of her husband's nephew who had become the ruler of Mangalore. This time Ullal was sacked and Abbakka was killed in battle. However, her daughter and then her granddaughter would keep up the resistance for the next four decades using light coastal vessels to strike at the larger European ships. They were the last known users of fire arrows in naval warfare.

There is surprisingly little written by scholars about the three queens although their exploits are well remembered in the oral histories of the Kanara coast and are recounted in numerous folk songs and in dance-theatre. The problem is that the folk tales often fuse the exploits of the three queens into one character that makes it difficult to work out the actual chronology. The warrior-queens are also mentioned in a few European accounts such as those of Pietro Della Valle but again we have only scraps of information that have not quite been pieced together. So, a full history of the remarkable queens of Ullal is yet to be written.[26]

9

Nutmegs and Cloves

The sixteenth century had belonged to Spain and Portugal and, when their crowns merged, it would have seemed that the combined empire would be unassailable for a long time. However, their supremacy would be challenged before the century was over by two newcomers—the Dutch and the English. In 1580, Francis Drake returned to England after circumnavigating the world. He not only brought back a ship filled with Spanish booty and spices from the Indies but also information that the Portuguese hold on the Indian Ocean was not as secure as had been previously thought. A few years later, the English sank the Spanish Armada and with it the myth of Iberian maritime supremacy.

The English decided that it was time to stake a claim on the spice trade. A fleet of three ships was sent out under the command of James Lancaster in 1591.[1] The ships bypassed India and made directly for the Straits of Malacca. The English did not even pretend to trade but simply plundered Portuguese and local ships before heading back. On the way home, however, disaster struck—two of the three ships were wrecked in a storm and all the ill-gotten cargo was lost. The smallest of the three ships somehow limped back with just twenty-five survivors, including Lancaster himself. Thus ended the first attempt by the English to insert themselves into the Indian Ocean.

Meanwhile, the Dutch also sent out a number of fleets and these consistently returned with valuable cargoes. English merchants watched this with envy and decided that it was worth another shot and Queen Elizabeth I was petitioned for a royal charter. It was granted on New Year's Eve in 1600 and set up as 'The Company of Merchants of London trading into the East Indies'; we know it now as the East India Company. The Dutch merchants similarly banded together to form the United East India Company (also known by its Dutch initials VOC). Both of these entities would grow to become among the largest and most powerful multinational companies ever seen.

The Dutch Hand

In February 1601, the English East India Company (EIC) sent its first fleet of four ships. Despite the disasters of the previous attempt, Lancaster was once more put in charge. He again bypassed India and headed directly for South East Asia but this time he landed in Aceh, on the northern tip of Sumatra. The English were received with great warmth by the Sultan. This should not be surprising given that the Portuguese, exhorted by the likes of Francis Xavier, had been making brutal raids on the Acehnese from their base in Malacca. The Sultan hoped that the English would provide a counterbalance to Portuguese naval power. Thus, Lancaster and his men were treated to buffalo fights, tiger fights, elephant fights and grand feasts. No doubt they also sampled the Acehnese aqua-party: the guests were seated on stools submerged in a river or lake with water up to their chests. Servants paddled between them serving spicy delicacies and fiery arrack. European visitors who attended these parties were known to die from 'a surfeit taken by immeasurable drunkenness'.[2]

The English fleet now made its way down the Straits of Malacca pillaging Portuguese ships along the way to Java. The Dutch already had a settlement in Java—at a place called Bantam, where they could control the alternative route through the Sunda Strait. Much to their annoyance, the local ruler also allowed the English to set up a base at the same place. Soon, the English were using Bantam to send out ships for the spice-growing islands further east. In 1610, an English ship made its way to the nutmeg-growing Banda islands. When the ship arrived at the main island of Neira, it found that the VOC had already set up shop and had forcibly imposed a monopoly on the locals.

Faced with Dutch hostility, the English decided instead to trade with two tiny outlying islands—Pulau Ai and Pulau Run—where the locals had so far resisted Dutch pressure. Just to provide some perspective on scale, Pulau Run was a mere 700 acres of nutmeg plantations and did not even have enough water or rice to sustain its small population. The local chiefs were so afraid of the VOC that they threw themselves under English protection. Thus, Ai and Run became the first colonies of the English East India Company! It is a measure of the commercial importance attached to these islands that King James I would proudly proclaim himself 'King of England, Scotland, Ireland, France, Puloway and Puloroon'.

The English soon discovered that their claims on the islands had to be actively defended against the VOC and its notoriously cruel Governor-General Jan Pieterszoon Coen. Made Governor-General at the age of thirty, Coen would lay the foundation for Dutch power in the East and was strongly opposed to English presence in the Spice Islands. In 1616, the English sent out an equally young Captain Nathaniel Courthope with two ships to the Bandas in order to establish a permanent presence. He and his men landed a battery of brass cannons on Pulau Run and proceeded to build a small fort using exposed coral rock. The Cross of St George was proudly flown to make a point to the incensed VOC Governor who watched the proceedings from Dutch-held Neira and Lonthor.

Despite this act of defiance by the English, it soon became clear that the Dutch had the muscle to impose a blockade on Pulau Run. As the months rolled by, supplies began to run low for not just the English garrison but also for the locals. Using local traders, Courthope sent back increasingly desperate appeals for help to his superiors in Bantam but, unfortunately, the East India Company's commanders were distracted by their own internal bickering and by a siege of the new VOC headquarters at Batavia (i.e. Jakarta). When the siege failed, most of the English fleet inexplicably sailed home without sending relief to Pulau Run. Thus, the blockade on Nathaniel Courthope and his men tightened. When a feeble attempt was eventually made to resupply them, the Dutch were easily able to block it. Matters became worse when rains failed in 1618. The island's water reserve fell precariously low and was teeming with so many tropical parasites and worms that it had to be drunk through clenched teeth. In this way, three and a half years passed and the English garrison continued to be depleted by disease and poor nutrition. It is a testimony to the young captain's leadership that his men and the locals stood by him despite the extremely strained situation. Indeed, the dwindling English garrison and its Bandanese allies were able to fend off repeated Dutch attempts to land troops on the island.[3]

Eventually, things became so desperate that Courthope decided to risk making a trip to a nearby Dutch-held island in order to secure food supplies from sympathetic islanders. Unfortunately, his small boat was discovered and he was killed. His men and local allies, however, continued to hold out till Coen arrived with a huge fleet in April 1621. His first targets were the Bandanese on the Dutch-held islands whom he accused of violating the VOC monopoly. What followed can only be described as genocide. Of the 15,000 islanders, barely a thousand survived death or deportation.[4] Many of those deported to Batavia would be tortured and killed.

Coen now turned his attention to Pulau Run where a dozen English soldiers were still holed up. Despite the willingness of the Bandanese to fight to the last man, the English had had enough and they surrendered when five hundred VOC soldiers landed on the island. This was the end of the EIC's first colony. Coen would continue to systematically tighten his control over the East Indies by using brutal tactics to terrorize both European rivals and the native population. In 1624, fifteen Englishmen based in Ambon, in the Maluku islands, would be tortured and decapitated on trumped-up charges. Known as the Ambon Massacre, it would cause a furore in England. In 1641, the Dutch would evict the Portuguese from Malacca and thereby secure control over both the routes to the Spice Islands.

The heroic resistance of Nathaniel Courthope, nevertheless, had established a territorial claim that would have a curious unintended consequence. When England and Holland signed the Treaty of Brenda in 1667, they agreed to swap two islands—the Dutch got Pulau Run in the East Indies in exchange for the somewhat larger island of Manhattan in North America. This brings us to one of the most important findings of history—never invest in real estate based on past performance. I can visualize how seventeenth-century real estate consultants, armed with two hundred years of data on nutmeg production, would have made the case that the Dutch got the better deal!

The Company Cities

The English East India Company had initially focused on South East Asia rather than on India. Other than the Dutch, its major problem was that there were few takers for English goods in the region. Given that the English were famous for their woollen broadcloth, one is puzzled as to why the EIC had such difficulty selling their wares in the steamy Spice Islands; perhaps a badly run advertising campaign for woollens. As a result, the English found that they had to constantly cough up bullion in exchange for spices. This was the same problem that the Romans had faced fifteen hundred years earlier. The EIC discovered, however, that South East Asia had an insatiable demand for Indian cotton textiles and that one could make a profit by participating in intra-Asian trade. Soon they also found a market for Indian textiles back in Europe. Indian cotton would become so popular that wool producers would force the imposition of tariff and non-tariff barriers on their import. Thus, more than black pepper, textiles were the reason that the EIC decided to build permanent establishments on the Indian mainland.

The English soon set up warehouses in Machilipatnam on the Andhra coast, Hugli in Bengal and Surat in Gujarat—all modest establishments. Sir Thomas Roe led an embassy to the court of Mughal emperor Jahangir. However, as business grew, the EIC decided that it was necessary to build fortified settlements that could be defended against both Indian rulers as well as European rivals. The first of these was Madras (now Chennai). As already mentioned, a small strip of coastline was acquired from the local ruler in 1639 by the EIC agent Francis Day. It was an odd choice as it was neither easily defensible nor did it have a sheltered harbour. Ships had to be anchored far from the shore and boats had to ferry people and goods through heavy surf. It was not uncommon for boats to overturn and cause the loss of life and property. Contemporary gossip had it that Day chose the site as it was close to the Portuguese settlement at San Thome where he kept a mistress. Thus, we must thank this unnamed lady for the location of one of India's largest cities.[5]

The English built a fortified warehouse on the site and grandly christened it Fort St George. However, it was initially a modest affair and the fortifications that one sees today were built in the eighteenth century. Visitors should definitely make a trip to the museum which contains a reasonably good collection of old maps, photos and cannons; it also explains how the fort evolved over time. The rest of the site is today a random mix of colonial-era buildings and government office blocks. Some of the old buildings are re-used in curious ways—for instance, the old armoury is now the canteen and one can sip coffee in a long, dark windowless hall with thick walls designed to withstand heavy bombardment. If you wander to the back of the fort, you will find that significant stretches of eighteenth-century ramparts have survived despite the neglect. I found a group of construction workers damaging a part of the old wall as they built a new toilet facility—symbolic at many levels.

The next major settlement was Bombay which was acquired from the Portuguese as part of the dowry when King Charles II married Catherine of Braganza. Bombay was then a group of small islands and the king leased them to the EIC in 1668 for ten pounds per annum. Unlike Madras, it already had a small but functioning settlement and also a good harbour. As a naval power, the English would have found its island geography easier to defend. Given the unpredictable demands of the Mughal governor in Surat and raids by Maratha rebels led by Shivaji, the EIC's agents soon preferred to operate out of Bombay. Thus, a more substantial fort was built on the main island—in the area still known as the Fort. However, a series of smaller fortifications were also maintained at various strategic points. One surviving example is Worli Fort that was built to defend the northern approach. To get there today one has to walk through the narrow lanes of a former fishing village but the fort itself has been recently restored. From the top one gets a panoramic view of Mahim Bay and of the recently built Bandra-Worli Sea-Link. One can immediately see why this would have been a good location for a cannon battery. I stood on the ramparts at sunset and imagined myself an English gunner keeping a suspicious eye on the Portuguese in Bandra.

The third major EIC settlement was built in Bengal. Yet again, the decision was taken because the English found their position in the old river port of Hugli untenable due to conflicts with the Mughal governor. When peace was finally declared after an abject apology from the English, they were allowed to return and set up a new establishment. In 1690, the EIC's agent Job Charnok returned to a site that he had identified on the westernmost channel of the Ganga and bought the rights to three villages from the local landlords, the Mazumdars, for Rs 1300.[6] This is how Calcutta (now Kolkata) was founded. Note that it was not a completely rural area and merchant families like the Setts and Basaks already had significant businesses here.

The English soon build Fort William—this is not the star-shaped eighteenth-century fort that is used today as the Indian Army's eastern headquarters but its predecessor that was built on the site now occupied by the General Post Office. Nonetheless, the proximity of the Mughals and later the Marathas made the EIC directors in London nervous. The humid, swampy terrain, moreover, took a heavy toll on the Europeans and even Job Charnok died within three years of founding the outpost. It is worth mentioning that each of the above EIC settlements soon attracted a sizeable population of Indian merchants, clerks, labourers, sailors, artisans, mercenaries and other service providers. Thus, Madras, Bombay and Calcutta each developed a thriving 'black town' where the Indians lived.

Of course, the English were not the only Europeans building trading posts during this period. The French East India Company, a relative latecomer, would build a number of outposts including a major settlement in Pondicherry (now Puducherry). This was established right next to the Roman-era port of Arikamedu although it is doubtful that eighteenth-century French colonizers knew or cared about this ancient link to Europe. Pondicherry would remain a French possession till the 1950s and still retains a strong flavour of French influence.

Nevertheless, my favourite example of a European settlement from this era is the Danish fort in Tranquebar. Yes, even the Danes were in the game. Tranquebar (or Tharangambadi) is south of Pondicherry and very close to the old Chola port of Nagapattinam. It was here that Danish admiral Ove Gjedde built Fort Dansborg in 1620, well before the English and French forts. Despite this early start, the Danish East India Company was never able to make a success of its operations in the Indian Ocean and Tranquebar sank into obscurity. Therefore, unlike Madras or Bombay which grew into large cities, Tranquebar retains the atmosphere of a remote outpost. Walking along the shore, one can still imagine a homesick Dane scanning the horizon for ships that would take him back.

Skull and Bones

The proliferation of these settlements may give the impression that the various East India Companies were well-oiled machines and always making large profits. The reality was that they made big profits in some years and large losses in others. Wars, shipwrecks and fluctuations in commodity prices poked holes in their balancesheets. The English East India Company, for instance, nearly went bankrupt on some occasions. One of its perennial problems was that its employees were often more interested in their private trade than in pursuing the company's larger interest. The EIC officially allowed some private trade in order to compensate for the low salaries it paid, but its agents often misused the company's infrastructure and networks to further private deals. Thus, the company bore the costs and individuals pocketed huge profits. This is how Elihu Yale, the Governor of Madras, amassed a large personal fortune before being removed from his post on suspicions of corruption. Part of this ill-gotten wealth was used to fund the university that bears his name. Thus, one of North America's leading universities is built on money garnered through dodgy deals in the Indian Ocean.

Towards the end of the seventeenth century, a new problem arrived in the form of European pirates operating in the Indian Ocean. Their origins were in the culture of privateering in the Atlantic where different European monarchs granted commissions to private parties to carry out acts of piracy against rival states. The English, for instance, would use privateers to great effect against the Spanish in the Caribbean. However, once this culture of piracy had been established, it was not long before well-armed European pirates began to expand their operations into the Indian Ocean, often out of bases in Madagascar. Perhaps the most successful of these was Captain John Avery (also known as Henry Every) who would become a legend and an inspiration for the likes of Captain Kidd and Blackbeard.[7]

Born in Plymouth, England, Avery had served as a junior officer in the Royal Navy. In 1693, he signed up for a privateering expedition aimed at French shipping in the Caribbean and was assigned to the forty-six-gun flagship. The owners of the ship, however, did not pay the crew on time and Avery led a mutiny that took over the ship and renamed it the *Fancy*. Using the ship's firepower, they now looted and pillaged their way down the Atlantic before heading for the secluded harbours of Madagascar. The original mutineers had been

British but along the way they had picked up Danish and French sailors who had volunteered to join the pirates. They now set their sights on the shipping that passed between India and the Yemeni port of Mocha (it was famous for its coffee exports).

The *Fancy* headed for Bab-el-Mandeb but when it arrived there it found small sloops, also flying English colours, waiting for the Mocha fleet. They were privateers from Rhode Island and Delaware with licences to raid enemy shipping in the Atlantic but had decided to try piracy in the Indian Ocean. Seeing *Fancy*'s firepower, they agreed to work for Avery and they hunted like a pack of wolves over the next few months. One of the ships they captured was the *Fath Mahmamadi*, bigger than the *Fancy* but armed with only six guns. The ship belonged to the wealthy Surat merchant Abdul Gafoor and yielded 50-60,000 pounds worth in gold and silver, enough to purchase the *Fancy* many times over!

Just two days later, the pirates came across the enormous *Ganj-i-Sawai*, owned by Mughal emperor Aurangzeb himself. The ship was heavily armed and confidently prepared to put up a fight. However, as the battle began, one of the Mughal cannons exploded and killed several of the ship's gunners. Just then, the *Fancy* fired a full broadside that knocked over the main mast of the *Ganj-i-Sawai* and turned the main deck into a disarray of rigging and sail. Amidst the confusion, the pirates boarded the crippled ship and took it over. The Mughal captain would later be accused of cowardice.

According to stories that would later circulate in the taverns in England, the ship was carrying the stunningly beautiful granddaughter of the Mughal emperor. Avery immediately proposed and, on receiving her consent, married her on board the captured ship. Her gaggle of beautiful handmaidens were similarly married off to various members of the pirate crew.[8] This is the origin of several Hollywood scripts. The reality was that Avery presided over an orgy of violence and several women preferred to kill themselves by jumping into the sea. The treasure they found on the *Ganj-i-Sawai* is said to have been worth 150,000 pounds in gold, silver, ivory and jewels. The pirate ships next headed for the island of Reunion where they shared out the loot before heading their separate ways. Avery and his crew would head for Nassau in the Bahamas where they too split up. Some of the pirates would be later apprehended but the captain himself simply vanished. Thus, Avery would become a legend. For the next couple of decades, rumours would circulate among the world's sailors that Avery made his way back to Madagascar where he lived with the Mughal princess in a heavily fortified pirate hideout. This legend would inspire a new generation of pirates.

Perhaps no one suffered more from all this piracy than Abdul Gafoor, the wealthiest merchant of Surat and owner of the largest trading fleet in the Indian Ocean. He repeatedly complained to the Mughal authorities who, in turn, accused the European companies of aiding the pirates. The *Ganj-i-Sawai* incident was the last straw and the Mughal governor of Surat demanded that the Dutch and English East India Companies provide ships to patrol the Mocha–Surat passage. The Europeans were also forced to pay compensation to Indian merchants who lost their ships to European pirates.[9] Sustained pressure did eventually have some impact on piracy and several pirates, including Captain Kidd, were executed in the early eighteenth century.

The Merchant's Daughter

One of the important power shifts of the seventeenth century was the decline of the Portuguese. This was partly due to the entry of other Europeans in the Indian Ocean and partly due to the fact that local rulers adopted cannons and learned to deal with European military tactics. The Portuguese lost Hormuz to the Persians in 1622 and shifted their base to Muscat in Oman that was defended by two mud forts—Mirani and Jalali—both built on craggy rock outcrops overlooking the harbour. The forts still exist and can be seen standing on either side of the Sultan's Palace. The palace is a relatively recent construction and old photos show that till the middle of the twentieth century, the old city spilled right up to the water's edge between the two forts.

Despite the shift to Muscat, the Portuguese found that their position was not secure. Led by Imam Nasir ibn Murshid, the Omanis had regrouped in the interiors and were steadily reclaiming the coastline. The Portuguese were left only with Muscat when Murshid died in 1649. He was succeeded by his cousin, the equally aggressive Sultan ibn Saif who wanted to capture this last outpost. Unfortunately, this proved difficult as long as the Portuguese controlled the harbour and could resupply themselves from Goa. This problem was solved by a very unusual turn of events.

The Portuguese depended on an Indian merchant called Naruttam to supply their provisions. He had a beautiful daughter that the Portuguese commander Pereira coveted. Naruttam and his daughter were not keen on the match but Pereira kept up the pressure. At last, under threat, the merchant agreed and requested some time to prepare for a grand wedding. Meanwhile, he convinced the authorities that Mirani fort needed to be cleared out so that he could do some repairs. Using this as the pretext, Naruttam removed all the provisions from the fort and then informed Sultan ibn Saif that the garrison was unprepared for a siege. The Omanis attacked immediately and took the fort and the town in 1650.[10] Thus, an Indian father's determination to protect his beloved daughter led to the demise of the Portuguese in Oman.

In India, the Portuguese were similarly squeezed out by the Mughals and later by the Marathas. Pushed out of their base in Hugli, they were reduced to piracy in Bengal and withdrew to Chittagong where they formed an alliance with the Arakanese king Thiri who believed that he was Buddha and destined to unite the world under him. Thus, we have yet another of those impossible combinations of history—a Burmese Buddhist imperialist and Portuguese Catholic pirates. Together they carried out murderous raids into the riverine delta of Bengal that would remain imprinted in local memory for generations. The Bengali expression 'harmad' meaning 'notorious freebooter' is said to be derived from the word 'armada'.[11]

As they lost control over the spice trade, the Portuguese were reduced to trading in African slaves although they were not above kidnapping Indian children and selling them in faraway markets. A particularly intriguing case is that of an eleven-year-old girl, Meera, who was kidnapped from India's west coast and then sold to the Spanish in Manila. She was then taken to Mexico where she is remembered as Catarina de San Juan. She came to be considered a popular saint although her veneration was explicitly prohibited by the Inquisition. Her life is an amazing tale of how a young girl adapted herself to survive all alone in a distant land and in very difficult circumstances.

The Portuguese had also established themselves in Sri Lanka and had built a strong base in Colombo. They even managed to baptize Dharmapala, the ruler of the nearby kingdom of Kotte (effectively a suburb of Colombo and now the official capital of the country). This success, however, led to growing resentment when Dharmapala confiscated all the lands owned by Buddhist and Hindu institutions and gifted them to the Franciscans. The anger rose when Dharmapala bequeathed his kingdom to the Portuguese crown.[12] The Sinhalese resistance was led by Rajasimha, the ruler of a rival kingdom, who united a sizeable part of the island under his rule before turning on the foreigners. Although he repeatedly pushed the Portuguese back to Colombo, he was unable to take the fort because it could be continuously resupplied by ship from Goa. After Rajasimha, however, the Sri Lankan resistance collapsed and the Portuguese were able to expand control over much of the coastline. The Sinhalese now withdrew to mountain strongholds around Kandy. They became even more isolated when the Portuguese took over the Tamil kingdom in Jaffna thereby cutting off communications with traditional allies in southern India.

Given its difficult situation, it is not surprising that the Kingdom of Kandy entered into an alliance with the Dutch in 1638. Together they evicted the Portuguese from Sri Lanka. However, as the Sinhalese may have feared from the beginning, they had only exchanged one foreign colonizer with another. Over the next century, the Dutch would use their base in Sri Lanka to slowly expand control over the Indian coast, especially the pepper ports of Kerala. Perhaps the VOC dreamed that in the long run it could extend control over large parts of India as it had done in Indonesia. However, the world's most powerful multinational company was thwarted by the remarkable Marthanda Varma, ruler of the small kingdom of Travancore in the southern tip of India.

The King and the Captain

Marthanda Varma is a little-discussed figure in history books but without his determined opposition to the VOC, it is possible that this book would have been written in Dutch rather than in English. He was born in the royal family of what was a very tiny kingdom. As per the matrilineal custom of the Nair clans, he inherited the crown from his maternal uncle in 1729 at the age of twenty-three. His problem was that the Dutch tightly controlled the pepper trade on which the prosperity of Kerala depended.[13] The locals were unable to put up any resistance because the region was divided into very small kingdoms. Even within the kingdoms, the king had limited say as power was dispersed among the Nair nobility.

Rather than rely on the old feudal levies, Marthanda Varma began by building a standing army drilled in modern warfare. He also began to take over neighbouring kingdoms one by one. Not surprisingly, the rulers of these kingdoms appealed to the Dutch who repeatedly warned Travancore. Eventually, the VOC Governor of Ceylon dispatched a sizeable force of Dutch marines that landed at the small port of Colachel and marched on the royal palace in Padmanabhapuram in 1741. Marthanda Varma was away but returned in time to defend his capital. The Dutch were now chased back to Colachel where they suffered a humiliating defeat. The Battle of Colachel was a turning point and Dutch power in the Indian Ocean would go into steady decline. Not till the Japanese navy defeated the Russians in 1905 would another Asian state decisively defeat a European power. Colachel is today a small nondescript fishing town and the site of the surrender is marked by a pillar. When I visited the town in December 2013, the pillar commemorating this major military victory was standing neglected amidst heaps of construction debris.

Marthanda Varma's palace at Padmanabhapuram has survived in better condition and is an excellent example of Kerala's traditional wooden architecture. It also contains a painting showing Marthanda Varma accepting the surrender of the Dutch commander Eustachius de Lannoy. Interestingly the king offered to hire Lannoy as a general provided he trained his army on European lines. The Dutch captain accepted the offer and would loyally serve Travancore for over three decades. He would not just modernize the army but also build a network of forts using the most advanced European designs of that time. One of the best preserved of these is Vattakottai Fort, just outside the town of Kanyakumari. Built at the edge of the sea, it provides excellent views of the surrounding coastline. One will see a large number of wind turbines turning nearby, an odd reminder of the windmills of Lannoy's country of origin.

The army trained by Lannoy would help Travancore further expand the kingdom to as far north as Cochin (Kochi) and would help break the Dutch monopoly. Half a century later, it would help Travancore defend itself against Tipu Sultan of Mysore. For his energetic leadership, Lannoy would earn the title of 'Valiya Kapithaan' or Great Captain from his men.[14] One can visit his grave at Udaygiri Fort that he built not far from the royal palace. The inscription is both in Latin and Tamil, a fitting reflection of his dual identities. Amazingly, an army unit that had fought for Marthanda Varma against Lannoy at Colachel survives in the Indian Army as the 9th Battalion of the Madras Regiment. According to newspaper reports, the regiment recently arranged to take better care of the memorial pillar.

Company's Empire

While the Dutch were being squeezed by Travancore, the English and the Portuguese were up against another source of indigenous resistance. After the death of Mughal emperor Aurangzeb in 1707, the empire had quickly unravelled and a large part of it was taken over by the Marathas. They had begun their rebellion against the Mughals as mountain guerrillas but were quickly developing capability in other forms of warfare. In 1712, Kanhoji Angre was appointed the Surkhail or Grand Admiral of the Maratha navy. He is often dismissed as a pirate in the writings of Europeans but he was a legitimate official of the Maratha empire and had every right to impose control over the Konkan coast. When the English resisted, he detained a number of EIC ships and forced them to pay a fine. He did the same to the Portuguese.

The reason Angre was able to impose his will on the Europeans was that the Marathas had learned to challenge them at sea. A favourite tactic was to use smaller but fast and manoeuvrable vessels to approach a European ship from astern in order to avoid the cannon broadside. Sometimes they would also tow a larger cannon-laden vessel that would direct its fire at the sails and rigging in order to disable the ship. While the European gunners were trying to extricate themselves from the tangle of rope and canvas, the faster Maratha boats would close in and board the ship.[15]

The EIC initially agreed to Angre's demands but were soon found to be violating various conditions. Accusations and counter-accusations flew thick and fast, and Bombay began to prepare for war. A large fleet was assembled in 1718 and sailed down to Angre's main base at Vijaydurg, a formidable fortress built on a rocky peninsula jutting into the Arabian Sea. The attack was a total failure and the siege was lifted after just four days. The English and the Portuguese would try repeatedly to capture Vijaydurg over the next few years without any success. Eventually, the EIC called for help from the Royal Navy and in 1722, Vijaydurg was attacked by the large combined fleet of the EIC, the Royal Navy and the Portuguese. Yet again, the attackers failed to make a dent and were forced to withdraw. Except for the English, the Europeans would make their peace with Angre one at a time.

Kanhoji Angre died in 1729 and his descendants would harass the EIC for the next two decades. On one occasion, Tulaji Angre would engage a fleet of no less than thirty-six ships. However, the internal politics of the Marathas came to the EIC's rescue. Tulaji Angre had been part of the faction opposed to Peshwa Balaji Baji Rao who was the supreme leader of the Marathas. In 1756, Vijaydurg found itself under siege with the EIC fleet blockading it from the sea and the Marathas from land. The fort and its harbour fell after heavy bombardment from land and sea. Although the Marathas would remain powerful on land for another half a century, they would no longer be a factor in the Indian Ocean.

By the middle of the eighteenth century, with the Portuguese and Dutch in decline, the British had emerged as the strongest naval power in the Indian Ocean. However, the directors of the EIC would have still baulked at the idea of a land empire beyond a few fortified bases along the coast. It was the French, their main rivals, who first attempted to control inland territory. The key person behind this new strategy was Joseph Francois Dupleix, the Governor of Pondicherry. Note that at this time, the British and the French were at war in Europe but their companies in India had initially refrained from attacking each other. This changed when a British fleet plundered French ships in the Straits of Malacca in 1745. Dupleix immediately requested support from the French naval base in Mauritius. When reinforcements arrived the following year, the French marched on Madras and captured it without much difficulty.

The EIC now complained to the Nawab of Arcot who was the Mughal governor of the area (although by this time the Mughal empire was rapidly dissolving). The Nawab arrived in Madras with a large force but was decimated by French cannon. It was a clear demonstration of the sharp improvements in military technology that were taking place in Europe as it approached the Industrial Revolution. With the largest British settlement under his control and the Indians in awe of his firepower, it would have seemed that Dupleix was in a position to dramatically expand the French territory. However, he was repeatedly undermined by his colleagues and superiors. In 1749, he was forced to hand back Madras to the British as part of a peace deal in Europe.

Dupleix was not yet done, however. Within a year he had managed to place his own candidates as rulers of Hyderabad and the Carnatic coast. Just when the Maratha navy was being tamed on the west coast, the French seemed to have taken control of the east coast. The two European companies began to prepare for war and both recruited a large number of Indian soldiers and drilled them in modern warfare. What followed was a series of engagements known as the Carnatic Wars. The mounting cost of these wars would eventually force the French to recall Dupleix. Meanwhile, the British hand would be strengthened by a decisive victory over the ruler of Bengal in 1757. The British would occupy the French settlement of Chandannagar in Bengal and a few years later would also take over Pondicherry. Both of them were later returned to French rule as part of a peace deal but they would never regain their former importance.

Anyone with even a passing interest in Indian history would have heard of the Battle of Plassey in 1757 where British troops led by Robert Clive defeated Siraj-ud-Daulah, the Nawab of Bengal. Clive had 800 European soldiers, 2200 Indian sepoys and a contingent of artillerymen. The Nawab's army had 35,000 infantrymen, 15,000 cavalry, 53 cannons and also a small French contingent. This would appear like a big numerical advantage except that a large segment of the Nawab's army, led by the turncoat Mir Jafar, did not take part in the battle. The French contingent put up some resistance, as did the men led by two loyalists Mir Madan and Mohanlal. However, unsure of how many troops he still controlled, Siraj-ud-Daulah fled the battlefield (later he would be captured and killed). The British losses were '4 English soldiers killed, 9 wounded, 2 missing, 15 sepoys killed, 36 wounded'.[16] One of the most decisive victories in history was not much more than a skirmish. Mir Jafar became the new Nawab of Bengal but no one was in any doubt that it was Robert Clive who was in charge. This is how the East India Company came to control a major chunk of Indian territory.

The Battle of Plassey has a curious but almost forgotten epilogue. On hearing about Clive's victory, the Dutch decided that they could revive their fortunes by making a surprise attack on Calcutta. It is quite possible that Mir Jafar had secretly encouraged them. So in 1759, the VOC sent a fleet of seven ships from Batavia (now Jakarta) carrying 300 European and 600 Malay soldiers. They made their way up the river but were routed by the British. It is not clear what the Dutch were thinking but it should have been obvious that Calcutta was not Pulau Run of a hundred years earlier.

Tipu Sultan—Tiger or Tyrant?

Despite their success in Bengal and control over the sea, the British were far from being the masters of India. The Marathas would remain the biggest threat to their hegemony for another half a century till they were finally defeated in the Third Anglo-Maratha War of 1817–18. The East India Company also had to contend with the hostility of a number of other rulers such as Tipu Sultan, the ruler of Mysore. Tipu is often portrayed as a great patriot in Indian history textbooks for having opposed British colonization but his record is not so straightforward. While it is true that he fought the British, he was constantly trying to subjugate other Indians—the Marathas, the Nizam of Hyderabad, Travancore, the Kodavas of Coorg to name just a few. He was also considered a usurper by many of his own subjects.

Tipu Sultan came to the throne in 1782 on the death of his father Hyder Ali. Hyder Ali had usurped the throne of Mysore from the Wodeyar dynasty that he served as a military commander. Over the next few years, Tipu crushed all dissent within his kingdom as well as took over the smaller kingdoms adjoining Mysore. The Karnataka coast and the Kodavas of Coorg (now Kodagu in Karnataka) soon found themselves under savage assault. The indiscriminate cruelty of Tipu's troops is not just testified in both Indian and European accounts but also in the letters and instructions that Tipu himself sent to his commanders on the field:[17]

> You are to make a general attack on the Coorgs and, having put to the sword or made prisoners the whole of them, both the slain and prisoners, with the women and children, are to

be made Mussalmans . . . Ten years ago, from ten to fifteen
thousand men were hung upon the trees of that district; since
which time the aforesaid trees have been waiting for men . . .

Around 1788, Tipu Sultan turned his attention on the Kerala coast
and marched in with a very large army. The old port city of Calicut
was razed to the ground. Hundreds of temples and churches were
systematically destroyed and tens of thousands of Hindus and
Christians were either killed or forcibly converted to Islam. Again,
this is not just testified by Tipu's Sultan's enemies but in his own
writings and those of his court historian Mir Hussein Kirmani.[18]
Interestingly, one of the things that Tipu loudly denounced in order
to justify his cruelty was the matrilineal customs of the region.

Not surprisingly, hundreds of thousands of refugees began to
stream south into Travancore. Tipu now used a flimsy excuse to
invade the kingdom founded half a century earlier by Marthanda
Varma. Travancore's forces were much smaller than those of Mysore,
but Lannoy had left behind a well-drilled army and a network of
fortifications. A few sections of these fortifications have survived to
this day and can be seen north of Kochi, not far from where the ancient
port of Muzeris once flourished. Tipu's army was repeatedly repulsed
by the Nair troops but Travancore knew that it was up against a much
larger military machine and was forced to ask the EIC for help.

The British responded by putting together a grand alliance
of Tipu's enemies that included the Marathas and the Nizam of
Hyderabad and, in 1791, they marched on Mysore. Within a few
months, the allies had taken over most of Tipu's kingdom and
were bearing down on his capital Srirangapatna. Eventually, he was
forced to accept humiliating terms—half his kingdom was taken
away and he was made to pay a big war indemnity. Given his record
of reneging on treaties, the EIC kept two of his sons hostage till he
paid the indemnity.

Friendless in India, Tipu now began to look for allies abroad.
It is known that he exchanged letters with Napoleon and had great
hopes of receiving support from the French. He also wrote to the

Ottoman Sultan in Istanbul and urged a joint jihad against the infidel British. The problem was that Napoleon had occupied Egypt and the Ottomans considered the French the real infidel enemies and the British as allies! The Ottoman Sultan's reply, later published in the Madras Gazette, makes the point clearly: 'We make it our special request that your Majesty will please refrain from entering any measure against the English.'[19]

British intelligence was fully aware of what Tipu was doing and decided to finish him once and for all. The allies again marched on Srirangapatna in 1799. The Mysore army was a shadow of its former self and the allies had little difficulty in reaching the capital. After three weeks of bombardment, the walls were breached. Tipu Sultan died fighting, sword in hand. The allies would restore Mysore to the old Wodeyar dynasty from whom Tipu's father had usurped the throne. Napoleon would do little to rescue his ally but the siege of Srirangapatna would bolster the reputation of a thirty-year-old British colonel named Arthur Wellesley. Now remembered as the Duke of Wellington, he would defeat Napoleon sixteen years later at Waterloo.

The Srirangapatna fort lies on a river island just off the Bangalore–Mysore highway. The final siege is so well documented that one can wander around the area and get a very good feel of how the last weeks unfolded. Tipu's personal effects were taken by the victors and most of them were shipped to England where they can be seen in various museums.

Tipu died a warrior's death, defending his fort to his last breath. Moreover, despite the extreme cruelty towards Hindus and Christians in Kerala and Coorg, there are also instances of his making generous grants to temples. His critics will argue that most of these were given after his defeat in 1791. It is difficult to say if this was a genuine change of heart or a tactical retreat by a cornered bully desperately looking for new friends. Still, given his record of brutality towards fellow Indians, it is difficult to think of him as a great freedom fighter. At best, he belongs to the shades of grey that mark a lot of history.

10

Diamonds and Opium

End of Dutch Spice Monopoly

Despite the failure to expand its empire into India, the VOC retained control over Sri Lanka and much of South East Asia till the end of the eighteenth century. However, its monopoly over the spice trade was about to be dealt a body blow by the emergence of plantations in other parts of the world. Over the years, many attempts had been made to grow expensive Asian spices outside their places of origin. Pepper, originally from south India, had spread to Sumatra and elsewhere but cloves and nutmeg had proved impossible to grow outside their original habitats. Moreover, the Dutch were aware that other Europeans wanted to break their monopoly and jealously guarded against any attempt to smuggle out seedlings.

The first systematic attempt at transplanting these spices was made by a French adventurer, Pierre Poivre, who had started life as a missionary in China and rose to become the administrator of Mauritius. Interestingly, his efforts were constantly opposed by Dupleix who may have been privately running a parallel effort to steal seedlings. Poivre personally captained a ship to the Spice Islands, narrowly escaped being exposed by a Dutch patrol ship, and procured a small number of seedlings. Unfortunately, the plants did not survive for long in Mauritius. A few years later, Poivre sent out a protégé called Provost to make a new attempt to procure seedlings. Sailing through VOC-controlled waters, the French managed to find a small island where the locals, unknown to the Dutch, had succeeded in transplanting clove and nutmeg. Provost procured seedlings from them before heading for Mauritius but was stopped by Dutch customs officials. The price for being caught smuggling was death, so this must have been a tense moment. However, the French managed to convince the officers that they had been blown off course and escaped a full inspection.[1]

Provost returned to Mauritius with four hundred rooted nutmeg trees and seventy rooted clove trees. Within a couple of decades there were spice plantations in Zanzibar, Madagascar and the Caribbean. The VOC's spice monopoly had been shattered. Poivre returned to France a very wealthy man. After his death, his widow would marry Pierre Samuel Dupont, a liberal politician and publisher. During the French Revolution, the couple would narrowly escape the guillotine and head for North America where Dupont would use his wife's wealth to set up a successful gunpowder factory near Wilmington, Delaware. Dupont's business would flourish and survives today as one of the world's largest chemical companies. In contrast, the VOC's fortunes would go into rapid decline and the company would be dissolved in 1799.

The transplanting of spices was by no means the only instance of economic espionage. Indian textile technology was also stolen and copied by the Europeans. Indian cottons, especially wood-block prints called 'chintz', were so popular in Europe that governments often imposed severe import restrictions and bans on usage. A French missionary called Father Coeurdoux managed to get some Indian weavers, whom he had converted to Christianity, to reveal the secrets of the technique to him. Over time, further details were sent back by agents of the French East India Company. Thus, by the 1760s, French and English factories were churning out chintz on an industrial scale.[2] Western countries today often accuse Asian economies of violating intellectual property rights but it is worth remembering that their own economic rise was based on stealing ideas from others.

The Free-Port of Singapore

Meanwhile, the English East India Company had a problem—it may have succeeded on the battlefield but its operations in India were not very profitable. The constant wars and the unscrupulous dealings of its agents meant that individuals became rich but the company suffered. Both Robert Clive and his successor Warren Hastings would be accused of corruption. By the late eighteenth century, trade with China was the only profitable part of the EIC's operations. However, the Chinese insisted on being paid in silver coins in exchange for tea, porcelain and other products coveted in Europe. As the trade gap grew, the British faced the same precious metals shortage faced by ancient Romans when trading with India. These are the problems that would have been debated by the EIC's directors sitting at the company headquarters on Leadenhall Street in London.

They found their solution in opium. Opium had been imported in small quantities into China from ancient times and used in traditional medicine. From the late eighteenth century, however, it became very fashionable to smoke it.[3] Depictions in popular culture tend to show sleazy opium dens but in reality, it was consumed at all levels of society and was seen as a sign of connoisseurship with its intricately carved pipes, silver heating lamps and reclining couches in red silk. As demand for opium boomed, the British found that they could use their control over India to grow poppies. The system of triangular trade was born: The British sold cheap mill-made textiles to the Indians and bought opium from them at artificially low prices. The opium was then sold to the Chinese in exchange for goods that were sold back in Europe. It solved the EIC's silver problem but destroyed the Indian economy. Cheap textiles made on an industrial scale by British mills devastated the old artisan-made textile industry. The shock was so great that a century later, the leaders of India's independence movement would choose the hand-turned spinning wheel as their symbol of protest. Meanwhile, farmers in EIC-controlled areas were forced to grow opium (along with indigo that was used as a dye) and sell it to company agents at artificially low prices. The adverse terms of trade impoverished the farmers but what made it worse was that they were often not free to grow food crops; a small fluctuation in weather conditions resulted in devastating famines.

Although the triangular system solved the payments problem of trade with China, it still left the British exposed to geopolitical risk. The sea route from India to China had to pass through the Malacca Straits and there was always the risk that the Dutch would use their control over the region to cut off the passage. The British had a couple of small holdings in the region—at Penang and Bencoolen (now Bengkulu)—but they knew that these were inadequate. Thus, when Napoleon took control of Holland, the British moved systematically to take over Dutch territories in the Indian Ocean: Cape Colony at the southern tip of Africa, Sri Lanka, the nutmeg-growing Banda Islands, clove-growing Ternate. With the mother country under occupation, the Dutch put up little resistance and by 1799, the VOC itself ceased to exist. The remaining Dutch territories were briefly managed by a French vassal state called the Batavian Republic but after a brief period of peace, the British took over the Dutch headquarters at Batavia (Jakarta) and occupied Java in 1811. Note that most of the British troops consisted of Indian soldiers who had become the backbone of British power in the East.

It was a column of Indian troops, led by a young officer called Thomas Stamford Raffles, that marched into central Java and stormed the palace of the Sultan of Yogyakarta. The palace still exists although many of the original buildings were damaged during the British attack and had to be substantially rebuilt. Wandering around the grounds and the airy pavilions of the palace, one is struck by how the influence of the Majapahit has survived to this day despite European colonization and the conversion to Islam. Raffles too was

amazed by the large numbers of remains of the ancient Hindu–
Buddhist kingdoms of Java. One of the sites that he 'discovered' was
Borobudur that he arranged to be cleared of the encroaching jungle
and to be surveyed. Raffles showed an extraordinary interest in the
natural and cultural history of the region and would be one of the
first to initiate its systematic study. A factor that may have driven his
interest in the temple ruins was that he had become a Freemason
and Masons during this period were very interested in the study
of ancient pagan sites.[4] One wonders if Raffles saw the panels in
Borobudur depicting the merchant ships, a reminder of another age
of globalization.

Raffles would return to England briefly before coming back as
the Governor of the tiny British colony of Bencoolen in Sumatra.
He soon realized that with Napoleon defeated, the Dutch would
ask the British to return their territories in the Indian Ocean. This
would mean that the sailing route to China through the Malacca
Straits would again be under threat. After surveying the area, Raffles
identified Singapore as a good place to set up a new outpost that
would ensure permanent British control over the passage. Using an
internal squabble within the royal family of Johor, Raffles managed
to gain control over the island in 1819. Crucially, he declared that
Singapore would be a free port: 'Our object is not territory, but
trade; a great commercial emporium, and a fulcrum, whence we
may extend our influence politically as circumstances may hereafter
require.'[5]

The idea of a free port under British protection was immediately
attractive and within a few weeks, thousands of Malays and Chinese
had shifted from Malacca to Singapore. The Dutch were furious and
lodged a protest with London claiming that the free port was within
their traditional zone of influence. The British Governor of Penang
also opposed Singapore as it undermined his turf. However, the new
settlement became so successful in such a short time that it could
not be ignored. The authorities in London and Calcutta grasped its
strategic importance at the tip of the Malay peninsula and eventually
backed Raffles. The Dutch, in any case, were too weak to push

their case too far. The Anglo-Dutch Treaty of 1824 gave the British control over Singapore and the Malay peninsula, including Malacca. The Dutch retrieved territories that we now know as Indonesia. As compensation for Singapore, the Dutch also got Bencoolen (proving once again that the British always trump the Dutch when it comes to urban real estate).

When the British first established their outpost in Singapore, the coastline was drastically different from what we see now. Beach Road is now far inland due to several rounds of land reclamation but, as the name suggests, it used to originally run along the beach. Thus, residents of the famous Raffles Hotel could sit on the veranda and look out to sea. Similarly, Telok Ayer Street which runs through today's central business district was once the waterfront. One of the most prominent buildings on the street is the Thian Hock Keng temple, established in the 1830s, that Chinese sailors visited as soon as they landed on firm land in order to give thanks for a safe sea voyage. Right next door is Nagore Dargah that was used by Indian Muslims for exactly the same purpose. The Hindus had also been given a plot on the street for a temple but would build the Mariamman temple on another site not far away. Thus, Singapore was a bubbling mix of cultures right from the beginning.

Kandy for the British

One of the Dutch territories occupied by the British during the Napoleonic wars was Sri Lanka. The Europeans had taken control of the coast but the mountainous interior was still under the kingdom of Kandy. The kingdom was then ruled by the Nayak dynasty who, interestingly, were not Sinhalese but were of south Indian origin. The last Sinhalese ruler of Kandy did not have any legitimate sons and, after his death in 1739, the throne was taken over by his queen's brother who came from the ruling family of Madurai (once the capital of the Pandyas). As one can see, the link between the Sinhalese and Madurai is a very deep and long-lasting one. Nonetheless, the Nayaks were aware of their foreign status and they strongly encouraged a Buddhist revival in order to cement their position.

Just as Tamils and Sinhalese had close links, we have seen how Hinduism and Buddhism were also very closely connected throughout the island's history. As already mentioned, virtually all old Buddhist temples in Sri Lanka have shrines dedicated to Hindu gods including the most sacred Temple of the Tooth Relic. Indeed, the Sinhalese hero Rajasimha, who had fought the Portuguese, would probably have described himself as a Hindu. In the same vein, it was an Indian dynasty that would heavily invest in reviving Buddhism on the island. By the eighteenth century, the institutions of Buddhism had long been in decline due to constant wars and the pressure from Christian missionaries. The Nayak kings, therefore, imported monks from Thailand to re-establish various institutions.[6] According to historian K.M. de Silva, the famous Esala Perahera procession of Kandy was originally a procession for Hindu gods under the Sinhalese dynasties but was repurposed for the Tooth Relic under the Nayak kings.

Meanwhile, having secured the coast, the British decided to attempt what both the Portuguese and the Dutch had failed to do—subjugate Kandy. In May 1803, an expeditionary force was sent into the mountains but on arrival found that the town had been evacuated. While the commanders were debating what to do next, the monsoons arrived and the British found themselves caught without supplies in a muddy and wet terrain. Eventually they decided to retreat to Colombo but were harassed constantly by Sinhalese guerrilla attacks as they made their way back through the slushy mountain passes. Almost all the British officers and men were killed. The episode is not dissimilar to the much better-known events relating to the retreat of the British army from Kabul during the First Anglo-Afghan War. As with the Afghans four decades later, the gains of the initial victory were not long-lasting. The British returned to Kandy in 1815 and, taking advantage of frictions between the king and the nobility, took over the kingdom with little resistance. Thus, the whole of Sri Lanka became part of the British empire.

The Haze of Opium

Although trade had been booming since the eighteenth century, Chinese authorities strictly restricted trade with the Europeans to a single port—Canton (i.e. Guangdong) in the Pearl River delta. Here business was controlled by a cartel of wealthy Chinese merchants known as the Hongs. During the trading season (September to January), Europeans were allowed to stay in the port in lodgings leased out by their Hong counterparts. Situated deliberately outside Canton's city walls, these 'factories' included warehouses and living quarters. Outside of these months, the foreigners were expected to either go home or withdraw to the Portuguese enclave of Macau.[7] In other words, the Chinese government kept the Europeans at arm's length.

Despite these restrictions, the East India Company and its agents benefited from its cosy long-term relationships with the Hongs. However, lobbying by its business rivals in Britain ended its monopoly over trade with the East and suddenly there were many new merchants trying to sell opium in China. Even the Americans entered the business. Many of the new entrants began to bypass the old arrangements and smuggle the drug into the mainland. As a result, the price of opium fell and its usage rose sharply in China. The flow of silver coins reversed and opium addiction became widespread.

The Chinese imperial government was eventually forced to take action and, in May 1839, the authorities confiscated and destroyed 20,000 chests of opium in Humen. This triggered a chain of events that resulted in the First Opium War. The British sent out fifteen barrack ships with 7000 soldiers, mostly from India. They were armed with modern rifles and were backed by the *Nemesis*, a steam-powered warship. The scattered and outdated Chinese army was completely outmatched as the British fleet pounded its way up the coast. The apparently magical ability of the *Nemesis* to move irrespective of wind direction caused panic. Ultimately the Manchu emperor was forced to accept the humiliating conditions of the Treaty of Nanjing by which several ports were forced open for foreign trade and the British gained control of Hong Kong. War reparations, including compensation for the confiscated opium, were also paid.

It is worth mentioning that when the Chinese were fighting British-led Indian soldiers along the eastern coast, they were simultaneously fighting Indian soldiers in Tibet! After establishing control over Ladakh, the famous general Zorawar Singh decided to march the Dogra army into Tibet in 1841. He pushed his way up to the sacred Mansarovar Lake but, despite his meticulous planning, was ultimately unable to sustain his supply lines through the harsh terrain. This allowed the Tibetans, along with Chinese reinforcements, to counter-attack. Zorawar Singh was caught defending an untenable position and was killed. The Dogras were now pushed back to Ladakh where they, in turn, defeated the Tibetan–Chinese army. At this point both sides seem to have been exhausted and peace was concluded under the Treaty of Chushul but this stretch of border between India and China remains disputed to this day.

The peace between the Chinese and the Dogras would last (till the Indo-Chinese War of 1962) but that with the British would unravel a few years later. Tensions began to simmer in 1856 but the British could not respond for the next couple of years because a large section of the British-Indian army was in revolt across northern India during 1857–58. Given the importance of Indian soldiers in policing the growing empire, the British were able to pay attention to China only after the revolt had been brutally suppressed. The Second Opium War started as a series of skirmishes. A large expeditionary force was finally dispatched in 1860. With the active support of the French and the Americans, the British repeatedly defeated the Chinese imperial army and marched into Beijing. The Qing emperor fled his capital and the Summer Palace was deliberately destroyed.[8] Yet again, Indian troops formed the bulk of British forces. They would return four decades later to help the British put down the Boxer Revolt in 1900–01.[9]

One can see how Indian soldiering was of such importance in world history. The British empire, in particular, was heavily dependent on it. This is why one stream of India's freedom movement would focus over several decades on undermining the loyalty of these soldiers.

The Tycoons of Bombay

The East India Company had built the British empire in Asia but by the middle of the nineteenth century it was effectively defunct. The incessant wars, rampant corruption and, ultimately, the loss of its monopoly had steadily eroded the company's profits. The Revolt of 1857–58 in India exposed its inability to govern the empire it had created. The Court of Directors met one last time on 1 September 1858 at the company's headquarters at Leadenhall Street. A few weeks later, its colonies were taken over by the Crown.[10] The building on Leadenhall Street that housed the EIC's headquarters, once the heart of the world's largest commercial enterprise, no longer exists. I walked up and down the street one winter afternoon, armed with old sketches to identify the place till I realized that the site is now occupied by the Lloyd's building which incongruously looks like a twentieth-century petrochemical refinery.

Even as the EIC's fortunes declined, it was replaced by new merchants and agency houses such as Forbes & Company and Bruce Fawcett & Company.[11] One of the largest of these operations was run by Jardine, Matheson and Company (which survives today as the conglomerate Jardine Matheson Holdings). It was set up by Charles Magniac, James Matheson and William Jardine who initially used technical loopholes to circumvent the EIC's monopoly in order to trade Indian cotton and opium in exchange for tea out of Canton. Business boomed after the EIC lost its monopoly in 1834 and they relocated their operations to Hong Kong after the First Opium War.

While most Indian farmers and weavers were hurt by the triangular trade system, some Indians also benefited from working for the European merchants as agents and brokers. Many of these were drawn from the Parsi community, descendants of Zoroastrian refugees who had come to India centuries earlier from Iran. From the late eighteenth century, many Parsis had migrated to Bombay where they prospered as suppliers, victuallers and shipbuilders. Opium exports were initially monopolized by Calcutta but Bombay gradually emerged as an alternative hub as cotton farmers in Malwa switched to growing opium. Soon, Parsi agents became an important part of the supply chain all the way to Hong Kong. This is why many of Hong Kong's old institutions have Parsi founders. The famous ferry between Hong Kong island and Kowloon, for example, was set up by Dorabjee Naorojee Mithaiwala. The Indian brokers and agents were known as 'shroffs' (derived from the Hindi word 'saraff' used variously for agent, broker or money changer). The term 'shroff' survives in Hong Kong but is now used mostly for parking-ticket collectors—one of those odd artefacts of history!

Arguably the most successful of the Parsi merchants of Bombay was Jamsetjee Jeejeebhoy. He was born in 1783 and is said to have moved from Navsari to Bombay when he was still a boy. Bombay was a much smaller settlement than Calcutta but, with the Maratha threat receding, it was witnessing rapid growth. In 1780, the population of Bombay was estimated at 47,170 but by 1814 it had risen to 162,570 and had further jumped to 566,119 by 1849.[12] Armed with a smattering of English and some knowledge of bookkeeping, the enterprising boy soon inserted himself into the city's trading community. Jamsetjee would steadily earn himself both a large business and a good reputation as a reliable partner.

In 1805, a few months before the British decisively beat the French navy at Trafalgar, Jamsetjee and William Jardine were taken prisoner by the French while sailing off the Sri Lankan coast. The captors later agreed to release the prisoners at a neutral Dutch outpost near the Cape of Good Hope at the tip of Africa. While this transfer was taking place, a sudden gale wrecked their ship near the Cape. Both Jamsetjee and Jardine survived, but the shared experience created a bond that became the basis of a long-term business partnership. Jamsetjee soon became the main Indian partner of Jardine, Matheson & Company and acquired a large fleet of ships. He also became a highly respected citizen of Bombay and was included by the EIC's Court of Directors in the Queen's Honours List. In an elaborate ceremony at the Governor's residence in May 1842, Jamsetjee Jeejeebhoy was knighted.[13]

Modern-day critics of Sir Jamsetjee Jeejeebhoy may say that he was no more than a drug lord who collaborated with a colonial power to enrich himself by engaging in a business that devastated the lives of many fellow humans, both Indian and Chinese. His supporters would argue that he was just a businessman who responded to the circumstances of his times. Moreover, they will point out the fact that Jamsetjee gave away a significant part of his fortune in charity. Mumbai is still served by the Jamsetjee Jeejeebhoy School of Art and the Jamsetjee Jeejeebhoy Hospital. Whatever one thinks of him on balance, he was certainly a remarkable man living at a remarkable time in Mumbai's history.

One of Jamsetjee's lesser-known contributions to Mumbai is the introduction of ice cream. This was made possible by the regular supply of ice from Boston from the 1830s. An 'ice-house' was built to store the ice but the stock often ran out due to melting or delays in the supply chain. Not surprisingly, the rich saw ice as a way to display their wealth and Jamsetjee began to serve ice cream at his dinner parties. The very first time he served it, it was alleged that everyone caught a cold![14] Social rivalries within the city's elite were just as intense in the mid-nineteenth century as they are today.

Another of Bombay's merchant princes was David Sassoon, a Baghdadi Jew who had fled the despotic rule of Daud Pasha.[15] When Sassoon arrived in Bombay in 1833, the city already had a significant Jewish population. He soon built a business empire trading in cotton and opium but the Sassoon family fortunes skyrocketed when the American Civil War cut off supplies of raw cotton between 1861 and 1865. The mills of Lancashire turned to India for raw material and Bombay witnessed a boom. David Sassoon died in 1864 but he is remembered through several institutions built by him and his sons in Mumbai and Pune.

Sassoon's palatial house survives as Masina Hospital in the neighbourhood of Byculla. Readers familiar with Mumbai may wonder why one of the city's richest residents built a house in such a crowded area but Byculla was in fact a fashionable suburb in the nineteenth century. The exterior of the main building is in good condition but the interiors have been haphazardly divided into cubicles for various medical activities. I did, however, find a grand wooden staircase that has survived largely unscathed and retains the feel of a merchant prince's house. The David Sassoon Library, built in Mumbai's Kala Ghoda area, is another elegant example of the period's architecture. The Sassoon Docks in Colaba were built by David's son Albert-Abdullah. It is now used to land Mumbai's daily supply of fish. This is the reason that on a hot day, when the wind is blowing from the east, Mumbai's expensive Cuffe Parade neighbourhood finds itself cloaked in a strong fishy odour.

Not all of Bombay's tycoons made their money from opium. Premchand Roychand would make, lose and regain his fortune in real estate and financial markets. His father had brought his family from Gujarat and had settled in a tenement in the densely packed Kalbadevi area. As a boy, Premchand would have heard about the exploits of David Sassoon and Jamsetjee Jeejeebhoy. By the 1850s, he had amassed a sizeable capital base as a cotton broker. Around the same time, a small group of Indian brokers began to trade financial securities and bullion under a banyan tree in front of Town Hall (this later evolved into the Bombay Stock Exchange).

It was in this milieu of speculation and risk-taking that Premchand Roychand began to promote land reclamation projects. By this time, the original seven islands of Bombay had already been connected through land reclamation into a single land mass but growing population and commercial activity argued for further reclamation. What added fuel to the fire was the cotton boom caused by the American Civil War. So when Premchand launched the Backbay Reclamation Company, its shares spiralled up in a frenzy of speculation. Soon, the city saw many new banks, companies and construction projects being launched and Premchand was involved in several of them. It was mania like never before and, inevitably, it ended suddenly when North American cotton supplies resumed in 1865. The shares of the Backbay Reclamation Company dropped from Rs 50,000 to Rs 2000 and that of Bank of Bombay from Rs 2850 to Rs 87. Many investors were ruined and the economic collapse was so large that the city's population dropped from 816,000 in 1864 to 644,000 in 1872![16]

Premchand Roychand not only lost everything but was also blamed for the wider financial mess. Nonetheless, he seems to have been stoic about the whole affair and, over the following decades, would repay his creditors and gradually build back his fortune. When he died in 1906, he would be remembered for his extraordinary resilience and the large sums he gave away to charity and public works. For instance, the Rajabhai Clock Tower, one of Mumbai's most iconic buildings, was built with funding from Premchand Roychand and is named after his mother.

The stories of these three tycoons give a good flavour of how Bombay evolved and expanded over the nineteenth century. These were larger-than-life figures who took big, even reckless risks but were also prepared to share their good fortune. Many of the city's most loved buildings and institutions were built by them or others like them. More importantly, they bequeathed the city a risk-taking spirit that remains alive to this day. David Sassoon, Jamsetjee and Premchand were all migrants who had made it big in the city. Mumbai's slums are still full of migrants who think they too can do it. This is why Mumbai slums are not places of hopelessness as one may expect but full of industry and enterprise despite all the squalor.

Oman to Zanzibar

Even as the Europeans were tightening their stranglehold on the Indian subcontinent and South East Asia, the Persian Gulf was witnessing its own geopolitical realignment. As we saw in the previous chapter, the Omanis had managed to evict the Portuguese in the mid-seventeenth century but a few decades later they found themselves under occupation by the Persians led by Nadir Shah (this is the same Nadir Shah who raided Delhi in 1739 and took away the famous Peacock throne from the Mughals). In 1747, Ahmad ibn Said united the various feuding Omani factions and then invited the Persian officers for a ceremonial banquet. At a pre-planned signal midway through the meal, the hosts suddenly attacked and massacred the guests.[17] The occupying Persian forces were leaderless and were pushed out with ease. Nonetheless, the Omanis knew that they remained under threat and therefore opted for a long-term strategic alliance with the British. The British, in turn, were keen on building up a local ally as a bulwark against the Wahhabis of the Arabian peninsula. This special relationship with Britain would remain alive till the late twentieth century.

In 1804, Sultan Said came to the throne. His fifty-two-year rule is often seen as the golden age by the Omanis. His success was based on naval power that he systematically built up over time. Sultan Said supported shipbuilding yards at Muscat, Sur, Mutrah and Shinas (the one at Sur still builds wooden dhows) but also imported a number of European-designed ships built in Bombay.[18] Using this growing fleet, and with implicit British support, the Omanis steadily expanded control over a maritime empire that extended from Gwadar on the Makran coast (now in Pakistan) to Zanzibar off the east African coast (now in Tanzania).

The economic engine of the empire was powered by cloves grown in Zanzibar and African slaves procured from the interiors. This meant that Sultan Said needed to maintain control over the Swahili coast. Recall that much of this coastline had been explored and settled by the Omanis in medieval times and some links had been intermittently maintained. Even before Sultan Said, the Omanis had nominal control over some parts of the coast but in the 1830s the Omani court moved to Zanzibar and tightened its grip. Many reminders of these times have survived on the island's Stone Town including the palaces of rich merchants and the Omani nobility. The hanging balconies look exactly like those one sees in the older parts of Muscat and Ahmedabad, a reminder of linkages across the Indian Ocean. One can also see remains of the dark hovels where newly procured slaves were kept. Climbing down into one of the underground slave prisons, one can still feel some of the terror that newly arrived slaves, chained together, must have felt as they waited for an uncertain fate.

The trade in slaves, however, was eventually abandoned under pressure from the British. The role of the Royal Navy in ending this despicable practice is indeed praiseworthy but let it be clear that British motivations were not entirely driven by altruism. The British economy had already gone through the Industrial Revolution and was less dependent than its rivals on mass deployment of unskilled labour. Coal and steam now provided much of the muscle of their economy. Moreover, the British also had access to an inexhaustible supply of cheap indentured labour from India where British policies had systematically impoverished the population. So, the anti-slavery position of the British at least partly aimed at undermining rivals and was self-serving.

The Omani nobility would continue to rule over Zanzibar till as late as 1964 when a revolution would overthrow them. Many would be killed in riots and most of the remaining Arabs would leave. Zanzibar would then merge with Tanganyika on the mainland to form Tanzania. The island's once thriving Indian community was also hurt by the revolution and most left for other shores. But I was pleasantly surprised to find a small group that still survives in the narrow lanes of Stone Town and maintains a handful of Hindu temples; a reminder of another age.

Steam Ships and Fishing Fleets

From the middle of the nineteenth century, the commercial and human dynamics of the Indian Ocean world suddenly went through a radical shift as Victorian-era transportation technologies began to reorder the landscape. Coal-powered railways and steam ships dramatically reduced the time taken to move goods and people over land and sea. It also changed the dynamics of naval war with the construction of steam-powered, armour-plated, iron-hulled warships. Amazingly, the very first such warship—*HMS Warrior* of the Royal Navy—has survived and has been beautifully restored. Maritime history enthusiasts can visit it in Portsmouth harbour. The design was still a hybrid as the *Warrior* also had masts for sails and its guns were lined along the sides for a broadside. Nonetheless, the contrast with the previous generation of ships is plainly visible if one compares it with *HMS Victory* that is also moored at Portsmouth harbour. The latter had been the most advanced war machine of its time and had participated in the Battle of Trafalgar as Nelson's flagship (indeed, Nelson would be killed on its deck). Interestingly, the *Warrior* never participated in a war. Its design was so successful that all ships were subsequently designed with steam power and metal hulls, and the *Warrior* itself rapidly became outdated.

The other major factor that changed the dynamics of the Indian Ocean was the Suez Canal. As we have seen, the idea of a canal was not new and various versions had been built since ancient times. However, all the earlier versions had focused on connecting the Red Sea to the Nile and, in each case, was choked by sand and silt after a few years. In contrast, the nineteenth-century canal built jointly by the French and the Egyptians connected the Red Sea directly with the Mediterranean. It was opened in 1869 under French control but faced severe financial difficulties. Their Egyptian partners eventually sold their stake to the British. Combined with steam power, the Suez Canal soon changed the logistics of Atlantic–Indian Ocean trade as ships no longer had to make the long and arduous journey around Africa. Aden re-emerged as a major hub after centuries of decline.

One of the less anticipated effects of the Suez Canal was the flood of young, unmarried European women who headed for India and other colonies in search of husbands.[19] Known as the 'fishing fleet', these women were drawn from all segments of society.

Depending on their class background, they would marry British civilian and military officers, merchants, clerks and so on. Some even found their way into the harems of native princes. While Victorian society was very conscious of class, it was possible for an enterprising woman to climb the ladder in the East. An average-looking girl from a modest background could become a sought-after beauty if she made her way to a sufficiently remote outpost. The arrival of so many women transformed the Europeans in Asia into an endogamous ruling caste that lived in enclaves with conventions and etiquette completely separate from those of the indigenous people. The stage was set for the numerous Raj-era books about tiger hunting, amateur theatricals, and tea parties in hill stations.

Meanwhile, the ships also carried increasing numbers of Indians across the Indian Ocean and beyond, but their experience was very different. A key factor driving this churn of people was the shortage of labour in sugar-growing colonies after the British abolished slavery in 1833. Within a year, there were fourteen ships engaged in transporting Indian indentured workers from Calcutta to Mauritius.[20] The original contracts were for five years at Rs 10 per month plus some food and clothing. An option of a free return passage was provided at the end of the contract. Soon Indian indentured workers were being transported to faraway places like the Caribbean and Fiji. Other European countries, such as France, also began to recruit workers. By the 1840s, the authorities began to encourage women to sign up so that self-perpetuating Indian communities could be created which in turn would reduce the need for constant replenishment from the mother country.

The recruitment of indentured workers was done by a network of Indian subagents who further contracted out their work. For example, Ghura Khan was British Guyana's subagent at Buxar and paid his recruiters Rs 5 to Rs 8 per month plus Rs 5 for a man and Rs 8 for a woman (evidently women were more difficult to recruit). The whole supply chain was riddled with false promises and rampant abuse but repeated famines in India pushed increasing numbers to risk the journey. During 1870–79 alone, Calcutta shipped out 142,793 workers, Madras 19,104 and Pondicherry 20,269.[21]

Indentured workers and soldiers were not the only Indians on the move. The late nineteenth century saw Indian merchant and financial networks come alive again after a hiatus of centuries. Tamil Chettiar merchants and moneylenders spread across South East Asia. In Malaya they lent to Chinese tin miners and European planters, and in Burma they supplied credit to farmers. They operated through a system of guild-like firms and agencies, usually run by members of the extended family. One of the largest of these firms, established by Muthiah Chetty in the early 1900s, was headquartered in Kanadukanta in Chettinad, Tamil Nadu, but with offices in Sri Lanka, Burma, Malaya and French Indo-China. Similarly, Gujarati traders and moneylenders established themselves along the coast from South Africa to Oman.

A significant concentration of Indians settled around Durban in South Africa. Some had come as indentured workers and stayed back while others came freely in search of economic opportunities. By the end of the nineteenth century, their numbers not only equalled that of the white population but they were successfully competing with the Europeans as accountants, lawyers, clerks, traders and so on. This led to a series of discriminatory laws aimed at protecting the interests of the whites. This was the milieu to which a young lawyer called Mohandas K. Gandhi arrived in 1893. He was brought to South Africa by a well-established Gujarati businessman Dada Abdoolah to assist in a personal matter. However, he was soon part of a movement to oppose anti-Indian laws. In 1894, the Natal Indian Congress was established with Gandhi as its secretary. Thus began a journey.

The Scramble for Africa

The nineteenth century was a tumultuous time for the African shores of the Indian Ocean. The Cape at the southern tip of Africa had long been a Dutch colony but it was taken over by the British during the Napoleonic wars. The treaty of 1814 confirmed British control but a sizeable community of Dutch settlers continued to live there. Known as Afrikaners or Boers, they were constantly suspicious of the motives of their new rulers. When the British outlawed slavery, the Afrikaners saw it as a ruse to undermine them. Eventually large numbers of them decided from the 1830s to take their families, livestock, guns and African slaves (now dubbed as servants), and trek into the interiors. As one trekker subsequently wrote:

> We abandoned our lands and homesteads, our country and kindred [because of] the shameful and unjust proceedings with reference to the freedom of our slaves: and yet it is not so much their freedom that drove us to such lengths as their being placed on an equal footing with Christians, contrary to the laws of God and the natural distinction of race and religion. . . . we rather withdrew in order thus to preserve our doctrines in purity.[22]

Just as the Afrikaners were moving into the interiors of what is now South Africa, the area was also witnessing a large influx of Bantu tribes from the north-east. A prolonged drought in the early nineteenth century had caused these groups to migrate but there was a more immediate cause—the rise of the Zulus. The Zulu tribe had been converted into a military machine by the famous leader Shaka. Using a combination of spears and fast-moving, disciplined units, the Zulus were even capable of taking on guns on occasion. As they expanded their territories, the other African tribes were forced to flee. This is known as the 'Mfecane' or The Scattering. The current location of various tribes in southern Africa is a direct outcome of this episode. Swaziland and Lesotho were both founded as a result of refugee groups banding together under powerful chiefs to defend themselves. The Xhosa (Nelson Mandela's tribe of origin) were among the worst affected as they were being crushed between the Zulus and white settlers.

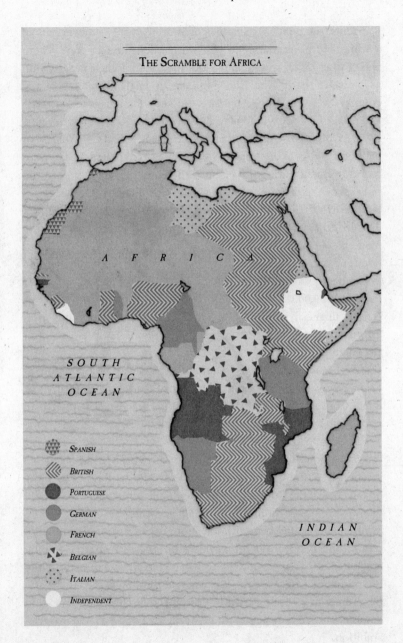

THE SCRAMBLE FOR AFRICA

A F R I C A

SOUTH
ATLANTIC
OCEAN

INDIAN
OCEAN

SPANISH

BRITISH

PORTUGUESE

GERMAN

FRENCH

BELGIAN

ITALIAN

INDEPENDENT

Thus, the political dynamics of South Africa was never simply a white and black matter (if you will pardon the bad pun). There was just as much rivalry and bloodshed within each racial group as between them. The Khoi-San, the original inhabitants of the country, were the sorriest victims—already marginalized, enslaved and dispersed, they would play almost no role in subsequent events.

The next twist in the story took place with the discovery of diamond and gold deposits in South Africa. Till new deposits were found in Brazil during the eighteenth century, India had been the only source of diamonds in the world. The quantity and quality of South African diamonds, however, was at a different level altogether. This led to a mad rush. Within just a year of the first claims being made in 1867, fifty thousand people were living in tents and other temporary shelters in Kimberley. By 1871, there were more people in Kimberley than in Cape Town![23] In that year alone, South Africa exported 269,000 carats of diamonds. With the boom came dubious claims, financial manipulation and large-scale gun running. It is estimated that 75,000 guns were sold in Kimberley between April 1873 and June 1874.

Eventually, order was restored and the entire operation at Kimberley was brought under the control of a single company; De Beers Consolidated Mines Limited was incorporated in 1888. The man behind this consolidation was Cecil Rhodes.

Rhodes had arrived in Kimberley as a dirt-poor teenager but, over time, had managed to establish himself as a formidable businessman and canny speculator. With the backing of wealthy financiers like the Rothschilds, he eventually came to control all the diamond mines of Kimberley. In 1890, he would become the Prime Minister of Cape Colony. Rhodes now began to use his immense wealth and political power to push the interests of large mining magnates as well as expand the British empire at the cost of both the Boers and the African tribes. It is said that Rhodes wanted to expand the empire from Cape Town to Cairo. The discovery of large gold deposits in 1886 only added to the heady mix of greed and imperial ambition.

The frictions between the British and the Afrikaners eventually led to the Second Anglo-Boer War (1899–1902). The Boers made pre-emptive strikes and laid siege on a number of towns including Kimberley. The British struck back with reinforcements shipped in from India. Indian soldiers would yet again play an important role in the course of events. Interestingly, Mohandas Gandhi also participated in the war by organizing a group of local Indian civilians into the Natal Indian Ambulance Corps that provided support to the British forces.

By the middle of 1900, Boer resistance had begun to crumble and the British had taken over their capital, Pretoria. The Boers now shifted to guerrilla tactics and continued to harass their adversaries. The British responded by creating large concentration camps where they herded in the families of the Boer guerrillas. At their height, the concentration camps held 112,000 inmates. Conditions in the camps were appalling and an estimated 28,000 Boers, mostly women and children, died over the course of a year from malnutrition and disease.[24] Reports of these civilian casualties would cause an uproar in Europe and embarrass the British government. Boer forces would eventually surrender in May 1902 and the two Boer republics were incorporated into the British empire.

Cecil Rhodes did not live to see the end of the war as he died in March of that year. He would leave most of his estate for the creation of the famous scholarship that now bears his name. The idea seems to have been to create an Anglo-Saxon elite, educated in Oxford, who would rule the British empire into perpetuity (there was also a hope that the United States would join the British in this grand enterprise). Rhodes lived during the high noon of British power and it would not have occurred to him that his beloved empire would cease to exist within half a century.

It is somewhat ironic that I owe most of my education to Francis Xavier and Cecil Rhodes. I attended a high school named after the former and my years at Oxford were financed by a scholarship named after the latter. I am quite aware that in both cases I was not the intended beneficiary. This brings us to the tricky question of how to judge individuals from history—do we judge them by their intentions or by the consequences of their actions? Do we judge them only by the standards of their times or by some absolute yardstick? I do not claim to know the answer but these are questions that scholars of history constantly grapple with.

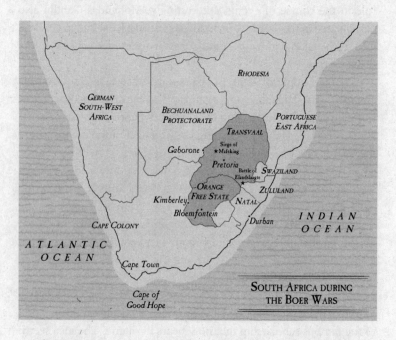

SOUTH AFRICA DURING
THE BOER WARS

Nonetheless, while researching this book, I was surprised to come across the following line in Rhodes' final will and testament: 'No student shall be qualified or disqualified for election to a Scholarship on account of his race or religious opinions.'[25] This is a remarkably liberal statement given the context of the times and Rhodes' reputation as a racist. Perhaps like Ashoka he wanted future generations to think well of him. Or perhaps he had more shades of grey than I had imagined. The first black Rhodes Scholar was elected as early as 1907 and this elicited such a backlash in the United States that American selection committees did not award the scholarship to another black student till 1963. The Rhodes Trust to its credit, however, persisted with its open policy in other parts of the world and non-whites continued to be elected (Queensland 1908, Jamaica 1910 and so on).

Note that the British were not the only Europeans occupying swathes of Africa in the late nineteenth century. In earlier times, Africa had been seen as an impediment on the way to Asia and occupation was limited to resupply outposts along the coast. The Suez Canal had reduced the need for re-supply ports but Africa's interiors were now seen as a source of raw materials to feed industrial economies and of easily conquerable territories to feed imperial egos. France took over large swathes of north and west Africa. Germany had only become a united country in 1870 but it lost no time in claiming territories that we now know as Tanzania, Rwanda, Burundi, Namibia, Togo and Cameroon. When the Omani Sultan of Zanzibar objected to the land grab in East Africa, Otto von Bismarck sent in his warships.[26] The Sultan had probably hoped that his British allies would help, but the British turned a blind eye and carried out their own land grab in what is now Kenya. A few years later, they placed their own candidate on the throne and effectively turned Zanzibar into a protectorate.[27] Even tiny Belgium got into the act and occupied a large swathe of central Africa, what is now the Democratic Republic of Congo.

The takeover of Africa had been so quick that colonial governments often struggled to keep up with it. For example, the British-held territory of Nyasaland (now Malawi) had a budget of just 10,000 pounds per year. This was just enough for ten European civilian officers, two military officers, seventy Sikh soldiers of the Punjab regiment and eighty-five porters from the Zanzibar coast.[28] This was all the resources available to run a territory of 94,000 square kilometres with a population of one to two million. Ignoring for a moment the morality of the colonial enterprise, one must admire the sheer scale and audacity of it. National borders across the continent are still marked by the arbitrary straight lines drawn on a map by various European powers to mark out their acquisitions. These boundaries made no geographical or cultural sense on the ground, but this would not have bothered European colonizers who had convinced themselves that Africans had no history or culture.

Denying a people's history and culture is an obvious way for a colonizing power to present everything preceding their arrival as the age of darkness and ignorance. Thus, the conquered territory can be termed as *Terra Nullius* or Nobody's Land, and the rights of the indigenous people can be denied. Indeed, the *Terra Nullius* argument was used in Australia till as recently as 1992 when the courts finally began to accept the land rights of the aborigines.

Not all the African tribes and kingdoms gave in without a fight, and in at least one instance the Europeans were beaten back. We have seen how the Ethiopians had preserved their independence in isolation for centuries despite being surrounded by the Arabs. Unfortunately, Ethiopia was one of the last independent territories left in Africa when the Italians too decided to join the scramble for Africa. In 1885, the Italians simply seized the port of Massawa on the Red Sea and turned Ethiopia into a landlocked country. Emperor Menelik protested against this but found no support from major world powers. Soon he was forced to sign a treaty that ceded Eritrea to Italy in return for recognizing his sovereignty over the highlands of the interior.

The Italians, however, had no intention of stopping with just the coast. They picked on some differences between the Italian and Amharic texts of the treaty and occupied northern Ethiopia. Menelik now began to smuggle in modern rifles and train an army. After a few initial skirmishes, the final battle took place at Adowa in March 1896. The Ethiopians inflicted a crushing defeat in which 3179 Italians and 2000 locally recruited auxiliaries were killed.[29] Many more were wounded or taken prisoner. At this stage, Menelik may have been able to march on Eritrea but he knew that his supply lines were stretched. Moreover, despite the victory, the Ethiopians had suffered 7000 dead and over 10,000 wounded. So, the emperor accepted a new, more favourable treaty that explicitly recognized his independence.

Thus, Ethiopia would be the only African country to successfully defend itself against the colonial onslaught. The Italians had retained Eritrea but had been made to look very foolish. Mussolini would try to erase the memory of this defeat by invading and briefly occupying Ethiopia in the 1930s but would lose control of it during World War II. Given their long history of defending their country against both the Arabs and the Europeans, often at great cost, the Ethiopians can be justly proud of their record of preserving their independence.

The End of Pretence

When the twentieth century dawned, almost all of the shores of the Indian Ocean were already under European control. The British controlled the Indian subcontinent, Burma, Malaya, Australia and large sections of the east African coast. The French had established themselves in Indo-China (what is now Vietnam, Laos and Cambodia). Even a latecomer like Germany had managed to find a territory to colonize in East Africa and in the north-eastern quarter of New Guinea. This probably left the Dutch feeling inadequate. They had once been the dominant power but had steadily lost influence and territory. The British had taken away their former holdings in South Africa, Sri Lanka and Malaya. Although they had tightened control over their remaining territories in the Indonesian archipelago, they must have felt that history had left them behind. So the Dutch did what all school bullies do when they are feeling down—they beat up the smallest kid in the class.

The small island of Bali was divided into a network of tiny kingdoms that, despite frequent Dutch interference, had remained effectively independent.[30] In 1906, the Dutch used a minor pretext to land a large force on the island armed with modern rifles and machine guns. They knew that the Balinese were armed with no more than spears, shields and a few muskets. They also had a handful of small cannons that can still be viewed at the Bali Museum at Denpasar. They are beautifully decorated with dragon-heads but are of an eighteenth-century design that would have been hopeless against modern weapons. In other words, both sides knew that the Balinese did not stand a chance.

The Dutch force landed on Sanur beach and faced little resistance as it marched inland. Along the way, it found that all settlements had been abandoned. Only when they approached the royal palace at Denpasar did they see signs of activity. There was no army to greet them but they could see a lot of smoke rising and hear drums beating inside the palace compound. The invading force took up positions and waited. After a while, a ceremonial procession emerged from the main gate including the king, his queens and children, priests, servants and retainers. They all wore funerary garments and their finest jewellery. The women next walked up to the lined soldiers and mocked them, flinging their jewellery and gold coins at them. Then a priest took out a *kris*, the traditional dagger, and stabbed the king to death in full view. This seems to have been the signal for the Balinese to pull out their krises and make a last charge. The Dutch machine guns and rifles mowed them all down within minutes. Waves of men, women and children kept coming out of the palace and the Dutch kept shooting them down. There were soon mounds of dead bodies, probably numbering over a thousand.

What the Dutch had just witnessed was the Balinese Hindu rite of 'Puputan' or the Last Stand (the Indian equivalent is called *jauhar*). This extraordinary event took place in the open field in front of what is now the Bali Museum in Denpasar. There is a memorial on the spot to commemorate it. I stood there for a long time trying to imagine the mental state of those who had preferred to die rather than live under foreign domination. The nearby museum has a few photographs that show the aftermath of the massacre.

The Dutch commanders, however, were not too impressed by what they had just witnessed. They only waited to allow the soldiers to collect all the jewellery and loot the palace before setting it on fire. They then marched to the next kingdom where they witnessed a similar sequence of events. They finally left after forcing the king of Klungkung, the senior most of Bali's rulers, to sign a humiliating treaty. Not surprisingly, the Balinese were seething with anger that would spill over into riots. This gave the Dutch the pretext to return in 1908 and attack Klungkung. Yet again, the Balinese opted to commit Puputan. The king charged out wielding his kris along with two hundred of his followers and they were all shot dead. His six queens committed ritual suicide; the palace was looted and razed to the ground.

The Dutch today take great pride in their liberal traditions but the history of their occupation of Indonesia tells a different story. When reports of the events in Bali finally reached Europe, it caused quite an uproar. It did not help that they had themselves photographed the atrocities. By now the supposed civilizing mission of the European colonial enterprise was sounding increasingly hollow. The incidents in Bali were merely the last nails in the coffin. Within a few years, the barbarity of the First World War would take away even the pretence of moral and civilizational superiority.

11

From Dusk to a New Dawn

The twentieth century began with the Indian Ocean rim firmly in the grip of European powers. Even the smallest independent enclave, such as Bali, had been brutally crushed. With the loss of many of their colonies in the Americas, the Europeans had greater control over the Indian Ocean than over the Atlantic. It had taken centuries of war and colonization to create this edifice and not many would have wagered that it would all dissolve within a few decades. The first hint of the turning tide was the Japanese victory over the Russians in 1905. This was the first time that Asians had scored a decisive victory over a European power since Marthanda Varma's victory over the Dutch. Although this victory may have encouraged later Japanese militarism, it also shattered the myth of European racial and cultural superiority. Then came the First World War.

The Raider

Most histories of the First World War (WWI) tend to ignore the Indian Ocean. While much of the action happened in the trenches of Europe and around the Mediterranean, the Indian Ocean rim also saw a number of important events that are often left out of the story and are now largely forgotten even in the countries where they took place. One of the fascinating episodes relates to the German light cruiser *Emden* that single-handedly paralysed Allied shipping in the Indian Ocean for several months.

When the war began in July 1914, the *Emden* was one of a handful of German vessels that found themselves stranded on the other side of the world at Tsingtao (Qingdao). This was a German-controlled enclave along the Chinese coast and is still famous for a beer brewery established by the Germans. It soon became clear that Tsingtao and other German colonies in the East were not defensible and the ships would have to find their way home. They left as a convoy to cross the Pacific in an attempt to get to the Atlantic by rounding South America. Karl von Muller, the commander of the *Emden*, however, asked for permission to head west to the Indian Ocean. Permission was granted and the *Emden* slipped through neutral Dutch-controlled waters into the Indian Ocean. Muller added a fake smoke funnel in order to disguise his ship as a British cruiser.

By early September, the *Emden* was in the Bay of Bengal where it began to systematically attack and sink ships belonging to the British and their allies. There was panic as no one knew what was happening; British intelligence had been under the impression that the *Emden* was in the Pacific along with the rest of the German fleet. Karl von Muller, interestingly, soon developed a reputation as a gentleman privateer because he minimized casualties, treated his prisoners well and let them go at the first opportunity.[1] It was only through information gleaned from the released crews that authorities in Calcutta realized what was happening.

On 22 September, the *Emden* unexpectedly appeared off the coast of Madras and proceeded to bombard the port. The raid lasted for barely half an hour but the 125-odd shells set ablaze oil containers and threw the city into chaos. The ship then disappeared as suddenly as it had appeared. Although the damage was limited, the raid had a major psychological impact on the city and for a generation the word 'Emden' would be used as Tamil slang to denote maverick cunning or resourcefulness. I was surprised, therefore, to find that few of Chennai's younger residents knew about this episode and not one could tell me the location of the plaque commemorating it. Eventually, I found it along the eastern wall of the High Court (across the road from the line of stalls selling mobile phones and other electronics). It marks the spot where one of the shells had landed.

The *Emden* now sailed down the coast towards Sri Lanka, capturing and sinking more ships along the way. Eventually, it headed for Diego Garcia, a remote British-held island in the southern Indian Ocean. Muller was pleasantly surprised to find that the islanders had not heard about the war! Modern communications technology had not yet connected every point on the planet. The *Emden* was, therefore, able to carry out repairs and refuel in peace. At this stage, Muller could have decided to head home around the Cape or make for an Ottoman-held port on the Red Sea, but he opted for his most audacious raid yet—an attack on Penang in the Malacca Straits.

The *Emden* slipped into Penang harbour at dawn on 28 October using the extra funnel to disguise itself. It soon spotted an old Russian cruiser that had stopped by for repairs. The Germans opened fire before the Russians could respond and destroyed the ship. The *Emden* was now engaged by a number of British and French ships but managed to fight its way out, sinking a French destroyer along the way. The Penang raid added to Muller's legend and was a big blow to the prestige of the Allies. Not only had a German ship made its way into the Malacca Straits but had also single-handedly caused so much damage before getting away. Now every warship in the Indian Ocean was pressed into looking for the *Emden*.

Muller now headed for the Coco Islands, south of Sumatra, where the Allies had a major wireless and cable communications station. The Germans planned to knock out the communications hub and a small party was sent ashore to destroy the equipment. Here Muller's luck finally ran out. One of the operators on the island was able to send out an SOS message and alert an Australian naval convoy that happened to be in the vicinity before the Germans captured the station. The convoy included a state-of-the-art cruiser *HMAS Sydney* that could outmatch the *Emden*'s firepower.

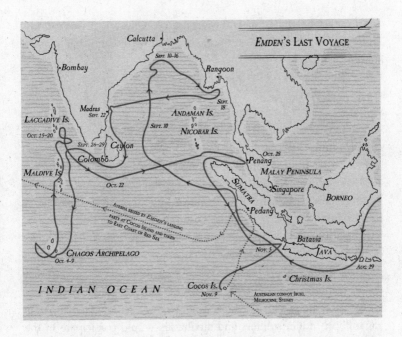

The sudden appearance of *Sydney* forced Muller to abandon the landing party and sail out to meet the enemy. The two cruisers bombarded each other but *Sydney* was both faster and had heavier guns. After a couple of hours of exchanging fire, Muller realized that his ship was sinking and was forced to beach it in order to save the remaining crew.[2] Sometime later he surrendered. Some of *Emden*'s guns were carried away as trophies and one is now displayed in Sydney's Hyde Park.

This was not the end of this story. Remember that a German landing party had been abandoned on one of the islands. This group managed to commandeer a schooner and sailed all the way to Yemen from where they fought their way past Bedouin tribesmen before making it to Turkish-controlled territory. The Turks arranged for them to travel by rail to Istanbul where they told their remarkable story. Meanwhile, Karl von Muller was taken as a prisoner of war and held in Malta till he returned home at the end of the war to a hero's welcome. Most of the remaining crew were held prisoners in

Singapore where their arrival caused quite a flutter. A few months
later they would be witness to major revolt by Indian soldiers based
on the island.

The Great War

As we have seen, Indian soldiers were the foundation on which the
British empire was built, but the colonial authorities were always
worried that the soldiers would switch loyalties; the memories of
1857 were still fresh. Under normal circumstances, all colonial powers
maintained a sizeable force of European regiments in the colonies as
backup but WWI had forced the withdrawal of many of these units.
The balance worsened as the British began to recruit Indian soldiers
on a large scale to fight in the war. They even managed to get Indian
political leaders like Mahatma Gandhi to support the recruitment
drive. Gandhi would initially recruit for non-combatant roles but
would later help with the recruitment of soldiers.[3] Approximately
1.3 million Indian soldiers and auxiliaries would participate in the
war and around 74,000 would lose their lives. It was Indian soldiers
who stopped the German advance at Ypres. Thousands would die in
the trenches of Europe and at Gallipoli. Sadly, their contribution is
barely remembered and recognized today even in India.[4] Even less
remembered are the battles they fought in the Indian Ocean rim.

One of the first places where Indian soldiers were deployed
was in German East Africa (now Tanzania) where they campaigned
against the spirited guerrilla tactics of Paul von Lettow-Vorbeck.
Despite being cut off from supplies and reinforcements, and with
British Indian troops in hot pursuit, the wily Lettow-Vorbeck and
his men would keep up German resistance in Africa till the end of
the war.

Recognizing the importance of India as a source for troops and
supplies, the Germans and the Turks were very keen to provoke a
revolt. One strategy was to instigate the Muslim population across
the Middle East and the subcontinent to rise up against the British.
The Ottoman Sultan's supposed position as the 'Caliph' of all

Muslims was played up. A German agent called Wilhelm Wassmuss slipped into the Persian Gulf to instigate the tribes of southern Iran to attack British interests in the region. He even spread rumours that the German Kaiser had converted to Islam and adopted the name 'Haji' Wilhelm Mohammad.[5] I am not making this up!

Wassmuss told the tribes that a grand Turko-German army would soon march through Iran into India and throw out the British infidels. Reports soon began to reach Quetta that a powerful Baloch chief was already in touch with the Germans. British intelligence took this threat seriously and an expeditionary force was sent out from India to Iraq in order to pre-empt the possible invasion. They would simultaneously use their own agent, T.E. Lawrence, better known as 'Lawrence of Arabia', to instigate the Arabs against the Turks.

The British Indian troops led by Major General Townshend initially won a series of easy victories in Iraq as they made their way inland. However, as they closed in on Baghdad in November 1915, the Turks put up an unexpectedly fierce resistance at Ctesiphon (once the capital of the pre-Islamic Persian empire). Townshend was forced to retreat to the town of Kut that he fortified while he waited for reinforcements. The Turks, meanwhile, surrounded the town and enforced a siege. It was a grim reminder of how Indian mercenaries fighting for the Shiite cause twelve centuries earlier had been surrounded and trapped at the battlefield of Karbala. With the evacuation of Gallipoli, the Allies suddenly found themselves in a difficult situation, and the Turks were able to fend off British relief columns that had got bogged down by floods on the Tigris. There was even a failed attempt by T.E. Lawrence to bribe the Turkish commanders.

The siege of Kut would last five agonizing months till the starving garrison finally surrendered on 29 April 1916.[6] The Turkish leader Enver Pasha celebrated the victory by declaring himself a *Ghazi* (Holy Warrior). Around 3000 British and 6000 Indian troops were captured and force-marched to Turkey as prisoners. Although Townshend would be treated quite well in captivity, many of his men would die from disease and ill-treatment. The Haider Pasha cemetery in Istanbul contains the graves and ashes of a few of these soldiers. One of the memorial stones reads: 'The following Hindu soldier of the Indian Army is honored here: Lance Naik Dhan Bahadur Limbu, 6th Gurkha Rifles.'

Few Indians today remember these men and their deaths in faraway lands but their stories were still fresh when civil servant and writer Dennis Kincaid wrote these words in the 1930s:

> When you are wandering around in the Maratha hills you chance upon a war memorial in some tiny hamlet; and it is moving to read that, say, eleven men went from that village to serve in Irak. Many of these village lads were at Kut. Very few men, once taken prisoner, returned or were heard of again. The clean fighting Turk saw to that.[7]

Few residents of Mumbai will be aware that the city has a memorial to Indian sailors who died in WWI. It's tucked away in a sailors' hostel in the old port area and almost no one visits it. Commodore Odakkal Johnson of the Indian Navy and I tracked it down amidst torrential monsoon rain and spent an hour reading the names of these long-forgotten sailors. It told an interesting pattern of how the British of that period recruited and deployed their Indian troops—the army casualties in Kut were mostly Hindu but here the naval casualties were largely Muslim.

The events at Gallipoli and Kut had resurrected the reputation and morale of the Turkish military. The British now needed a decisive victory and a formidable force of 150,000 men was assembled. These men were put under the command of Sir Stanley Maude, one of the most experienced generals in the British empire. In early 1917, this huge army pushed towards Baghdad against determined Turkish resistance. Finally, on the night of 10 March, the British forward positions witnessed a bright glow over Baghdad. The Turks were burning everything of military or economic value before retreating. By noon the next day, General Maude's troops had occupied the city. Despite the city's romantic associations, they found Baghdad in shattered ruins—almost all major government buildings had been burned down, shops and homes had been looted, rotting corpses lay everywhere.

The fall of Baghdad also meant that the German agent Wassmuss found himself isolated in southern Iran. Few tribesmen now believed his story of a grand Turko-German army marching to India. However, his greatest failure was not his fading ability to rouse the Tangistani tribesmen but a small error that had major consequences for the German war effort. During his adventures in southern Iran, Wassmuss had been captured on one occasion by a pro-British tribe. Although he made a daring escape, he was forced to leave behind his belongings which included the German diplomatic code book. This code book eventually made its way to 'Room 40'—the specialist code-breaking unit in London.

Armed with Wassmuss's code book, the cryptographers uncovered a German plan to unleash all-out submarine warfare against the Allies while simultaneously bringing Mexico and Japan into the war. The Germans had promised the Mexicans that if they entered the war, they would be helped to recover Arizona, Texas and New Mexico from the United States. The British gleefully passed this information to the Americans. On 1 March 1917, newspaper headlines across the United States revealed the story to an outraged American public.[8] The sinking of American merchant ships by U-boats over the next few weeks made it clear that the United States could no longer remain neutral. On 6 April, President Wilson declared war on Germany. The fate of the Central Powers was now sealed. Thus, a small mistake by a secret agent in the Persian Gulf had a big influence on the course of world history; the flapping of a butterfly's wings had caused a hurricane.

The Grand Conspiracy

As already mentioned, many senior leaders of Indian National Congress, including Mahatma Gandhi, opted to collaborate with the British during the First World War. There was an expectation that this would be rewarded with major political concessions after the war. However, not all Indians agreed with this approach and many felt that the war provided a golden opportunity to throw off the colonial yoke. At the forefront of this alternative effort to free India were revolutionaries who believed in using armed rebellion to defeat the British. Most conventional history books and textbooks give the impression that India's independence movement was a uniquely peaceful one led by Mahatma Gandhi and the Indian National Congress. The role of the revolutionaries is usually left out or mentioned as a footnote. As we shall see, they too played a very important role in how events unfolded.

Punjab and Bengal were the two main hubs of the revolutionary movement although there were several others scattered across the country, most notably Varanasi. The movement was initially made up of a number of autonomous groups working in isolation but before the outbreak of war they were already getting networked due to the efforts of Rash Behari Bose and his young lieutenant Sachindra Nath Sanyal. They were also in touch with like-minded activists among the expatriate Indians scattered around the world. One of them was Har Dayal who was studying at St John's College, Oxford (incidentally, I would attend the same college eight decades later). While in England, Har Dayal was influenced by the ideas of Vinayak Damodar 'Veer' Savarkar, a revolutionary then operating out of India House in London.

Savarkar was arrested in 1910 and, despite a dramatic escape attempt in Marseilles, was sent off to prison in Port Blair in the Andamans. Recognizing the risks, Har Dayal shifted to California where he continued to organize support for revolutionary activities among the newly arrived Indian students and immigrants, especially Sikhs from Punjab. In other words, an elaborate revolutionary network was already in place before war was declared. Indeed, the revolutionaries had nearly managed to kill Lord Hardinge, the Viceroy, in December 1912 while he rode on a ceremonial elephant through Delhi's Chandni Chowk. The Viceroy sustained severe injuries from the bomb but survived; none of the attackers were caught.

When war was declared and it became clear that the British would have to rely heavily on Indian troops, the revolutionaries immediately came up with a plan to take advantage of the situation by instigating a coordinated revolt by Indian regiments. Rash Behari Bose and Sachin Sanyal set about making elaborate arrangements on the ground. They coordinated a large number of clandestine participants—Sikhs returning from North America, revolutionaries in Bengal and regiments primed for mutiny from Punjab to Burma. The date of what would be known as the Ghadar uprising was set for 21 February 1915.

Unfortunately, the uprising unravelled before it began. It had been planned that the sequence of events would be triggered by the regiments in Mian Mir on the north-west frontier and Punjab first rising in revolt. However, just five days before the revolt, an informer called Kirpal Singh revealed the plans to the colonial authorities in Lahore. Bose now decided to bring forward the date to 19 February in order to deny the authorities time to react but by now British intelligence was already on full alert. Police raids captured several of the conspirators, and Indian guards at all armouries were replaced by British ones. The element of surprise had been totally lost. Seeing such decisive action, the soldiers lost their nerve and momentum simply melted away.

The only place that saw a full-scale revolt was Singapore where predominantly Muslim regiments mutinied on 15 February and took over large parts of the island.[9] They also freed the Germans captured from *Emden* and asked them to join the battle but were refused. It took the authorities a full week of fighting, backed by reinforcements, to quell the uprising. Dozens of mutineers would be lined up against a wall on Outram Street and publicly executed by a firing squad.

With his plans unravelling and the authorities closing in, Bose first sought refuge in the narrow lanes of Varanasi where the Sanyal clan could use its network of family and friends to temporarily hide a fugitive. However, as police raids mounted, he decided to escape to Japan where he would keep up his efforts for the next three decades. Sachin Sanyal saw him off at Calcutta's docks in May but stayed back to organize the remaining revolutionaries.[10] They received a morale boost when they heard that the German war machine had decided to back them. A body called the Indian Revolutionary Committee was set up in Berlin and was given full embassy status. Since the United States was still neutral at this stage, the German embassy in Washington DC acquired 30,000 rifles and pistols (plus ammunition) and began to secretly arrange for them to be sent to India.[11]

Two vessels—a schooner called *Annie Larsen* and a tanker called *Maverick*—were hired to take the weapons across the Pacific to Asia where they would be divided into smaller vessels to be carried to India. The idea was that well-armed revolutionaries would capture Calcutta on Christmas Day, 1915. Again, things did not go according to plan. The two ships failed to make their rendezvous on the agreed date and location. Worse, a German agent named Vincent Kraft was arrested in Singapore; he agreed to tell everything in exchange for a large sum of money and being allowed to emigrate to the US under a new identity. Boats carrying weapons to India through Thailand and the Bay of Bengal were intercepted. Finally, in a series of lightning raids, 300 conspirators were arrested in Calcutta and Burma. The Christmas Day plot had been crushed.

As one can see, the Ghadar uprising and the Christmas Day plot were very large-scale plans to overthrow British colonial rule in India. Although they failed, they had both come closer to being executed than most people realize and, with a bit of luck, could well have worked. Ex ante, they were no more audacious than T.E. Lawrence's exploits in Arabia but Lawrence succeeded while Wassmuss and Bose did not. Even allowing for possible differences in individual competence, it is an illustration of how small twists of fortune can sway the flow of history. Nonetheless, as we shall see, the dynamics set in motion by the revolutionaries did not end here but would influence events in the Second World War and eventually contribute to India gaining freedom in 1947.

Imprisoned by the Black Waters

By early 1916, the colonial government in India had managed to capture a large number of revolutionaries. Several of them were hanged while others were given long prison sentences. This included Sachindra Nath Sanyal who was sentenced to life imprisonment in the dreaded Cellular Jail in Port Blair in the Andaman Islands. It was where the British held those whom they considered the most dangerous—hardened criminals as well as political prisoners considered a serious threat to the empire. It was known in India as 'Kala Pani' or the Black Waters.

The Andaman and Nicobar Islands are a string of Indian islands in the Bay of Bengal. Although separated from the mainland by a large body of water, it was somehow colonized by humans at a very early stage and some local tribes still carry the genetic imprint of the earliest human migrations. Given their location close to major maritime trade routes, it is not surprising that the islands were known to ancient and medieval mariners and are mentioned in several old texts. It is thought that the name 'Andaman' is derived from the Malay pronunciation of 'Hanuman', the Hindu monkey-god. In the eighteenth century, the Danes, of all people, came to control these islands but failed to establish an economically viable settlement. Eventually they handed over the islands to the British who decided to use it as a penal colony. The Cellular Jail complex was built for this purpose. Barindra Ghosh, younger brother of the famous spiritual leader Sri Aurobindo, would be sent there in 1909 for his revolutionary activities and would spend over a decade there. He has left us vivid descriptions of life inside the prison:[12]

> Each room has a door closed by iron bars only, with no door leaf. On the back wall of the room, at a height of four cubits and a half, there is a small window, closed also with iron rails two inches apart. Of furniture in the room there is a low bedstead one cubit and a half wide and in one corner an earthen pot

painted with tar. One must have a most vigilant sleep on such a bed, otherwise even the least careless turn would land the sleeper with a bang on the floor. And the tarred pot is a most marvelous invention to produce equanimity of the soul with regard to smell, for it is the water closet. . . .

It is amazing that Barindra Ghosh was able to write with a sense of humour about a place where he languished for so many years. He tells us that prisoners were made to do hard physical labour—making coir ropes, turning the oil press and so on. However, the prisoners, especially the revolutionaries, were constantly subject to mental and physical torture. This was not done directly by the British warden but through his Pathan subordinates, particularly a certain Khoyedad Khan. These petty officers further recruited enforcers from among the criminals in the prison in order to maintain their writ. The idea was to systematically break the will of the revolutionaries. Ghosh tells us how the petty officers and their enforcers would often sexually assault and rape the teenagers and younger men: 'The very shame of it prevents them from complaining to the authorities; and even if they do, it is more often than not crying in the wilderness.'

Mahatma Gandhi and the Indian National Congress had expected major concessions after the war but they soon realized that Indians would get little in return for their cooperation. Instead, the British introduced the draconian Rowlatt Act in 1919 that gave the authorities sweeping powers to arrest and detain activists. It was the colonial government's response to fears that the returning Indian soldiers would be susceptible to revolutionary ideas. The law elicited strong protests and, amidst the deteriorating political climate, culminated in the Jallianwala Bagh massacre in April 1919. Like the massacre perpetrated by the Dutch in Bali, the cold-blooded murder of so many unarmed men, women and children ended British claims of civilizational superiority.

The colonial government tried to retrieve the situation by giving a general amnesty to several of the revolutionaries including

Sachindra Nath Sanyal. The returning revolutionaries now agreed to work with Mahatma Gandhi on a movement of non-violent non-cooperation. The protests spread very quickly and brought the subcontinent to a standstill. It looked like the British authorities had finally been cornered but, just as some form of victory seemed imminent, Gandhi unilaterally suspended the movement. The proximate reason for the decision was an incident in Chauri-Chaura where a mob of protesters set fire to a police station and killed several policemen. Gandhi argued that this incident had violated the principle of non-violence but it caused a permanent schism with the revolutionaries who saw it as hypocrisy. Why did Gandhi have to make such a fuss over a single incident of violence, they argued, when he had been recruiting soldiers for the British just a couple of years earlier?

What particularly incensed the Indian revolutionaries was that only a few weeks earlier the Irish had managed to force the British to sign the Anglo-Irish Treaty paving the way for an independent Irish Republic. If a tiny country like Ireland could gain freedom under the nose of the British, why did a large and faraway country like India have to wait? Sachin Sanyal now reverted to organizing the various revolutionary groups under an umbrella organization called the Hindustan Republican Association in 1924 and under it began to build the Hindustan Republican Army. The choice of names shows how the success of the original Irish Republican Army (not to be confused with later versions) had inspired Indian revolutionaries of that time. The Irish influence on India's freedom struggle is barely recalled today.

It was during this period that Sachin Sanyal came in contact with a young, rising star in the Congress party—Subhash Chandra Bose, later to be known simply as 'Netaji' (literally, The Leader). Sanyal would be sent back to prison a few years later and many of his followers would be killed or executed, but Subhash Bose would leverage the international networks pioneered by the revolutionaries in his attempt to build an armed revolt against the British during the Second World War.

The Fall of Singapore

Countless Hollywood films have led us to believe that the attack on Pearl Harbour marks Japan's entry into the Second World War. In reality, the very first shots were fired at 10.20 p.m. on 7 December 1941 on the beaches of Kota Bharu on the north-eastern corner of the Malay peninsula.[13] Given the differences in time zones, this took place a little before the first bombs fell on Pearl Harbour. Despite resistance from Indian troops in the area, the Japanese were soon storming the beaches and landing men and equipment. By 4.30 a.m., Japanese bombers were making raids on Singapore.

To be fair, British commanders in Malaya had anticipated the possibility of such an attack but had thinly spread their troops as they did not know exactly where the landing would take place. Moreover, the best Indian regiments had already been deployed on the other side of the Indian Ocean in Africa where they evicted the Italians from Ethiopia before engaging Rommel's Afrika Korps in Libya.[14] The Allied troops in Malaya were inexperienced new recruits from India and Australia who, in many cases, had not completed their basic training. What made it worse was they were not backed either from the air or from the sea. The small number of outdated aircraft based in Asia would prove no match against the Mitsubishi Zero.

Soon the Japanese were landing troops at will and making their way down the peninsula. The defence crumbled so quickly that in many areas the invading force cycled over long distances without encountering serious resistance. When British Prime Minister Churchill realized what was happening, he ordered that Singapore should be defended to the last. This was based on a widely held belief that the island was an impregnable fortress. He also ordered the cruiser *HMS Repulse* and the battleship *HMS Prince of Wales* to sail to Singapore. Their arrival in Singapore on 2 December brought some cheer to the defenders but military strategists should have realized that they were sitting ducks without air cover. By 10 December, both of them had been sunk by torpedo bombers.

Recognizing the deteriorating situation, Lieutenant General Arthur Percival ordered his remaining troops to fall back on Singapore. Nonetheless, there was still a sense of confidence that Singapore would hold. Even as the Japanese were closing in on the island in mid-January 1942, Robinson's department store was still advertising 'Snappy American Frocks for day and afternoon wear $12.50' and the Raffles Hotel was still organizing dances. P&O was even running regular passenger services to Calcutta—$185 for first class and $62 for second class.[15]

By the first week of February, however, the Japanese had taken over Johor and were bombarding the island from the air and by artillery. There is an oft-repeated legend that Singapore's big guns pointed south towards the sea in anticipation of a naval assault and could not be turned around against attackers from the north. This is not entirely accurate. The problem was that they were supplied with armour-piercing ammunition meant to be used against ships and were not effective against infantry. So, although the guns could be turned 360 degrees, there is an element of truth in the old legend.

Percival now had to guess where Japanese commander Tomoyuki Yamashita would make his main assault. Eventually, he decided to place his best troops to the north-east. This proved to be a big mistake as the main Japanese landing took place from the north-west where the Johor Strait is at its narrowest. Overcoming resistance from Australian units defending this sector, the Japanese were soon closing in on the city. On 13 February, the 1st Malay Regiment attempted a last desperate defence of Pasir Panjang ridge. A colonial-era bungalow on the ridge is now a museum dedicated to their last stand (most of the hand-to-hand combat happened just below the museum in what is now the car park).

By this point the centre of the city, including the underground command centre at Fort Canning, was being pounded constantly and civilian casualties were mounting. The situation was clearly hopeless and on 15 February, Percival drove to the Ford Motor factory in Bukit Timah to personally discuss the terms of surrender with Yamashita. It says something of the dire situation that Percival had to borrow a car from the Bata Shoe Company in order to go for his meeting. Thus began the Japanese occupation of Singapore. For the Chinese population, in particular, this would be a period of extreme hardship. The Indians would face hardship too but for them the period has a different significance. Another example of how the same history can have different meanings for different people.

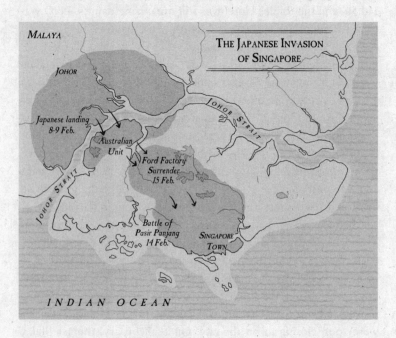

The Indian National Army

When the Second World War broke out, the British again looked to India for troops and support; some 2.5 million Indians would participate in the Allied war effort. However, having learned from the experience of the previous war, Mahatma Gandhi and the Indian National Congress decided not to cooperate with the colonial government and launched the non-violent Quit India movement. Note that not all Indian leaders agreed with the decision to launch the Quit India movement as they felt that opposition to Fascism was the greater cause. Still others felt that the war had produced a second golden opportunity to throw off colonial rule through armed revolt. By this time the senior revolutionary leaders from the previous war had mostly been killed or were in prison, so it fell on Netaji Subhash Bose to take up this cause.

Subhash Bose had drifted away from the Congress but the British still considered him a dangerous leader and had placed him under house arrest in Calcutta. In early 1941, he made a dramatic escape and made his way in disguise through Afghanistan and the Soviet Union to Germany where he requested help from the Nazi government. He was treated well and given a patient hearing but he soon realized that the Germans were unwilling or unable to commit large resources to his cause.

While Netaji was wondering about his next move, he received news of the fall of Singapore. Soon he heard that veteran revolutionary Rash Behari Bose was organizing surrendered Indian soldiers into the Indian National Army (INA) that would fight alongside the Japanese (recall that Rash Behari had escaped to Japan in 1915 after the collapse of the Ghadar uprising). Netaji next travelled by submarine around the Cape of Good Hope to Singapore where the older Bose handed him the command of the INA on 4 July 1943. The handover ceremony took place at the Cathay Cinema theatre where Netaji delivered a rousing speech. The next day he reviewed the INA troops at the Padang grounds in the middle of the city. Of the 40,000 Indians who had surrendered in Singapore, the majority opted for the INA.[16] S.R. Nathan, a future President of Singapore, would witness many of these events as a boy.[17]

Some of the landmarks related to Netaji's stay in Singapore can still be discerned. The Cathay theatre has been turned into a shopping mall but part of the old facade has been preserved. The open grounds of Padang and several of the surrounding buildings are still around. So is the old Ramkrishna Mission compound where he frequently withdrew to meditate. The bungalow where Netaji lived, No. 61 Meyer Road, has been pulled down and replaced by a high-rise condominium. It was here that he wrote down the

Proclamation of the Provisional Government of Free India. The neighbourhood is popular with expatriate Indians today, perhaps some sort of subliminal memory of its historical links!

Meanwhile, the Japanese had taken over the Andaman and Nicobar Islands and handed *de jure* control to Netaji. This would be the only piece of Indian territory that the Provisional Government would ever control but, given its associations with the revolutionaries, it had great symbolic value. The INA now joined the Japanese on their march through Burma to the eastern gates of India. The British responded by rushing a large number of troops to defend the line. Through the summer of 1944, the two sides simultaneously fought ferocious battles in Kohima (now capital of the state of Nagaland) and in Imphal (capital of Manipur). These are considered among the most hard-fought battles of the Second World War.[18] The climax was a closely fought hand-to-hand struggle over a tennis court in Kohima. The Japanese lost and the tide of war turned in favour of the Allies. The campaign would cost the Japanese side 53,000 in dead or missing while the Allies lost 16,500.

Churchill's Dirty Secret

From an Indian perspective, the tragedy of these battles was that Indian soldiers fought and died bravely on both sides, sacrificing their lives for someone else's empires. Even worse was the famine that killed 3 million people in Bengal in 1943. Crop failure and the disruption of rice supplies from Burma may have initially triggered the problem but the British colonial government did little to provide relief. Instead, they commandeered all the boats in order to deny the invading army the means to traverse the riverine terrain. This meant that locals could not even fish.

Meticulous research by writer Madhusree Mukerjee shows how Churchill was fully aware of the dire situation but seems to have deliberately delayed and diverted supplies as part of a scorched earth strategy against the advancing Japanese.[19] He is reported to have remarked that Indians were a 'beastly people with a beastly religion' and that the famine was caused by Bengalis who 'bred like rabbits'. There is a strong case for terming this genocide.

As the Japanese retreated, the INA fought against the Allied advance in Burma but by early 1945 it had effectively disintegrated. A day after Japan surrendered on 15 August, Subhash Bose flew from Singapore to Taiwan. What happened next is a mystery. The official line is that he died in a plane crash in Taiwan but the story was disputed right from the start. It is beyond the scope of this book to evaluate the evidence for and against various theories except to say it remains a highly controversial matter to this day.

Netaji's decision to ask Axis powers for help also remains controversial but this is unfair. First of all, the British had behaved appallingly from the Jallianwala massacre to the Bengal famine and, from an Indian perspective, there was little to morally distinguish the Allies from the Axis. They were just two sets of evil empires and Netaji cannot be faulted for trying to use every available opportunity to free his enslaved people.

Secondly, he was following up on international support networks established by the revolutionaries a generation earlier. We know that Subhash Bose repeatedly met Sachin Sanyal in the late 1930s when the latter was briefly out of prison. The links between the two are not widely known but Sachin Sanyal's son, then a teenager, was witness to these clandestine meetings and personally recounted them to me. On one occasion, the Japanese counsel was also present. In other words, one cannot judge Netaji's actions and the formation of the INA without taking into account the longer history of the revolutionary movement and its long-standing connections with Germany and Japan. This was not a case of developing a sudden love for Fascism.

The Decisive Rebellion

From the Ghadar plot to the INA, the revolutionaries had made several attempts to incite a revolt among Indian troops on whom the British empire relied. So far, they had not succeeded but their efforts did eventually bear fruit. The general public had been largely unaware of the activities of the INA due to wartime censorship but it caused a sensation when the prisoners of war were brought back and put on trial. As their stories circulated among the troops, rumblings of discontent began to grow. It culminated in the Royal Indian Navy Mutiny of 18–23 February 1946.[20]

The episode was triggered by a minor altercation in Bombay over the quality of food being served to sailors but, given the overall mood, it blew quickly into a full-fledged revolt. The sailors stopped obeying their officers and took control of a number of ships and shore establishments. Remember that the sailors were not novices; this was just a few months after the war and the British were dealing with battle-hardened veterans. Soon they had taken over the wireless communications sets on their ships and were coordinating their actions. As the news spread across the city, students, industrial workers and others went on strike and marched in support of the mutineers. Next, sailors in Calcutta and Karachi also mutinied. At its height, the unrest involved seventy-eight ships, twenty shore establishments and 20,000 sailors. When Baloch and Gurkha troops in Karachi were sent in to quell the revolt, they flatly refused to fire on the sailors. Officers and pilots of the Royal Indian Air Force similarly refused to help the authorities.

Unfortunately for the mutineers, they received no support from the Indian political leadership of the time. Both the Indian National Congress and the Muslim League asked them to surrender.[21] Subhash Bose was missing, and the senior revolutionary leaders Har Dayal, Rash Behari Bose and Sachin Sanyal, who had tried so hard to trigger exactly such a mutiny, were no longer alive. Lacking political leadership, the sailors eventually surrendered. Despite various assurances, large numbers of sailors would be court-martialled and dismissed (note that none of the dismissed would be reinstated by the governments of Pakistan and India after Independence).

Although the episode ended peacefully, the British colonial administration must have realized that they were rapidly losing control over their Indian soldiers. Just a week after the naval mutiny, the signals unit of the army in Jabbalpur also rebelled.[22] It was quite clear that another large-scale revolt was only a matter of time. The Indian soldier was one of the bulwarks of the British empire and once his loyalty had been undermined, the British empire began to unwind not just in the Indian subcontinent but worldwide. The revolutionaries had finally succeeded.

It is quite telling that the role of the revolutionaries in India's freedom struggle is barely presented as a footnote in official Indian histories. Having come to power in 1947, the Indian National Congress would ensure that story would be told in a way that focused exclusively on its own role. The Naval Mutiny is almost never mentioned and I learned about it accidentally after stumbling across a memorial tucked away in Colaba, Mumbai. The dominance of the Congress party's narrative was helped by the fact that it fitted the face-saving British account that they had peacefully granted freedom to India at the end of a successful 'civilizing' mission. This is not to suggest that Mahatma Gandhi and the Indian National Congress did not play an important role but merely to point out that India's freedom struggle was made up of many streams.

The Majapahit Dream

The Dutch had simply crumbled when the Japanese invaded their colonies in the East Indies and had put up very little resistance. For their own interests, the Japanese had in turn encouraged a number of nationalists like Sukarno during their occupation. So, two days after Japan surrendered, the Indonesian leaders made a proclamation of independence. There were a number of groups that had emerged in the political vacuum including Islamists and Communists but Sukarno's Republicans were the strongest. The problem was that the Dutch had every intention of returning and claiming back their colonies. For the moment, however, they did not have the resources to reoccupy the islands and so they asked for help from the British who landed a large contingent of Indian troops near Surabaya.[23] This resulted in heavy fighting and the British commander, General Mallaby, was assassinated. The Indonesians were eventually pushed out but there had been significant casualties on both sides. The episode further added to growing dissatisfaction among the Indian troops who did not see why they should risk their lives for such a cause. Some of them switched sides. As the unrest continued to spread across the islands, the Allies were forced to deploy surrendered Japanese troops in order to maintain control.[24]

An important factor that bolstered Indonesian resolve was that events seemed to be playing out an ancient prophecy. The twelfth-century Javanese king Jayabaya is said to have prophesied that three centuries of rule by white men would end with the coming of short yellow men who would leave after just one harvest. Other than the minor discrepancy that the Japanese had stayed for three harvests, the prophecy seemed to be coming true.

In early 1946, the Dutch began to land thousands of troops on Bali backed by support from the air. They faced fierce resistance from a small guerrilla force organized hurriedly by Ngurah Rai. The guerrillas were eventually cornered and Ngurah Rai ordered the Puputan. Yet again, the Balinese fought to the last man. The international airport in Bali is named after the guerrilla leader who was killed during the last stand.

Over the months, the Dutch managed to take over many of the main towns with the support of Allied troops but the Republicans continued to control the countryside. Realizing that the Republicans were too well entrenched to be wished away, the Dutch finally accepted the Linggadjati agreement on 15 November 1946 which gave the Republicans authority over the islands of Sumatra, Java and Madura. The two sides also agreed to work towards the establishment of the United States of Indonesia. Unfortunately, the Dutch were merely buying time in order to organize themselves. In May 1947, their troops occupied large parts of Java and Sumatra and cut the Republican forces into small enclaves. The country descended into war. An attempt by the United States to force a compromise also failed.

Amidst the chaos, a daredevil pilot from Odisha called Biju Patnaik flew secret missions into Java and rescued two key

Indonesian rebel leaders from being captured (he would later go on to become the chief minister of Odisha).[25] Prime Minister Nehru, meanwhile, organized the Asian Conference in New Delhi that pressured the UN Security Council to take action against the Dutch. It is remarkable that the first foreign policy action taken by newly independent India was to support Indonesia's freedom movement. It was as if an ancient civilizational kinship had been suddenly rekindled. It was also appropriate that someone from Kalinga had played an important role in the sequence of events. It is said that Sukarno named his daughter Megawati, meaning 'Goddess of the Clouds' in Sanskrit, in honour of Biju Patnaik's heroics in the sky.

The UN had forced a ceasefire but the Dutch were still not prepared to leave. They tried to instigate different parts of the archipelago against the Republicans using the bogey of Javan domination. Finally, the United States threatened the Dutch with cutting off Marshall Plan aid and forced them to accept a provisional government with Sukarno as President and Mohammad Hatta as Prime Minister on 27 December 1949. Sukarno would spend the next decade securing the territorial claims of his fledgling country against secessionists, communist rebels and the continued interference of the Dutch. It is said that he was driven by a vision of re-establishing the Majapahit empire and that a map of the medieval empire hung in his office.[26] It is another example of how current events are often influenced by civilizational memories that reassert themselves after being buried for centuries.

The Unravelling

Once India gained independence in 1947, the whole colonial project in the Indian Ocean began to unwind. One by one, all the countries in the region began to demand independence and the Europeans were soon reduced to fighting a rearguard action. Their reduced status was clearly demonstrated by the Suez Crisis of 1956. The sequence of events was triggered by Egyptian leader Gamal Abdel Nasser who nationalized the Suez Canal Company. The British, with support from the French and the Israelis, invaded Egypt in order to take control of the canal. Although the invaders succeeded militarily, they faced severe criticism from the United States and the Soviet Union and were forced to withdraw meekly. The episode can be said to mark the end of Britain's reign as a world power.[27]

Within the next fifteen years, the British and other colonial powers would free virtually all their colonies in the Indian Ocean rim. The withdrawal was far from peaceful and involved many conflicts including anti-communist operations in Malaya and the Mau Mau uprising in Kenya. Tens of thousands of Europeans went back 'home', including those who had been born in the colonies and many of mixed parentage. Nevertheless, there were exceptions. In South Africa and Rhodesia (now Zimbabwe), a dominant white minority was strong enough to remain in power for several years after the departure of colonial backing. In Australia, of course, those of European origin had replaced the indigenous population as the majority.

Perhaps the most determined attempt to retain colonial possessions was made by the French in Vietnam. In the political vacuum left by Japan's surrender, the Viet Minh led by Ho Chi Minh had taken over Hanoi and declared independence. Nonetheless, the country was occupied by Allied troops—British in the south and Chinese in the north—and the French were soon given back control of the administration. The French made several promises about granting freedom but it became apparent that they had no intention of leaving. Things dragged on till 1954 when the French assembled a large military force, backed from the air, in order to expel the Viet Minh from the north of the country. However, the Vietnamese outwitted and trapped the colonial army in the Battle of Dien Bien Phu and inflicted a devastating defeat. After this, the French departed quickly leaving the north of the country in the hands of Ho Chi Minh and the south with a puppet regime backed by the Americans.

The departure of the Europeans unfortunately did not mean that the Indian Ocean rim became a postcolonial utopia. Instead, the region would experience years of war and genocide. The Vietnam War would consume the country till North Vietnamese tanks finally crashed through the gates of the presidential palace in Saigon in April 1975. Next door in Cambodia, almost two million people were killed by the Khmer Rouge regime between 1975 and 1978 in a brutal attempt to create a communist agrarian paradise. In East Pakistan, the West Pakistani army perpetrated a genocide that killed as many as three million Bengalis and pushed ten million as refugees into India. This resulted in the Indo-Pak War of 1971 and the creation of Bangladesh. In the western Indian Ocean, Ethiopia and Eritrea would fight a long, bitter war that only ended in 1991. Yemen would be locked in a civil war between the north and the south.

The Solomonic dynasty in Ethiopia had outlived the Arab and the European expansionism but it did not survive the social forces unleashed by modernity. An aging Haile Selassie was removed from the throne in a military coup in 1974. Polish journalist Ryszard Kapuscinski, in his classic book *The Emperor*, has left us a vivid account of the last days of a medieval court struggling to cope with changing times.[28] A few years later, Kapuscinski would witness the Iranian revolution and write about the fall of Mohammad Reza Pahlavi, the last Shah of Iran.

The unwinding of the European empires also disrupted the commercial and human networks that had been created under the colonial umbrella. The Indian communities scattered across the region were particularly vulnerable. For instance, there were over a million Indians in Burma and they accounted for more than half the population of Rangoon in the 1930s. After the military coup in 1962, their businesses were forcibly nationalized and large numbers were expelled. The Indians in Uganda were similarly given ninety days to pack up and leave by Idi Amin in 1972. They were allowed to take only 55 pounds with them. Some went back to India but many went to the United Kingdom where they would rebuild their lives.[29]

Under French rule, Saigon too had been home to a significant number of Indians. They were not expelled but as economic conditions deteriorated during the war, they gradually drifted away. There are still two prominent Hindu temples in the middle of Saigon (now Ho Chi Minh City). They have been maintained quite well by the government. There was a lady official deputed to act as the priest at the Mariamman temple when I visited it in 2015. She took her job quite seriously and, despite the language barrier, solemnly carried out her own interpretation of Hindu rituals. I wondered if she was a descendant of Kaundinya and the Naga princess.

Singapore, Alone

The first subregion in the Indian Ocean rim to witness rapid economic change was the Persian Gulf. Commercially viable oil was first discovered at Well Number One at Masjid-e-Suleiman, Iran, in 1908. Bahrain was producing oil by 1932 followed by Dammam in Saudi Arabia and Kuwait by 1938.[30] By the 1970s, the wealth accumulated from oil exports had transformed the economic and social fabric of the region. The boom sucked in construction workers, engineers, clerks, corporate managers, nurses, teachers and other service providers from the rest of the world, particularly the Indian subcontinent. The small port of Dubai, once known for the pearl trade, did not itself have much oil. Nonetheless, it positioned itself as the key commercial hub in the region and evolved over the next few decades into the glitzy city we see today. In contrast to the oil-driven success of the Gulf states, nevertheless, the most remarkable economic transformation in the Indian Ocean rim was arguably achieved by a tiny, crowded island with so few natural resources that it even had to import water: Singapore.

In 1963, the British colonies of Singapore, Sarawak and North Borneo (Sabah) agreed to enter into a federation with the states of the Malay peninsula in order to form Malaysia.[31] The main objection came from Indonesia's Sukarno who saw it as a 'neocolonial plot' to thwart his plan of rebuilding the Majapahit empire. Trouble began to brew soon afterwards as the Malay politicians in Kuala Lumpur looked with suspicion at the Peoples' Action Party (PAP) led by a firebrand socialist called Lee Kuan Yew. They worried that he would leverage his base in Singapore to gain inroads into Sabah, Sarawak and the Chinese population in the peninsula. Matters were further complicated by widespread race riots in Singapore that killed twenty-three people. Dr Mahathir Mohamad, then a young backbencher, accused the PAP of being 'positively anti-Malay'.[32] Many readers will be surprised to know that this champion of Malay rights was himself not a pure Malay but of Indian origin; a Nandi Varman in reverse!

Given this atmosphere of suspicion, the Malay politicians decided to squeeze Singapore out of the federation and, on the morning of 9 August 1965, the city state's proclamation of independence was announced over the radio. Later that day, Lee Kuan Yew broke down in tears at an emotional press conference. The future of the tiny, slum-ridden island looked grim. The British added to the prognosis by announcing that they would be shutting down their military base—they no longer had an empire and had no need to control the Malacca Straits.

Lee Kuan Yew, now Prime Minister, knew that he needed to quickly find a new economic engine for his city state. He decided to ask multinational companies to set up their manufacturing hub in Singapore by offering them rule of law, ease of doing business and low taxes. This was not only a break from his early socialist rhetoric, but was very different from what other newly independent countries were doing at that time (and much more in tune with the ideals of Stamford Raffles). Foreign capital financed capacities in sectors ranging from ready-made garments to oil refining. The Singaporeans also used the naval facilities abandoned by the British to build out a shipbuilding and repair cluster. The economic strategy was so successful that, despite a setback during the Oil Shock of 1974, Singapore soon needed to import workers!

Nonetheless, the experience of the Oil Shock taught the government that the economy needed to be diversified and upgraded. Thus, in the 1980s, new industries like electronics and pharmaceuticals were brought in. Meanwhile, the government invested in top-quality infrastructure and public housing. All of this turned Singapore into a first world country by the time Lee Kuan Yew stepped down as Prime Minister in 1990 (although he would remain in the Cabinet as a mentor). This was a truly remarkable achievement.

Things went well till the Asian Crisis of 1997 devastated the economies of South East Asia. Although Singapore was not itself in crisis, it was impacted as the main financial centre for the region. This was followed by a series of shocks—the bursting of the information technology bubble in 2000, the 9/11 attacks in New York and the panic over the SARS epidemic in 2002. All of these events hurt Singapore and there were many observers who argued that Singapore had run out of luck and would face long-term stagnation. Singapore was too expensive to compete in most traditional sectors and a new growth dynamic was needed.

The government decided to take a gamble and turn Singapore into Asia's 'Global City'.[33] It was an audacious idea. Other global cities like London and New York had evolved organically over a very long time but Singapore would attempt to deliberately turn into one by strategically encouraging sectors like higher education, entertainment and international finance. Within a decade, the skyline was transformed by iconic towers and 'super-trees', while the influx of professionals for the new sectors pushed the population to 5.5 million (more than double the 1.9 million at independence). Somehow the plan worked. When Lee Kuan Yew passed away in 2015, he left behind a city that was arguably the most advanced in the world. Those unfamiliar with Singapore's history tend to assume that its success is due to the efficient implementation of a grand plan. Far from it, modern Singapore is the result of constant adaptation and tinkering in order to deal with a complex and evolving world.

A New Dawn

The years 1990–91 witnessed major shifts in world history. The Soviet Union, till then considered a superpower, collapsed without a shot being fired. The Indian Ocean rim too saw major changes. After decades of being stifled by the socialist economic model imposed by Nehru, India finally began to liberalize its economy. As discussed in my first book, *The Indian Renaissance*, this would have profound implications for India's economic and social trajectory.[34] Meanwhile in South Africa, the apartheid regime finally began to crumble. Nelson Mandela was released from prison in February 1990 after twenty-eight years. He had been sent to prison in 1962 and at one point had faced execution for fomenting armed rebellion. Yet, he had kept the faith for all those years and on three occasions had rejected conditional offers of release. After his release, he took over as the leader of the African National Congress and began the difficult process of negotiations that would finally end white minority rule.[35]

My first visit to South Africa was in the tumultuous summer of 1993.[36] I was then a student at Oxford University and had somehow managed to get myself funded to work on a development project in a remote tribal 'homeland' for three months. My passport still read 'Not valid for the Republic of South Africa' although the Indian government had removed restrictions just a few weeks earlier. My visa was not stamped on the passport but given on a separate sheet of paper. The South Africa I visited was still heavy with the remnants of the apartheid era. Racial segregation had been abolished only a few months earlier but public toilets still read 'White' and 'Coloured'. Nelson Mandela had been freed but the white-run government was still in place. I lived and worked in the tribal homeland of KaNgwane along the Swaziland border—one of the many nominally autonomous reservations created for the black population (it is now part of the province of Mpumalanga). However, even in the remote savannah grassland and hills of the Low Veld, there was palpable tension in the air.

To the outside world, South Africa's internal tensions appeared as black-versus-white but the situation on the ground was much more complicated. The white population was split between those who favoured the changes and those who clung on to hopes of some form of return to segregation. There were also the old suspicions between English-speaking whites of British origin and Afrikaans-speaking Boers of Dutch origin. The wounds of the Boer wars of 1880–1881 and 1899–1902 had still not been completely healed. The black population was similarly divided on tribal lines. The Zulu nationalist Inkatha Freedom Party was suspicious of the African National Congress (Nelson Mandela and many ANC leaders are from the rival Xhosa tribe). As the apartheid regime crumbled, these rivalries increasingly spiralled into bloodshed. In just one of the incidents, dubbed the Boipatong massacre, forty people were killed and many more were injured. By the summer of 1993, all sides were stockpiling arms. The camp where I stayed was on the route used to smuggle arms from nearby Mozambique and on one occasion my pick-up truck (locally called a Bakkie) was hijacked at gunpoint. Luckily I was not driving it at that time but my co-worker had to walk back many miles to camp. The vehicle was found abandoned a few days later, probably after being used to smuggle guns.

As if this was not complicated enough, there were still other groups including Indians and those of mixed race. The latter formed a large segment of the population in the western half of the country, but found themselves stuck in a cultural and political no man's land. The Indian population was scattered but formed a significant concentration around the eastern city of Durban. Although it had faced discrimination under apartheid, the industrious community had come to control much of the country's retail and wholesale trade and had become fairly prosperous. Not surprisingly, all other groups resented them. In fact, virtually every group suspected that the Indians were funding its rivals!

Over that summer, I witnessed riots at Witwatersrand University in Johannesburg, attended political rallies in seething townships, and listened to the hum of distant gunfire. A white-supremacist group even managed briefly to take over the World Trade Centre, Kempton Park, where multiparty negotiations were taking place. South Africa was a country on the boil and I met worried white families who were making plans of leaving the country and moving to the United States, Britain or Australia.

As I look back to that period, I realize how easily the country could have gone into a spiral of violence and retribution. The South Africa we see today owes much to the philosophical evolution and personal example of one man. It would have taken very little for the country to have turned out as another Zimbabwe or even another Somalia. It is Nelson Mandela's extraordinary achievement that he was able to somehow reconcile the country's many internal contradictions and carry people along with him. Equally commendable is the fact that, unlike many leaders of newly freed countries, he did not yield to the temptation of holding on to power till his death or starting a dynasty. He became President in 1994 and stepped down in 1999 after just one term. Modern historians tend to be dismissive of the 'Great Man Theory' of history but Mandela and Lee Kuan Yew are proof that individuals do matter. It is noteworthy that, despite being very determined leaders, both of them allowed their philosophies and ideas to evolve with changing circumstances. Therein may lie the secret of their success.

Bombay to Mumbai

The evolution of Mumbai encapsulates the social and economic changes witnessed by India since independence. When India became a Republic in 1950, Calcutta was no longer the capital but it was still the most important commercial and cultural centre. With a population of 2.6 million, it was by far the largest urban cluster in the country. Bombay was India's second largest city with a population of almost 1.5 million. Madras was much smaller at 0.8 million.[37]

Bombay's financial and commercial heart was still in and around the old Fort area although an extension had been added in the form of Ballard Estate during the First World War. Further north, the cotton mills of Lower Parel hummed with activity and attracted migrants. Although modern innovations like telephones and automobiles were leading to changes in how business was done, this was still a world that would have been recognizable to Premchand Roychand. The first big shift came in the 1970s with the construction of Nariman Point on reclaimed land near the southern tip of the island (not far from Fort). It was an unfortunate period in history for a construction boom and Nariman Point became home to a collection of exceptionally ugly office towers. Nonetheless, it created a cluster of relatively modern corporate offices. Its success in attracting corporate offices was helped by the decline of Calcutta which was wracked by violence from left-wing extremists (dubbed 'Naxalites') and militant trade unionism in the 1970s and '80s. As the old capital declined, one by one, companies shifted their headquarters to Bombay. It too witnessed a period of labour unrest which led to the closure of many mills in the Lower Parel area but Bombay's overall business culture remained intact and it emerged as India's commercial capital.

In 1990–91, India's socialist economic model collapsed and the crisis forced the country to start liberalizing the economy. The corrupt system of industrial licensing was dismantled and rules were eased for foreign investment. As foreign banks and multinationals entered the country, they bid up prices of the limited stock of commercial real estate and, within a few years, Nariman Point had some of the most expensive real estate in the world. This was ironical as many of the office blocks were shoddy and crumbling, and had elevators that were so slow and unreliable that it was often preferable to use the tobacco-spit stained stairs. Still, the country's business elite was a small club and everyone who mattered lived and worked in the southern tip of Bombay in the 1990s. Anyone sitting in the lobby of the Oberoi hotel in Nariman Point would have seen the who's who of India's business elite cutting deals with foreign investors. Self-important consultants walked hurriedly to meetings with neatly bound presentations tucked under their arms while speaking into their newly acquired Nokia phones.

The socialist period, despite the rhetoric, had effectively perpetuated the privileges of a small elite. In Delhi, this elite lived in the centre of the city, dubbed Lutyens' Delhi. In Bombay, the elite lived and worked in the southern tip—Malabar Hill, Cuffe Parade and Marine Drive, all within easy reach of Nariman Point and Fort.

This meant that better urban amenities—bars, restaurants, colonial-era clubs, schools and so on—were also concentrated in the southern tip. In turn, this imposed a peculiar socio-economic hierarchy on the city where one's position in the pecking order determined the distance one lived from Nariman Point (only Bollywood was exempt from this as it had its own cluster in Bandra–Juhu).

Given the spiralling real estate prices, a poor migrant had little choice other than to live in a slum but even a white-collar newcomer, with a well-paying job, would have to either rent a room as a 'paying guest' or opt for a far-off northern suburb like Borivali or Kandivali. Since jobs were concentrated in the southern tip, the office day began with a long journey in a tightly packed train followed by a hop by 'share-taxi' to one's office; in the evening one did the same thing in reverse. This rough commute still defines the experience of many but taught me one of the crucial lessons in life: Never get into the Virar Fast if you only want to go as far as Bandra. Readers from Mumbai will instantly know what I mean.

By the turn of the century, however, the dynamics of the city began to change. The old, derelict mills of Lower Parel were gradually converted into offices, condominiums and malls. The Phoenix Mills complex, now a popular entertainment and shopping hub, was one of the first to experience this change. Further north, a new financial district emerged in Bandra-Kurla. This created new hubs of activity in the middle of the city. Office towers and five-star hotels mushroomed even further north near the international airport. Within a decade, most banks and corporates shifted from Nariman Point to the glass-and-chrome towers of these new clusters. In many ways, these changes democratized the city as the old elite gave way to a confident new middle class; the South Bombay accent simply counted for less. Thus, Bombay became Mumbai.

The Churn of History

The long history of the Indian Ocean is one where the unfolding of events is the result of complex interactions between myriad factors—the monsoon winds, geography, human migrations, technology, religion, culture, the deeds of individuals and perhaps occasionally the whims of the gods. It followed no predetermined path or grand plan, but is the story of long cycles, dead ends and unintended consequences, of human triumphs and extraordinary bravery but also of treachery and inexplicable human cruelty. There are many shades of grey along the way.

The complex, adaptive nature of history is a warning that a linear narrative based on a unidimensional framework is necessarily misleading. This is true even when the narrative is based on 'scientific' evidence such as genetics. For example, if we tried today to reconstruct the history of the British Raj in India based solely on genetic data, we would find plenty of evidence of Gujarati and Punjabi genes in Britain but very little British DNA in India. A lazy researcher would then jump to the conclusion that it was India that colonized Britain!

A corollary is that the path of history flows neither from nor to Utopia. Indeed, the attempts to 'civilize' others and impose utopias have been the source of much human misery and are almost always based on some unidimensional interpretation of history. This book has been written at a time that the Indian Ocean rim is enjoying a period of peace and prosperity after many centuries of colonization, war and famine. However, the failed state of Somalia and renewed hostilities in Yemen remind us how fragile this peace can be.

It is also remarkable how many continuities remain through all these centuries of change. The monsoon winds may no longer dictate where ships can sail but they are still important to the economic lives of hundreds of millions who depend on them for the annual rains. Some continuities run so deep that we hardly notice them. For instance, certain ancient cultural ideas continue to impact us to this day despite layers of later influences. We saw how matrilineal customs were an important aspect of history in the eastern but not in the western Indian Ocean rim. Perhaps this explains why we have seen so many female leaders in countries ranging from the Philippines to the Indian subcontinent: Corazon Aquino, Megawati Sukarnoputri, Aung San Suu Kyi, Indira Gandhi, Sheikh Hasina, Sirimavo Bandaranaike to name just a few. Notice how these women leaders were able to occupy positions of power irrespective of ethnicity, culture and religion. While it is true that many of them inherited their position, the contrast is stark when one compares this with the almost complete absence of female leaders in the western Indian Ocean rim from the Persian Gulf, down to the Swahili coast to southern Africa. Even the exceptions—Madagascar and Mauritius—prove the rule as their cultural roots derive from the eastern Indian Ocean.

While researching this book I also came across numerous instances of how the lives of ordinary individuals had been impacted by the churn of people and empires in the Indian Ocean. Take, for instance, the story of Odakkal Mohammad who was born on 15 August 1927 in Mundappalam (now in the state of Kerala). His family claimed descent from Yemeni merchants who had settled here in the fourteenth century. In 1942, when barely fifteen, he was thrown out of school for wearing a black badge in protest against the arrest of Mahatma Gandhi. Too scared of being scolded by his father for this, Mohammad decided to run away from home and eventually ended up in the Royal Indian Navy as an electrical artificer.

The Second World War was raging at that time and Mohammad saw action on a number of occasions. After the war, he was posted to Bombay where he would participate in the Naval Revolt of 1946. When the mutiny was suppressed, he was dismissed from the navy with a certificate that read: 'Discharged in Disgrace from His Majesty's Service'. Mohammad tore up the paper and flung it at the British officer. The following year, India became independent on his twentieth birthday. Since the mutineers were never reabsorbed into the navy, Mohammad tried his hand at many jobs before getting involved in protests against Portuguese rule in Goa in 1955. He was arrested by the Portuguese and spent some time in prison before being released. After several more adventures, including cycling across India, he became a tour guide in Agra where he met and married a Christian nurse Mariamma on 15 August 1964. Decades later he would return to his village in Kerala where he was living at the time this book was written. This extraordinary story was narrated to me by his son Commodore Odakkal Johnson as we hunted, amidst torrential monsoon rain, for an almost forgotten memorial for WWI sailors in Mumbai's old port area.

This book is concerned with the past but the wheels of history roll relentlessly forward. What does the future hold? Even as I was completing this book, there were signs that the Indian Ocean may become the theatre of a new geopolitical rivalry between India and China. Those who remember history will know that the Indian Ocean has seen the likes of Rajendra Chola and Zheng He before. They will also know to expect the unexpected. After all, no one who saw Zheng He's magnificent Treasure Fleet would have believed that, a few decades later, a small country in the Iberian peninsula would open the Indian Ocean to centuries of European domination. If there is one lesson from this history it is this: Time devours the greatest of men and the mightiest of empires.

Notes

1. Introduction

1. D. Dennis Hudson, *The Body of God: An Emperor's Palace for Krishna in Eighth Century Kanchipuram* (OUP, 2008).
2. K.A. Nilakanta Sastri, *A History of South India* (New Delhi: OUP, 1975).
3. The idea that the Naga princess came from Sri Lanka may have something to do with the use of the lion in the royal insignia by some Pallava kings. This is perhaps taken to signify a link with the Sinhalese. However, the use of the lion as a royal symbol is so common across the world that it may not signify anything specific. In any case, several Pallava kings preferred other symbols such as the bull.
4. T.S. Subramanian, 'Remnants of a Relationship', *The Hindu* (20 August 2010).
5. Robert D. Kaplan, *Monsoon: The Indian Ocean and the Future of American Power* (Random House, 2011).
6. Tim Mackintosh-Smith (ed.), *The Travels of Ibn Battutah* (Picador, 2002).
7. Shaman Hwui Li, *The Life of Hiuen-Tsiang*, translated by Samuel Bean (1911, reprinted by Asian Education Services, 1998).
8. John Reader, *Africa: A Biography of the Continent* (Penguin, 1998).
9. Eric Hobsbawm, *On History* (Abacus, 1997).
10. There is some doubt about whether or not Mark Twain actually said this, but the quote sums up my point nicely.
11. T. Ramachandran, 'Indian Death Toll Highest in UN Peacekeeping Operations', *The Hindu* (30 October 2014). http://www.thehindu.com/opinion/blogs/blog-datadelve/article6547767.ece.

12. Alexander Stark, 'The Matrilineal System of Minangkabau and Its Persistence through History', *South Asia: A Multidisciplinary Journal* (2013).

13. D.G.E. Hall, *A History of South-East Asia* (Macmillan, 1981).

14. Nicholas Tarling (ed.), *The Cambridge History of South-east Asia*, Vol. 1, Part 1 (CUP, 1999).

2. Genetics and Ice

1. Subir Bhaumik, 'Tsunami Folklore Saved Islanders', BBC News (20 January 2005). http://news.bbc.co.uk/2/hi/south_asia/4181855.stm.

2. John C. Briggs, 'The Biogeographic and Tectonic History of India', *Journal of Biogeography* (2003).

3. Helen Shen, 'Unusual Indian Ocean Earthquakes Hint at Tectonic Breakup', *Nature* (Sepember 2012). http://www.nature.com/news/unusual-indian-ocean-earthquakes-hint-at-tectonic-breakup-1.11487.

4. The Commonwealth Scientific and Industrial Research Organisation (CSIRO) data. http://www.cmar.csiro.au/sealevel/sl_hist_intro.html.

5. Yuval Noah Harari, *Sapiens: A Brief History of Humankind* (Harvill Secker, 2014).

6. Yu-Sheng Chen (et al.), 'mtDNA Variation in the South African Kung and Khwe—and Their Genetic Relationships with Other African Populations', *American Journal of Human Genetics* (2000). http://www.ncbi.nlm.nih.gov/pmc/articles/PMC1288201/.

7. Nicole Maca-Meyer (et al.), 'Major Genomic Mitochondrial Lineages to Delineate Early Human Expansions', *BMC Genetics* (2001).

8. Rakesh Tamang (et al.), 'Complex Genetic Origin of Indian Populations and Its Implications', *Journal of Biosciences* (2012).

9. Jeffrey Rose, 'New Light on Human Prehistory in the Arabo-Persian Gulf Oasis', *Current Anthropology* (Chicago University, 2010).

10. Stephen Oppenheimer, 'Out-of-Africa, the Peopling of Continents and Islands: Tracing Uniparental Gene Trees across the Map', *Philosophical Transactions of the Royal Society* (2012).

11. Clive Finlayson (et al.), 'Gorham's Cave, Gibraltar—the Persistence of a Neanderthal Population', *Quarterly International* (2008).

12. 'Neanderthal DNA Hides in Genes Dictating Our Hair, Skin', Associated Press (29 January 2014); Sriram Sankararaman (et al.),

'The Genomic Landscape of Neanderthal Ancestry in Present-Day Humans', *Nature* (January 2014).

13. Yuval Noah Harari, *Sapiens: A Brief History of Humankind* (Harvill Secker, 2014).

14. *Guardian*, http://www.theguardian.com/science/2014/oct/08/cave-art-indonesia-sulawesi

15. *Telegraph*, http://epaper.telegraphindia.com/details/112778-173917265.html

16. Findings of the Human Genome Organization's Pan-Asian SNP Consortium: http://www.hugo-international.org/blog/?p=123.

17. Rakesh Tamang, Lalji Singh and Kumarasamy Thangaraj, 'Complex Genetic Origin of Indian Populations and Its Implications', published online by Indian Academy of Sciences (November 2012).

18. *Nature*, http://www.nature.com/ejhg/journal/v23/n1/full/ejhg201450a.html

19. John Reader, *Africa: A Biography of the Continent* (Penguin, 1998).

20. John Reader, *Africa: A Biography of the Continent* (Penguin, 1998).

21. Ainit Snir (et al.), 'The Origin of Cultivation and Proto-Weeds, Long Before Neolithic Farming', Israel Science Foundation (July 2015). http://journals.plos.org/plosone/article?id=10.1371/journal.pone.0131422.

22. Max Engel (et al.), 'The Early Holocene Humid Period in North-West Saudi Arabia—Sediments, Microfossils and Paleo-hydrological Modelling', *Quarterly International* (July 2012). http://www.sciencedirect.com/science/article/pii/S1040618211002424.

23. Report of Dr S. Badrinarayan, National Institute of Ocean Technology. http://archaeologyonline.net/artifacts/cambay.

24. Shi Yan (et al.), 'Y Chromosomes of 40% Chinese Descend from Three Neolithic Super-Grandfathers', *Quantitative Biology* (2013).

25. Peter Underhill (et al.), 'The Phylogenetic and Geographic Structure of Y-chromosome R1a', *European Journal of Human Genetics* (2014). http://www.nature.com/ejhg/journal/vaop/ncurrent/full/ejhg201450a.html.

26. *Nature*, http://www.nature.com/ejhg/journal/v23/n1/full/ejhg201450a.html

27. Peter Underhill (et al.), 'Separating the post-Glacial Coancestry of Europeans and Asian Y Chromosomes within R1a', *European Journal of Human Genetics* (2010).

28. Viola Grugni (et al.), 'Ancient Migratory Events in the Middle East: New Clues from the Y-Chromosome Variation of Modern Iranians', University of Cambridge (2012), Creative Commons.

29. Marc Haber (et al.), 'Afghanistan's Ethnic Groups Share a Y-Chromosomal Heritage Structured by Historical Events', *PLoS ONE* 7 (3) (March, 2012). http://journals.plos.org/plosone/article?id=10.1371%2Fjournal. pone.0034288.

30. Gerard Lucotte, 'The Major Y-Chromosome Haplotype XI— Haplogroup R1a in Eurasia', *Hereditary Genetics* (2015). http://www. omicsonline.org/open-access/the-major-ychromosome-haplotype-xi- -haplogroup-r1a-in-eurasia-2161-1041-1000150.pdf.

31. 'Europeans Got Fair Skin Only 7000 Years Ago: Study', IANS, *Times of India* (27 January 2014).

3. The Merchants of Meluhha

1. Upinder Singh, *A History of Ancient and Early Medieval India* (Pearson, 2009).

2. Upinder Singh, *A History of Ancient and Early Medieval India* (Pearson, 2009).

3. Upinder Singh, *A History of Ancient and Early Medieval India* (Pearson, 2009).

4. Upinder Singh, *A History of Ancient and Early Medieval India* (Pearson, 2009).

5. Nick Brooks, 'Cultural Responses to Aridity in the Middle Holocene and Increased Social Complexity', *Quarterly International* (2006). http://www.academia.edu/463993/Cultural_responses_to_aridity_ in_the_Middle_Holocene_and_increased_social_complexity.

6. Readers interested in the debate over the Saraswati should read Michel Danino's *The Lost River: On the Trail of the Sarasvati* (Penguin, 2010).

7. Rohan Dua, 'Haryana's Bhirrana Oldest Harappan Site, Rakhigarhi Asia's Largest: ASI', Times of India (15 April 2015). http://timesofindia. indiatimes.com/city/chandigarh/Haryanas-Bhirrana-oldest-Harappan- site-Rakhigarhi-Asias-largest-ASI/articleshow/46926693.cms.

8. Anindya Sarkar (et al.), 'Oxygen Isotope in Archaeological Bioapatites from India: Implications to Climate Change and Decline of Bronze Age Harappan Civilization', Scientific Reports, *Nature* (2016). http:// www.nature.com/articles/srep26555.

9. Mary R. Edward, *Maritime Heritage of Gujarat, Kathiawad and Kutch*, Maritime History Society (2013).

10. Penn Museum, http://www.penn.museum/research/research-near-east-section/804-the-jiroft-civilization-a-new-culture-of-the-bronze-age-on-the-iranian-plateau.html

11. Massimo Vidale and Dennys Frenez, 'Indus Components in the Iconography of a White Marble Cylinder Seal from Konar Sandal South (Kerman, Iran)', *South Asian Studies* (Routledge, 2015).

12. Edward Alpers, *The Indian Ocean in World History* (OUP, 2014).

13. Rajiv Rajan and Anand Prakash, 'Internationalisation of Currency: The Case of the Indian Rupee and Chinese Renminbi', RBI Staff Studies (2010).

14. Massimo Vidale, 'Growing in a Foreign World: For a History of the "Meluha Villages" in Mesopotamia in the 3rd Millennium BC', Proceedings of the Fourth Annual Symposium on Assyrian and Babylonian Intellectual Heritage Project, A. Panaino and A. Piras (eds) (October 2001).

15. Upinder Singh, *A History of Ancient and Early Medieval India* (Pearson, 2009).

16. Ralph Griffith, *The Hymns of the Rig Veda* (Motilal Banarasidass, 2004).

17. Yama Dixit (et al.), 'Abrupt Weakening of the Summer Monsoon in Northwest India 4100 Years Ago', *Geology*, (February 2014). http://geology.gsapubs.org/content/early/2014/02/24/G35236.1.full.pdf+html.

18. Adapted from http://faculty.washington.edu/lynnhank/The_Curse_of_Akkad.html

19. Anindya Sarkar (et al.), 'Oxygen Isotope in Archaeological Bioapatites from India: Implications to Climate Change and Decline of Bronze Age Harappan Civilization', Scientific Reports, *Nature* (2016). http://www.nature.com/articles/srep26555.

20. Priya Moorjani (et al.), 'Genetic Evidence for Recent Population Mixture in India', *American Journal of Human Genetics* (2013).

21. Priya Moorjani (et al.), 'Genetic Evidence for Recent Population Mixture in India', *American Journal of Human Genetics* (2013).

22. Analabha Basu (et al.), 'Genomic Reconstruction of the History of Extant Populations of India Reveals Five Distinct Ancestral Components and a Complex Structure', National Institute of Biomedical Genomics (January 2016).

23. B.R. Ambedkar, *Castes in India: Their Mechanism, Genesis and Development* (Columbia University, 1916). http://www.columbia.edu/itc/mealac/pritchett/00ambedkar/txt_ambedkar_castes.html.

24. Jhimli Mukherjee Pandey, 'Varanasi Is As Old As Indus Valley Civilization, Finds IIT-KGP Study', *Times of India* (25 February 2016).

25. Siddharth Tadepalli, 'Rare Discovery Pushes Back Iron Age in India', *Times of India*, 18 May 2015.

26. George Rapp, *Archaeomineralogy* (Springer, 2009).

27. Vibha Tripathi, *History of Iron Technology in India* (Rupa and Infinity Foundation, 2008).

28. Priya Moorjani (et al.), 'Genetic Evidence for Recent Population Mixture in India', *American Journal of Human Genetics* (2013).

29. Payam Nabarz, *The Mysteries of Mithras: The Pagan Belief that Shaped the Christian World* (Inner Traditions, 2005). Also see, http://www.historytoday.com/matt-salusbury/did-romans-invent-christmas.

30. Val Lauder, *When Christmas was against the law*, CNN (24 December 2014). http://edition.cnn.com/2014/12/24/opinion/lauder-when-christmas-was-against-law/.

31. Robert Hoyland, *Arabia and the Arabs* (Routledge, 2001).

32. Edward Alpers, *The Indian Ocean in World History* (OUP, 2014).

33. John Reader, *Africa: A Biography of a Continent* (Penguin, 1998).

34. Rebecca Morelle, 'Ancient Migration: Genes Link Australia with India', BBC World Service (January 2013). http://www.bbc.com/news/science-environment-21016700.

35. Pedro Soares (et al.), 'Climate Change and Postglacial Human Dispersals in South east Asia', *Molecular Biology and Evolution* (Oxford Journals, 2008). http://mbe.oxfordjournals.org/content/25/6/1209.long.

36. India's north-east would witness many later migrations, such as those of the Tibeto-Burmans. For the sake of simplicity, I have left them out of this book as their impact was more on the history of the Himalayan region than the Indian Ocean.

37. Yves Bonnefoy, *Asian Mythologies* (University of Chicago Press, 1993).

38. Patrick Nunn and Nick Reid, 'Indigenous Australian Stories and Sea-Level Change', Proceedings of the 18th Conference of the Foundation for Endangered Languages (2014).

39. Gyaneshwer Chaubey (et al.), 'Population Genetic Structure in Indian Austroasiatic Speakers: The Role of Landscape and Sex-Specific

Admixture' (May 2012). http://www.ncbi.nlm.nih.gov/pmc/articles/
PMC3355372/.

40. Note that Ulupi's Naga tribe may not relate to tribes living in modern-
day Nagaland as they probably came into this area at a much later date.
However, the term 'Naga' or 'serpent' was used loosely from an early
period to refer to people of South East Asian origin both by Indians and
by the groups themselves.

4. Kharavela's Revenge

1. *The Origins of Iron-Working in India*, Report of Rakesh Tewari, Director,
UP State Archaeological Department (2003). http://antiquity.ac.uk/
projgall/tewari/tewari.pdf.

2. Sanjeev Sanyal, *Land of the Seven Rivers* (Penguin, 2012).

3. Sushanta Patra and Benudhar Patra, Archaeology and the Maritime
History of Ancient Orissa, *OHRJ*, Vol. 2. http://orissa.gov.in/
e-magazine/Journal/Journal2/pdf/ohrj-014.pdf.

4. Lanka Ranaweera (et al.), 'Mitochondrial DNA History of Sri Lankan
Ethnic People: Their Relations within the Island and with the Indian
Subcontinental Population', *Journal of Human Genetics* (2013). http://
www.nature.com/jhg/journal/v59/n1/full/jhg2013112a.html.

5. 'Simplified Version of *Mahavamsa*', http://mahavamsa.org/
mahavamsa/simplified-version/princess-of-vanga/

6. Robert Knox, *An Historical Relation of the Island Ceylon, in the East Indies*,
published by Joseph Mawman (1817); reprinted by Asian Educational
Services (2011).

7. Herodotus, *The Histories* (Wordsworth Classics, 1996).

8. A. Azzaroli, *An Early History of Horsemanship* (E.J. Brill Leiden,1985).
This early Indian version of the stirrup seems to have consisted
of leather straps where the rider could slip in his big toe. These are
depicted in several sculptures. The true stirrup was invented several
centuries later in Central Asia.

9. Agnes Savill, *Alexander the Great and His Time* (Barnes & Noble,
1993).

10. Konstantin Nossov, *War Elephants* (New Vanguard, 2008).

11. Charles Allen, *Ashoka* (Little Brown, 2012).

12. Nayanjot Lahiri, *Ashoka in Ancient India* (Permanent Black, 2015).

13. Prafulla Das, 'Exploring an Ancient Kingdom', *Frontline* (September 2005). http://www.frontline.in/static/html/fl2220/stories/20051007000106500.htm.

14. Upinder Singh, *A History of Ancient and Early Medieval India* (Pearson Longman, 2009).

15. John Strong, *The Legend of King Asoka: The Study and Translation of the Asokavadana* (Princeton University Press, 2003).

16. For more see: 'Ashoka, the Not So Great', Sanjeev Sanyal, *Swarajya* magazine (22 November 2015). http://swarajyamag.com/culture/ashoka-the-not-so-great.

17. See more on this in, 'Why India Needs to No Longer Be an Ashokan Republic, but a Chanakyan One', Sanjeev Sanyal, *Economic Times* (26 January 2016). http://blogs.economictimes.indiatimes.com/et-commentary/why-india-needs-to-no-longer-be-an-ashokan-republic-but-a-chanakyan-one/.

18. Kautilya, *The Arthashastra*, L.N. Rangarajan (trans.) (Penguin, 1987).

19. Ashoka's Edict XIII, Routledge online resources, http://cw.routledge.com/textbooks/9780415485432/5.asp.

20. Several authors like Nayanjot Lahiri have claimed that some of the Barabar and Nagarjuni caves were built by Ashoka for the Ajivikas and therefore suggest that he patronized them. However, note that the only king mentioned by name in the inscriptions is Dasharatha and there is no mention of Ashoka. The confusion is due to the fact that Dasharatha uses language very similar to his predecessor and, like Ashoka, calls himself 'Beloved of the Gods'. The generic title may have also been used by Ashoka's father, Bindusara, who is known to have Ajivika links (in which case the Barabar caves would be the only known structure from his rule). Even if one accepts that Ashoka built the Barabar cave shelters for Ajivikas, the fact is that they were never finished and one can see that the term 'Ajivika' in the inscription was later deliberately vandalized. Clearly, there was some religious tension in the air. The point is that the matter is not as settled as mainstream historians claim and is largely a matter of interpretation. See Lahiri's *Ashoka in Ancient India* (Permanent Black, 2015).

21. Upinder Singh, *A History of Ancient and Early Medieval India* (Pearson Longman, 2009).

22. *The Hindu*, http://www.thehindu.com/features/friday-review/ history-and-culture/satvahana-site-to-be-reexcavated/article6842796. ece?ref=sliderNews

23. 'Translation of Hathigumpha Inscription', *Epigraphica Indica*, Vol. XX (1933). http://www.sdstate.edu/projectsouthasia/upload/ HathigumphaInscription.pdf.

24. Note that Kharavela seems to have followed both Jain and Vedic rituals. He uses salutations derived from the Jain tradition but also mentions Vedic fire sacrifices including the Rajasuya. Interestingly there is no reference to Buddhism. The Odiya probably still resented it as an Ashokan imposition.

5. Kaundinya's Wedding

1. Nicholas Tarling (ed.), *The Cambridge History of Southeast Asia*, Vol. 1 (CUP, 1999).

2. D.G.E. Hall, *A History of South-East Asia* (Macmillan, 1981).

3. Karuna Sagar Behera (ed.), *Kalinga–Indonesia Cultural Relations* (Orissan Institute of Maritime and South East Asian Studies, 2007).

4. Nicholas Tarling (ed.), *The Cambridge History of South-east Asia*, Vol. 1 (CUP, 1999).

5. As quoted in Upinder Singh, *A History of Ancient and Early Medieval India* (Pearson Longman, 2009).

6. A. Shrikumar, 'A Dead City Beneath a Living Village', *The Hindu* (19 August 2015).

7. K.A. Nilakanta Sastri, *A History of South India* (OUP, 1975). It should be pointed out that the formalizing of Sanskrit grammar was also done by an 'outsider', Panini, from what is now North-West Frontier Province, Pakistan, and eastern Afghanistan rather than someone from the Gangetic heartland.

8. K.A. Nilakanta Sastri, *A History of South India* (OUP, 1975).

9. K.M. de Silva, *A History of Sri Lanka* (Penguin, 2005).

10. Adapted from: Senake Bandaranayake, *Sigiriya* (Central Cultural Fund publication, 2005).

11. Wilfred Schoff (trans.), *The Periplus of the Erythraean Sea* (Longmans, Green & Co, 1912).

12. Raoul McLaughlin, *The Roman Empire and the Indian Ocean* (Pen and Sword, 2014).

13. P.J. Cherian (et al.), 'Interim Report of the Pattanam Excavations/ Explorations 2013' (Kerala Council of Historical Research, 2013).

14. K.A. Nilakanta Sastri, *A History of South India* (OUP, 1975).

15. Pius Malekandathil, *Maritime India* (Primus Books, 2015). It is possible that the story of St Thomas is due to a mix-up with Thomas of Cana about whom there is more reliable information.

16. Raoul McLaughlin, *The Roman Empire and the Indian Ocean* (Pen and Sword, 2014).

17. Sanjeev Sanyal, *Are We Entering a Post-Dollar World?*, The Wide Angle Series (Deutsche Bank, 2011); Sanjeev Sanyal, *The Age of Chinese Capital*, The Wide Angle Series (Deutsche Bank, 2014).

18. Raoul McLaughlin, *The Roman Empire and the Indian Ocean* (Pen and Sword, 2014).

19. Murray Cox (et al.), 'A Small Cohort of Island South-east Asian Women Founded Madagascar' (The Royal Society, 2012).

20. Richard Hall, *Empires of the Monsoon* (HarperCollins, 1996).

21. Philip Beale, 'From Indonesia to Africa: Borobudur Ship Expedition', *Ziff Journal* (2006). http://www.swahiliweb.net/ziff_journal_3_files/ziff2006-04.pdf.

22. Sen Li (et al.), 'Genetic Variation Reveals Large-scale Population Expansion and Migration During the Expansion of Bantu-speaking People' (The Royal Society, September 2014). http://rspb.royalsocietypublishing.org/content/281/1793/20141448.

23. John Reader, *Africa: A Biography of the Continent* (Penguin, 1998).

6. Arabian Knights

1. Upinder Singh, *A History of Ancient and Early Medieval India* (Pearson Longman, 2009).

2. Samuel Beal (trans.), *Travels of Fa Hian and Sung Yun* (reprinted by Asian Education Services, 2003).

3. *Times of India*, http://timesofindia.indiatimes.com/city/kolkata/Dum-Dum-mound-may-rewrite-Kolkata-history/articleshow/45244284.cms

4. Ramshankar Tripathi, *History of Ancient India* (Motilal Banarasidass, 1992).

5. Sandeep Unnithan, 'Feat Beneath the Ground', *India Today* (May, 2005). http://indiatoday.intoday.in/story/discovery-of-temples-at-mahabalipuram-gives-twist-to-seven-pagodas-folklore/1/193608.html

6. Ananth Krishnan, *Behind China's Hindu Temples, a Forgotten History* (*The Hindu*, July 2013). http://www.thehindu.com/news/national/behind-chinas-hindu-temples-a-forgotten-history/article4932458.ece

7. Robert Hoyland, *Arabia and the Arabs* (Routledge, 2001).

8. Saheed Adejumobi, *The History of Ethiopia* (Greenwood Press, 2007).

9. Robert Hoyland, *Arabia and the Arabs* (Routledge, 2001).

10. Robert Hoyland, *Arabia and the Arabs* (Routledge, 2001).

11. Georg Popp and Juma Al-Maskari, *Oman: Jewel of the Arabian Gulf* (Odyssey Books, 2010).

12. As quoted in *Oman in History*, Ministry of Information, Sultanate of Oman (Immel Publishing, 1995).

13. Karen Armstrong, *Islam: A Short History* (Phoenix Press, 2000).

14. Richard Hall, *Empires of the Monsoon* (HarperCollins, 1996).

15. Richard Hall, *Empires of the Monsoon* (HarperCollins, 1996).

16. The mosque is also linked to a legend about the last Chera king. Although the legend is probably untrue, the early date for the mosque's construction is plausible given the well-established maritime links between India and Arabia.

17. Sir Richard Burton, *The Arabian Nights* (The Modern Library NY, 2001).

18. Mahomed Kasim Ferishta, *History of the Rise of Mahomedan Power in India*, John Briggs (trans.) (Sang-e-Meel Publications, 2004).

19. Shahpurshah Hormasji Hodivala (trans.), *The Qissa-i-Sanjan* (Studies in Parsi History, Bombay, 1920). http://www.avesta.org/other/qsanjan.pdf.

20. Niraj Rai (et al.), 'H1a1a-M82 Reveals the Likely Origin of the European Romani Population', *PLoS One* (November 2012).

7. Merchants, Temples and Rice

1. D.G.E. Hall, *A History of South-East Asia*, (Macmillan, 1981).

2. Nicholas Tarling (ed.), *The Cambridge History of South-east Asia*, Vol. 1, Part 1 (CUP, 1999).

3. D.G.E. Hall, *A History of South-East Asia* (Macmillan, 1981).

4. *VOA News*, http://www.voanews.com/content/thailand-cambodia-clash-at-border-115266974/134501.html
5. D.G.E. Hall, *A History of South-East Asia*, (Macmillan, 1981).
6. Charles Higham, *The Civilization of Angkor* (Phoenix, 2003).
7. Charles Higham, *The Civilization of Angkor* (Phoenix, 2003).
8. Upinder Singh, *A History of Ancient and Early Medieval India* (Pearson Longman, 2009).
9. Herman Kulke, K. Kesavapany and Vijay Sakhuja (eds), *Nagapattinam to Suwarnadwipa* (ISEAS, 2009).
10. Herman Kulke, K. Kesavapany and Vijay Sakhuja (eds), *Nagapattinam to Suwarnadwipa* (ISEAS, 2009).
11. B. Arunachalam, *Chola Navigation Package* (Maritime History Society, Mumbai, 2004).
12. Upinder Singh, *A History of Ancient and Early Medieval India* (Pearson Longman, 2009).
13. Kanakalatha Mukund, *Merchants of Tamilakam* (Penguin, 2012).
14. K.M. de Silva, *A History of Sri Lanka* (Penguin, 2005).
15. As quoted in Edward Alpers, *The Indian Ocean in World History* (OUP, 2014).
16. Edward Alpers, *The Indian Ocean in World History* (OUP, 2014).
17. John Reader, *Africa: A Biography of the Continent* (Penguin, 1998).
18. Maryna Steyn, 'The Mapungubwe Gold Graves Revisited', *South African Archaeological Bulletin* (2007). http://repository.up.ac.za/bitstream/handle/2263/5791/Steyn_Mapungubwe(2007).pdf?sequence=1
19. R. Coupland, *Kirk on the Zambezi* (Clarendon Press, 1928).
20. Nitish Sengupta, *Land of Two Rivers* (Penguin, 2011).
21. Nitish Sengupta, *Land of Two Rivers* (Penguin, 2011).
22. Marco Polo, *The Travels* (Penguin, 1958).
23. Upinder Singh, *A History of Ancient and Early Medieval India* (Pearson Longman, 2009).
24. Tim Mackintosh-Smith (ed.), *The Travels of Ibn Battutah* (Picador, 2003).
25. Tim Mackintosh-Smith (ed.), *The Travels of Ibn Battutah* (Picador, 2003).

8. Treasure and Spice

1. D.G.E. Hall, *A History of South-East Asia* (Macmillan, 1994); Nicholas Tarling (ed.), *The Cambridge History of South-east Asia*, Vol. 1 (CUP, 1999).

2. Louise Levathes, *When China Ruled the Seas* (OUP, 1994).

3. Louise Levathes, *When China Ruled the Seas* (OUP, 1994).

4. Louise Levathes, *When China Ruled the Seas* (OUP, 1994).

5. Robert Hefner, *Hindu Javanese* (Princeton University Press, 1985).

6. D.G.E. Hall, *A History of South-East Asia* (Macmillan, 1981).

7. Prof. Sakaya's formal Vietnamese name is Truong Van Mon but he prefers his Cham name Sakaya.

8. Brendan Buckley (et al.), 'Climate as a Contributing Factor in the Demise of Angkor, Cambodia', (National Academy of Sciences, United States, 2009). http://www.pnas.org/content/107/15/6748.full.

9. Richard Hall, *Empires of the Monsoon* (HarperCollins, 1996).

10. Richard Hall, *Empires of the Monsoon* (HarperCollins, 1996).

11. Richard Hall, *Empires of the Monsoon* (HarperCollins, 1996).

12. As quoted in Richard Hall, *Empires of the Monsoon* (HarperCollins, 1996).

13. Charles Corn, *The Scent of Eden* (Kodansha International, 1998).

14. As quoted in Gillian Tindall, *City of Gold: The Biography of Bombay* (Penguin, 1992).

15. Jonathan Gil Harris, *The First Firangis* (Aleph, 2015).

16. William H. Rule, *The Brand of Dominic: Or Inquisition at Rome* (Carlton & Phillips, 1852).

17. http://verna.mahalasa.org/

18. William H. Rule, *The Brand of Dominic: Or Inquisition at Rome* (Carlton & Phillips, 1852).

19. Jonathan Gil Harris, *The First Firangis* (Aleph, 2015).

20. John Fritz and George Michell, *Hampi* (India Book House, 2003); Robert Sewell, *A Forgotten Empire* (Swan Sonnenschein & Co, 1900).

21. John Fritz and George Michell, *Hampi* (India Book House, 2003).

22. Extract adapted from John Fritz and George Michell, *Hampi* (India Book House, 2003).

23. Anish Shah (et al.), 'Indian Siddis: African Descendants with Indian Admixture', *American Journal of Human Genetics* (July, 2011). http://www.sciencedirect.com/science/article/pii/S0002929711002230

24. Robert Sewell, *A Forgotten Empire* (Swan Sonnenschein & Co, 1900). Note that there is another theory that the name Chennai is derived from the name of a local temple. The story related in the main text, however, is the more popular explanation.

25. Archana Garodia Gupta, *The Admiral Queen*, Swarajya (October, 2015).
26. I am told that a full history exists in Kannada but was unable to source a translation in English or Hindi.

9. Nutmegs and Cloves

1. Tirthankar Roy, *The East India Company* (Penguin, 2012).
2. John Keay, *The Honourable Company: A History of the English East India Company* (HarperCollins, 1991).
3. For a more detailed narration of these events read: Giles Milton, *Nathaniel's Nutmeg* (Sceptre, 1999).
4. Charles Corn, *The Scent of Eden* (Kodansha International, 1999).
5. John Keay, *The Honourable Company* (HarperCollins, 1991).
6. Tirthankar Roy, *The East India Company* (Penguin, 2012).
7. Colin Woodard, *The Republic of Pirates* (Pan Books, 2007).
8. Colin Woodard, *The Republic of Pirates* (Pan, 2007).
9. Ashin Das Gupta, *India and the Indian Ocean World* (OUP, 2004).
10. Georg Popp and Juma Al-Maskari, *Oman: Jewel of the Arabian Gulf* (Odyssey Books, 2010).
11. Nitish Sengupta, *Land of Two Rivers* (Penguin, 2011).
12. K.M. de Silva, *A History of Sri Lanka* (Penguin, 2005).
13. Ashin Das Gupta, *India and the Indian Ocean World* (OUP, 2004).
14. Jonathan Gil Harris, *The First Firangis* (Aleph, 2015).
15. John Keay, *The Honourable Company* (HarperCollins, 1991).
16. As quoted in Nitish Sengupta, *Land of Two Rivers* (Penguin, 2011).
17. As quoted in S. Balakrishna, *Tipu Sultan: The Tyrant of Mysore* (Rare Publications, 2013).
18. Francois Gautier, *The Tyrant Diaries*, Outlook (15 April 2015); Mir Hussein Ali Khan Kirmani, *Neshani Hyduri* (W.H. Allen & Co.).
19. Translated by J.A. Grant, *Madras Gazette*, 1799; as quoted in S. Balakrishna, *The Tyrant of Mysore* (Rare Publications, 2013).

10. Diamonds and Opium

1. Charles Corn, *The Scent of Eden* (Kodansha International, 1998).
2. Giorgio Riello and Tirthankar Roy, *How India Clothed the World: The World of South Asian Textiles, 1500–1850* (Brill, 2009).

3. Julia Lovell, *The Opium War* (Picador, 2011).

4. Nigel Barley, *In the Footsteps of Stamford Raffles* (Penguin, 1991).

5. Nigel Barley, *In the Footsteps of Stamford Raffles* (Penguin, 1991).

6. K.M. de Silva, *A History of Sri Lanka* (Penguin, 1981).

7. Julia Lovell, *The Opium War* (Picador, 2011).

8. Julia Lovell, *The Opium War* (Picador, 2011).

9. *The Hindu*, http://www.thehindu.com/features/friday-review/history-and-culture/the-forgotten-history-of-indian-troops-in-china/article2208018.ece

10. Tirthankar Roy, *The East India Company* (Penguin, 2012).

11. Lakshmi Subramanian, *Three Merchants of Bombay* (Penguin Allen Lane, 2012).

12. Amar Farooqui, *Opium City* (Three Essays Collective, 2006).

13. Lakshmi Subramanian, *Three Merchants of Bombay* (Penguin Allen Lane, 2012).

14. Gillian Tindall, *City of Gold: The Biography of Bombay* (Penguin, 1992).

15. Diane Mehta, 'Kings Have Adorned Her', *Paris Review* (7 November 2013). http://www.theparisreview.org/blog/2013/11/07/kings-have-adorned-her/.

16. Sachin Mampatta and Rajesh Bhayani, 'How Abraham Lincoln Triggered India's First Stock Market Crash' *Business Standard*, 11 July 2015. http://www.business-standard.com/article/beyond-business/150-years-later-115071001354_1.html.

17. Georg Popp and Juma Al-Maskari, *Oman: Jewel of the Arabian Gulf* (Odyssey Books, 2010).

18. *Oman in History* (Ministry of Information, Sultanate of Oman, 1995).

19. Anne de Courcy, *The Fishing Fleet: Husband Hunting in the Raj* (Weidenfield & Nicholson, 2012).

20. Brij Lal (ed.), *The Encyclopedia of the Indian Diaspora* (Didier Millet and NUS, 2006).

21. Brij Lal (ed.), *The Encyclopedia of the Indian Diaspora* (Didier Millet and NUS, 2006).

22. As quoted in John Reader, *Africa: A Biography of the Continent* (Penguin, 1998).

23. John Reader, *Africa: A Biography of the Continent* (Penguin, 1998).

24. John Reader, *Africa: A Biography of the Continent* (Penguin, 1998).

25. Anthony Kenny (ed.), *The History of the Rhodes Trust* (OUP, 2001).

26. Bismarck was known to have been opposed to creating colonies in remote locations but pressure from the German public and the Kaiser probably tipped the balance. Ironically, the administrative and financial burden of managing these far-flung colonies was among the factors that would lead to him being pushed into retirement.
27. Richard Hall, *Empires of the Monsoon* (HarperCollins, 1996).
28. John Reader, *Africa: A Biography of the Continent* (Penguin, 1998).
29. John Reader, *Africa: A Biography of the Continent* (Penguin, 1998).
30. The Dutch seem to have already had a presence on the north of the island.

11. From Dusk to a New Dawn

1. Nitya Menon, '100 Years On: Remembering Emden's Generous Captain', *The Hindu*, 24 September 2014. http://www.thehindu.com/news/cities/chennai/chen-society/100-years-on-remembering-emdens-generous-captain/article6439360.ece.
2. 'The Exploits of the Emden', *Advertiser* (10 November 1928); '100th Anniversary of the *HMAS Sydney* Sinking *SMS Emden* in Battle of Coco Islands', Australian War Memorial (October 2014). https://www.awm.gov.au/media/releases/100th-anniversary-hmas-sydney-i-sinking-german-raider-sms-emden-battle-cocos-island/.
3. Christian Bartolf, *Gandhi and War: The Mahatma Gandhi—Bart de Ligt Correspondence*, (Satyagraha Foundation for Non-violence Studies).
4. Shashi Tharoor, 'Why the Indian Soldiers of WW1 Were Forgotten', *BBC Magazine* (July, 2015).
5. Peter Hopkirk, *On Secret Service East of Constantinople* (John Murray, 1994).
6. Peter Hopkirk, *On Secret Service East of Constantinople* (John Murray, 1994).
7. Dennis Kincaid, *Shivaji: The Grand Rebel* (Rupa, 2015).
8. Peter Hopkirk, *On Secret Service East of Constantinople* (John Murray, 1994).
9. Sho Kuwajima, 'Indian Mutiny in Singapore 1915: People Who Observed the Scene and People Who Heard the News', *New Zealand Journal of Asian Studies* (2009). It remains unclear to what extent the Singapore mutiny was connected to the Ghadar conspiracy and to what extent it was an independent event caused by Muslim soldiers

being unhappy at the possibility of being sent to fight co-religionists in the Middle East.

10. P.C. Mitra, 'A Forgotten Revolutionary', *Sunday Amrita Bazar Patrika* (11 September 1983).

11. Peter Hopkirk, *On Secret Service East of Constantinople* (John Murray, 1994).

12. Barindra Kumar Ghosh, *The Tale of My Exile* (Arya Office, 1922).

13. Timothy Hall, *The Fall of Singapore* (Mandarin Australia, 1990).

14. Srinath Raghavan, *India's War* (Penguin, 2016).

15. Timothy Hall, *The Fall of Singapore* (Mandarin Australia, 1990).

16. It should be noted that many Indian soldiers refused to switch sides. They would face harsh treatment as prisoners of war or even execution. Many would end up in camps in New Guinea and there are reports that some were used as live targets for practice shooting. http:// timesofindia.indiatimes.com/india/Japanese-ate-Indian-PoWs-used-them-as-live-targets-in-WWII/articleshow/40017577.cms.

17. *Netaji Subhas Bose: The Singapore Saga*, (Nalanda-Sriwijaya Centre, ISEAS, Singapore, 2012).

18. 'Britain's Greatest Battles: Imphal & Kohima', National War Museum website, http://www.nam.ac.uk/exhibitions/online-exhibitions/britains-greatest-battles/imphal-kohima.

19. Madhusree Mukerjee, *Churchill's Secret War: The British Empire and the Ravaging of India during WWII* (Basic Books, 2010).

20. Ajeet Jawed, 'Unsung Heroes of 1946', *Mainstream Weekly* (1 October 2008); Dhananjay Bhat, 'RIN Mutiny Gave a Jolt to the British', *Tribune*, 12 February 2006; G.D. Sharma, *Untold Story 1946 Naval Mutiny: Last War of Independence* (VIJ Books, 2015).

21. Only the Communists seem to have provided some limited support to the mutineers but they were not a major political force in the country.

22. Saikat Dutta, 'Radioactive Rebels', *Outlook* (20 April 2009).

23. D.G.E. Hall, *A History of South-East Asia* (Macmillan, 1981).

24. Christopher Bayly and Tim Harper, *Forgotten Wars* (Penguin, 2008).

25. 'Biju Patnaik: Obituary', *The Economist* (April, 1997).

26. D.G.E. Hall, *A History of South-East Asia* (Macmillan, 1981).

27. Richard Hall, *Empires of the Monsoon* (HarperCollins, 1996).

28. Ryszard Kapuscinski, *The Emperor* (Penguin, 1983).

29. Brij Lal (ed.), *The Encyclopedia of the Indian Diaspora* (Didier Millet, 2006).

30. Edward Alpers, *The Indian Ocean in World History* (OUP, 2014).

31. C.M. Turnbull, *A History of Modern Singapore 1819–2005* (NUS Press, 2009).

32. C.M. Turnbull, *A History of Modern Singapore 1819–2005* (NUS Press, 2009).

33. Sanjeev Sanyal, 'Singapore: The Art of Building a Global City' (IPS Working Paper, January 2007). http://lkyspp.nus.edu.sg/ips/wp-content/uploads/sites/2/2013/06/wp17.pdf.

34. Sanjeev Sanyal, *The Indian Renaissance: India's Rise After a Thousand Years of Decline* (Penguin, 2008).

35. Biographical details taken from the Nelson Mandela Foundation website, https://www.nelsonmandela.org/content/page/biography.

36. A version of this section was published as: Sanjeev Sanyal, 'Great Men Do Make History', *Business Standard* (8 December 2013).

37. *Lands and Peoples*, Vol. 4 (The Grolier Society, 1956).

Index